YOUR RIGHT TO CHILD CUSTODY, VISITATION, AND SUPPORT

Mary L. Boland
Attorney at Law

Sphinx® Publishing
A Division of Sourcebooks, Inc.®
Naperville, IL • Clearwater, FL

First edition, 2000

Published by: **Sphinx® Publishing, A Division of Sourcebooks, Inc.®**

Naperville Office	Clearwater Office
P.O. Box 4410	P.O. Box 25
Naperville, Illinois 60567-4410	Clearwater, Florida 33757
630-961-3900	727-587-0999
Fax: 630-961-2168	Fax: 727-586-5088

Interior Design and Production: Amy S. Hall and Edward A. Haman, Sourcebooks, Inc.®

This publication is designed to provide accurate and authoritative information in regard to the subject matter covered. It is sold with the understanding that the publisher is not engaged in rendering legal, accounting, or other professional service. If legal advice or other expert assistance is required, the services of a competent professional person should be sought.

From a Declaration of Principles Jointly Adopted by a Committee of the American Bar Association and a Committee of Publishers and Associations

This product is not a substitute for legal advice.

Disclaimer required by Texas statutes.

Library of Congress Cataloging-in-Publication Data
Boland, Mary L.
    Your right to child custody, visitation, and support / Mary L. Boland. -- 1st ed.
        p.   cm.
    Includes index.
    ISBN 1-57248-097-1 (pbk.)
    1. Custody of children--United States Popular works.
2. Visitation rights (Domestic relations)--United States Popular works.   3. Child support--Law and legislation--United States Popular works.   I. Title.
KF547.Z9B65   1999
346.7301'73--dc21

99-35179
CIP

Printed and bound in the United States of America.

HS Paperback — 10 9 8 7 6 5 4 3 2

CONTENTS

USING SELF-HELP LAW BOOKS

Before using a self-help law book, you should realize the advantages and disadvantages of doing your own legal work and understand the challenges and diligence that this requires.

THE GROWING TREND

Rest assured that you won't be the first or only person handling your own legal matter. For example, in some states, more than seventy-five percent of the people in divorces and other cases represent themselves. Because of the high cost of legal services, this is a major trend and many courts are struggling to make it easier for people to represent themselves. However, some courts are not happy with people who do not use attorneys and refuse to help them in any way. For some, the attitude is, "Go to the law library and figure it out for yourself."

We write and publish self-help law books to give people an alternative to the often complicated and confusing legal books found in most law libraries. We have made the explanations of the law as simple and easy to understand as possible. Of course, unlike an attorney advising an individual client, we cannot cover every conceivable possibility.

COST/VALUE ANALYSIS

Whenever you shop for a product or service, you are faced with various levels of quality and price. In deciding what product or service to buy, you make a cost/value analysis on the basis of your willingness to pay and the quality you desire.

When buying a car, you decide whether you want transportation, comfort, status, or sex appeal. Accordingly, you decide among such choices as a Neon, a Lincoln, a Rolls Royce, or a Porsche. Before making a decision, you usually weigh the merits of each option against the cost.

When you get a headache, you can take a pain reliever (such as aspirin) or visit a medical specialist for a neurological examination. Given this choice, most people, of course, take a pain reliever, since it costs only pennies; whereas a medical examination costs hundreds of dollars and takes a lot of time. This is usually a logical choice because it is rare to need anything more than a pain reliever for a headache. But in some cases, a headache may indicate a brain tumor and failing to see a specialist right away can result in complications. Should everyone with a headache go to a specialist? Of course not, but people treating their own illnesses must realize that they are betting on the basis of their cost/value analysis of the situation. They are taking the most logical option.

The same cost/value analysis must be made when deciding to do one's own legal work. Many legal situations are very straight forward, requiring a simple form and no complicated analysis. Anyone with a little intelligence and a book of instructions can handle the matter without outside help.

But there is always the chance that complications are involved that only an attorney would notice. To simplify the law into a book like this, several legal cases often must be condensed into a single sentence or paragraph. Otherwise, the book would be several hundred pages long and too complicated for most people. However, this simplification necessarily leaves out many details and nuances that would apply to special or unusual situations. Also, there are many ways to interpret most legal questions. Your case may come before a judge who disagrees with the analysis of our authors.

Therefore, in deciding to use a self-help law book and to do your own legal work, you must realize that you are making a cost/value analysis. You have decided that the money you will save in doing it yourself outweighs the chance that your case will not turn out to your satisfaction. Most people handling their own simple legal matters never have a problem, but occasionally people find that it ended up costing them more to have an attorney straighten out the situation than it would have if they had hired an attorney in the beginning. Keep this in mind while handling your case, and be sure to consult an attorney if you feel you might need further guidance.

LOCAL RULES
AND PROCEDURES

The next thing to remember is that a book which covers the law for the entire nation, or even for an entire state, cannot possibly include every procedural difference of every jurisdiction. Whenever possible, we provide the exact form needed; however, in some areas, each county, or even each judge, may require unique forms and procedures. In our state books, our forms usually cover the majority of counties in the state, or provide examples of the type of form which will be required. In our national books, our forms are sometimes even more general in nature but are designed to give a good idea of the type of form that will be needed in most locations. Nonetheless, keep in mind that your state, county, or judge may have a requirement, or use a form, that is not included in this book.

You should not necessarily expect to be able to get all of the information and resources you need solely from within the pages of this book. This book will serve as your guide, giving you specific information whenever possible and helping you to find out what else you will need to know. This is just like if you decided to build your own backyard deck. You might purchase a book on how to build decks. However, such a book would not include the building codes and permit requirements of every city, town, county, and township in the nation; nor would it include the lumber, nails, saws, hammers, and other materials and tools you would need to actually build the deck. You would use the book as your guide, and then do some work and research involving such matters as whether you need a permit of some kind, what type and grade of wood is available in your area, whether to use hand tools or power tools, and how to use those tools.

Before using the forms in a book like this, you should check with your court clerk to see if there are any local rules of which you should be aware, or local forms you will need to use. Often, such forms will require the same information as the forms in the book but are merely laid out differently or use slightly different language. They will sometimes require additional information.

CHANGES IN THE LAW

Besides being subject to local rules and practices, the law is subject to change at any time. The courts and the legislatures of all fifty states are constantly revising the laws. It is possible that while you are reading this book, some aspect of the law is being changed.

In most cases, the change will be of minimal significance. A form will be redesigned, additional information will be required, or a waiting period will be extended. As a result, you might need to revise a form, file an extra form, or wait out a longer time period; these types of changes will not usually affect the outcome of your case. On the other hand, sometimes a major part of the law is changed, the entire law in a particular area is rewritten, or a case that was the basis of a central legal point is overruled. In such instances, your entire ability to pursue your case may be impaired.

To help you with local requirements and changes in the law, be sure to read the section in chapter 1 on "Finding the Law: Legal Research."

Again, you should weigh the value of your case against the cost of an attorney and make a decision as to what you believe is in your best interest.

INTRODUCTION

The issues of custody and visitation arise most often in divorce proceedings and can be the biggest contest between parents. About fifty percent of marriages end in divorce, affecting about one million children every year. Because of the importance of the decision and the possible need for expert witnesses, child custody battles are often a very expensive part of a divorce. Custody may also be an issue when the parents have never married. Roughly one million children are born to unwed mothers each year. Marriage or not, child support can not only be a hotly contested issue, but can also lead to long term enforcement problems. Knowledge of the legal process, and an understanding of the laws in this area, can help reduce the acrimony involved in these cases and ultimately increase the willingness of both parents to be actively committed to their children emotionally, physically, and financially.

The goal of this book is to help you consider your options in deciding custody, visitation, and child support questions by giving you a broad overview of the factors that courts examine when determining these issues. While every family has the same basic needs, every family is also unique. Perhaps the overriding concept in this area of law is that decisions, whether based on an agreement of the parents or determined after trial, should be made with the maximum flexibility to accommodate a particular family's needs within certain minimum guidelines.

Thus, as you read the chapters that follow, do not seek out a "boiler-plate" answer to fit every situation. Rather, considering your needs and desires, this book provides you with the necessary ingredients to be successful in working towards your goals, whether they be for full custody, a joint arrangement, flexible visitation, or appropriate child support. Additionally, keep in mind that there are no absolute "winners" in these cases. Your objective is to be heard and to have your concerns considered fairly, especially in a contested case where each parent would be seen by a court as a potentially appropriate caretaker and supporter of a child. The most important consideration of any decision in this area is that it be in the best interests of your child.

PRELIMINARY CONSIDERATIONS 1

PARENTAL RESPONSIBILITIES

The birth of a child brings long-term responsibilities to the parents. All parents, married or not, have a duty to provide reasonable care, financial support, and disciplinary guidelines for their child. Even so, not all parents share the same views on child rearing, and not all parents define the word *responsible* the same way. It is also true that parents often disagree on how much financial support is necessary, especially when it's the subject of a court order.

If the parents have been married, these differences are heightened during divorce proceedings, when custody, visitation, and child support all become issues to be resolved. If the parents have never been married, these differences may be even greater, since the parents may have never even considered or shared their views on children with one another. The "father" may not even be certain that he is, in fact, the father. Also, an unmarried parent may feel little responsibility for a child not in his or her daily care. This is most often the case with a father, especially if his relationship with the child's mother ends during, or shortly after, the onset of her pregnancy.

THE ROLE OF THE LAW

Once a child custody, visitation, or support matter is brought to the courts, there is a continuing duty under the law for the court to "watch over" the child, almost like a "super parent." The good news is, though, that parents who agree on the terms of care and support for their child will usually see a court adopt their agreement. Ultimately, the law in your jurisdiction will govern what kinds of agreements you can make and what kinds of orders are entered.

When parents contest these matters, courts have developed various strategies to address the difficult task of considering a unique relationship and weighing what is in the best interests of the child. However, there are nearly as many variations within the legal guidelines in custody, visitation, and support provisions as there are families.

The legal factors and guidelines are intentionally broad and generalized because the parent-child relationship is not so easily captured on paper with set times, places, and amounts. Yet, to some extent, that is what the law of child custody, visitation, and support is about—the effort to reduce the intangible relationships between parent and child to some definable level of interaction and support. This is why it is important, whenever possible, to try to work out an agreement which recognizes that both of you want the best for your child and which provides the maximum flexibility under the law to allow you to succeed in being good parents and observing what is in the best interests of your child. A great number of contested custody cases can be resolved with an agreement when the parents are willing to discuss the options.

FINDING THE LAW: LEGAL RESEARCH

Every state has passed a set of *statutes* or *codes* which contain the laws passed by the legislature. A portion the statutes or codes will set forth the standards for determining custody, visitation, and child support. The laws relating to custody, visitation, and support in each state are listed and summarized in appendix A of this book. To find the laws for your state and to properly prepare the necessary paperwork, you will need to do some basic legal research.

LAW LIBRARIES   A large public library may carry some legal books, but a specialized *law library* will have the most up-to-date version of your state's laws, as well as other types of research materials not found in a regular public library. Law libraries can usually be found at or near your local courthouse—your court clerk's office should be able to tell you where to find the law library. Also, any law school will have a law library.

Contact the closest law library to determine hours and directions. Also ask if there are any restrictions on use of the library by members of the general public. Some law libraries may have limitations (such as limited hours or days) for non-attorneys; and law school libraries may have similar (or stricter) restrictions for non-students.

STATUTES OR   Your first step will probably be to find the basic law in your state's
CODES   statutes or codes. The actual title of the set of books containing the statutes or codes is very important. For example, *Arizona Revised Statutes Annotated* or *Delaware Code Annotated*. Refer to the listing for your state in appendix A to find the title of the set of books for your state. Reference librarians are also very good and can help you find the correct set of books. Once you find the proper set of books, look for the section, title, or other numbers listed for your state in appendix A in order to find the exact provisions of the law.

For example, if you look at the listing for Illinois in appendix A, you will see the following notation after the heading "The Law": "West's Illinois Compiled Statutes Annotated, Chapter 750, Article 5, Section 602 (750 ILCS 5/602)." This gives you the title of the set of books (*West's Illinois Compiled Statutes Annotated*). You will also note the following notation under the heading "Custody": "750 ILCS 5/602." This tells you that the the portion of the Illinois law relating to custody is found in Chapter 750 of the set of books called the *Illinois Compiled Statutes* and begins with Article 5, Section 602. The legal *citation* (abbreviation) for this would be: "750 ILCS 5/602," where "750" refers to Chapter 750, "ILCS" is the abbreviation for Illinois Compiled Statutes, and "5/602" refers to Article 5, Section 602. Once you locate the specific laws for your state, check to see if there is a more current version available. This may be in the form of an update inserted in the back of the volume, a separate update volume, or in some other format. If necessary, ask a reference librarian for assistance in order to be certain you have the most recent version. The statutes may also be annotated with short summaries of court decisions which have interpreted the statutes.

CASE REPORTERS If you wish to find the court's entire decision, it will be included in a state or regional *case reporter*. A state case reporter, such as the *Illinois Reporter*, contains court opinions from the courts of a single state. A regional reporter, such as the *Northeastern Reporter*, contains cases from the courts of several states in a certain geographic area. To find a case, carefully copy down the case name and the numbers which follow it (called the *citation*) or make a copy of the page containing the case information. Next, locate the case reporters in the library. Many states have more than one reporter in which the same case can be found. Again, ask a librarian for assistance. The citation often looks as follows:

In re Marriage of Kern, 245 Ill.App.3d 575, 615 N.E.2d 402 (1993)

NAME OF CASE	STATE CASE REPORTER	REGIONAL REPORTER	YEAR PUBLISHED

Once you find the proper state or regional reporter, the case is found using the following method:

245	Ill.App.	3d	575
VOLUME	STATE REPORTER	SERIES VERSION	PAGE NUMBER

Thus, you will find the Illinois appellate court opinion in the case of *In re marriage of Kern* in volume 245 of the state reporter titled *Illinois Appellate Reporter, Third Series*, on page 575. After a point, instead of continuing to increase the volume numbers, publishers have started over with volume one of a subsequent *series* of the reporter. In our example, you would actually find three sets of books on the library shelves: one titled *Illinois Appellate Reporter*; another titled *Illinois Appellate Reporter, Second Series*; and a third titled *Illinois Reporter, Third Series*. Each set begins with "Volume 1." The *Third Series* contains the most recent cases.

INTERNET
RESEARCH

Increasingly, the Internet is becoming a resource to obtain legal information specific to the various states. Many states include their statutes (and selected cases) on their government web pages. One easy way to find available web information on the laws of your state is to begin by searching the LawCrawler search engine by Findlaw. Type in http://findlaw.com., then choose state cases and codes to search your state. The listings for each state's Child Support Enforcement Agency can be found in appendix A. Also, the Internet site for the Office of Child Support Enforcement at http://www.acf.dhhs.gov/programs/cse provides links to states that have their own child support home pages. Some states also include family law forms on the Internet.

Researching on the Internet can be much faster than looking up your state's laws in the books, but online research produces only a screen snapshot at a time, so you may need to open several pages to see the whole picture of your state's custody, visitation, or support laws. When working online, be sure to review all of the relevant website information, then download or print the portion of the law in which you are interested.

LEGAL
ENCYCLOPEDIA

You should also be able to find sets of books called *legal encyclopedias* at a law library. These are similar to a regular encyclopedia, in that you look up the subject (such as "Custody" or "Divorce"), and it gives you a summary of the law on that subject, along with citations to court cases which relate to that subject. There are two national legal encyclopedias:

one is *American Jurisprudence* (abbreviated *Am.Jur.*), and the other is *Corpus Juris Secundum* (abbreviated *C.J.S.*). Many states also have their own encyclopedia, such as *Florida Jurisprudence* (*Fla.Jur.*) and *Texas Jurisprudence* (*Tex.Jur.*). Like the case reporters, these may also have a second series.

DIGESTS

Another type of book found in law libraries is called a *digest*. Like a legal encyclopedia, you look up the subject and instead of giving you a summary of the law, it gives you summaries of court cases discussing that subject of the law. Although a national digest exists, it involves a very time-consuming search. You should look for a digest that is specific for your state. For example, *California Digest*. Again, there may be a second series.

FORM AND PRACTICE MANUALS

All law libraries also have certain form and practice manuals that include the law, procedures, and forms used in your state. These can be most helpful in both preparing your forms and finding forms you may need that are not included in this book. Never hesitate to ask a reference librarian for assistance in finding the practice section for family law in your local legal library.

For more detailed information about conducting legal research, see the book *Legal Research Made Easy*, by Suzan Herskowitz, available at most bookstores or directly from Sphinx Publishing by calling 1-800-226-5291.

THE ROLE OF LAWYERS

Cases involving child custody, visitation, and support are considered *civil* cases (as distinguished from *criminal* cases). For many years, if a party wanted a lawyer in a civil case, the party would have to get and pay for one themselves. That is still often true today. In some cases, though, the effort to make parents responsible for child support has led to collection laws enforced by government attorneys. The issues of custody and visitation may also be decided as part of the process. Additionally, in cases where the parents have not married, the parentage of the child may first need to be established in order to proceed with the custody, visitation, and support issues. (See appendix A and later chapters on child support for more information.)

For most parents, cases involving the issues of child custody and visitation are filed by the parties without the assistance of a government attorney. In these cases, it is still up to the parties to decide whether or not they want to be represented by a lawyer. When choosing a lawyer, recognize that the law is a business as well as a profession. This usually means that if you want a lawyer to help you obtain custody or visitation or help you seek to establish or collect child support, you will usually have to pay for one. However, if you are without funds to pay for an attorney, a court may order the parent with the most financial resources to pay for the attorney's fees of the other parent. Be sure to discuss this issue with any lawyer you consider hiring. If the lawyer believes you may qualify, he or she will file the necessary papers to ask the judge to order the other party to pay for your lawyer.

As you are analyzing your options with a lawyer, the lawyer is likely to be evaluating your case. Lawyers decide whether to take cases based on a number of factors, which include not only the costs, time, and effort, but also their potential for collection of fees.

LAWYERS AND CONFIDENTIALITY

To encourage people to speak freely to their lawyers, the law provides confidentiality protection for clients. This is called the *attorney-client privilege*. This privilege prevents a lawyer from disclosing your information under most circumstances, so be honest in disclosing all the facts, even those facts about your marriage, your relationship with the other parent, or yourself which may be embarrassing or humiliating. The lawyer may need this information to properly evaluate the case and to effectively represent you.

FINDING A LAWYER

The search for a lawyer can take some time and perseverance. Just as other professions are becoming more specialized, it is becoming rarer today to find a lawyer that has a general practice. Make sure that the lawyer you choose has some kind of experience with child custody and support cases. Many lawyers limit their practice to *family law* cases, which include cases involving divorce, custody, visitation, and child support. Some states certify lawyers as specialists. For example, California qualifies certain lawyers as specialists in family law.

Recommendations from friends. Many times a lawyer is chosen on the strength of recommendations by family or friends. These recommendations can be helpful because the good experience of your family member or friend may provide reliable information on the quality of service provided by the lawyer.

Referral services. If you do not personally know a lawyer and do not have a recommendation from a trusted friend or family member, you can look to other sources. In most cities, there are organizations called *bar associations* to which many attorneys will belong. Many local or state bar associations offer a referral service.

Yellow Pages and other advertisements. You may also search for a lawyer by examining advertisements. Sometimes lawyers list their practice in the Yellow Pages of the phone book under "Lawyers" or "Attorneys." Some may advertise in newspapers, or even on billboards; or you may read about a lawyer's representation of another child custody, visitation, or support case in the newspaper or see something about it on television.

Prepaid legal plans. If you are a member of a prepaid legal plan, you may be covered for family law matters. Under such a plan, you may qualify for a certain number of options such as a certain amount of hours of consultation or services, a reduced payment fee for certain services, or coverage for certain basic services like an uncontested divorce.

Websites. Another place to search for a lawyer is on the Internet. Some lawyers now have web pages and list their services and contact information. Even if you do not have access to the Internet at home, many public libraries have Internet computers for use by library patrons.

Legal clinics. In cities with larger populations, there are often legal clinics which provide lower-cost legal representation in family law matters. Low-income persons may also qualify for free legal representation.

Law schools. Some law schools maintain clinical programs which take cases. Be sure to check with any local law schools to see if any programs exist and whether your case would be eligible for the service. If the clinic does accept your case, you fee may be waived or your payment may be based on a sliding fee scale according to your income level.

Attorney registration. Every state maintains a registration of lawyers who practice law within that state. To find the phone number and address of any lawyer within your state, contact the bar association or any other attorney registration office within your state.

INITIAL CONTACT

The selection of a lawyer usually begins with a phone call to the lawyer's office. In this first contact with the lawyer, be sure to ask some preliminary information questions. Write down the information as it is given to you. Some questions to ask are: Does this lawyer charge for a consultation? How long will the first meeting be? How much does the lawyer usually charge for his or her services? Compare the answers given by all the lawyers to whom you have spoken and then decide which one to meet with for an introductory consultation.

FIRST INTERVIEW

The first interview with a lawyer is very important. Remember that you have not agreed to anything other than the terms of the initial visit. Do not be intimidated by the thought of meeting with the lawyer. You are under no obligation to sign or agree to anything at this time, and you can take any written documents home to think about before you sign. Also, be sure to write down any information you obtain from the lawyer. It will help you remember who said what later.

Follow your instincts and trust your evaluation of the lawyer when you meet. Do you like this lawyer? Do you feel that he or she is listening to you? Does he or she appear to understand your situation? Are you treated with respect during your visit by the office staff? Your "gut" is the most reliable source in deciding whether you wish to proceed further with this lawyer.

In telling the lawyer about your case, be as clear and concise as possible. You will want to bring any relevant documents (see chapters 5 and 10) which will help the lawyer to understand the facts of your case. Discuss what the lawyer thinks the projected costs will be, how you will be billed for those costs, and what payment arrangements can be made.

FEE
ARRANGEMENTS

In most family law cases, attorneys charge hourly fees in addition to the expenses of the case. Most attorneys are expensive, charging more than $100 per hour, and may require a substantial initial payment (sometimes called a *retainer*) from you to begin the case.

If a retainer is to be paid, make sure that you and your lawyer agree what minimum services are to be provided for that sum. For example, for a retainer of $500 or more, the lawyer should at least prepare and file your case and have the initial papers (usually a petition or complaint and a summons) served on the other parent. What you want to avoid is a situation where you pay your lawyer a retainer, he or she writes a letter and makes a few phone calls to the other parent (or the parent's attorney), then tells you the retainer is used up and more money is required from you to continue your case.

In collection of past due child support, some states permit attorneys to charge a percentage of the judgment collected (usually one-third). If no monies are collected, no fees will be due (but you will still be responsible to pay for the expenses of filing the documents, photocopying, telephone charges, postage, transcript, reporter, and service fees).

However your fee is arranged, make sure that you have it in writing so that there will be no confusion as to what is and what is not included in the attorney's fee, what is owed, and when and how it should be paid.

WORKING WITH
THE LAWYER

Once you decide to hire the lawyer and the lawyer agrees to take the case, be sure to let the lawyer know what kind of client you are. How involved do you want to be in the case? Do you want to be informed of each step in the case? Would you like copies of each document the lawyer files or receives in your case? Realize that you may be expected to pay for photocopies. Alternatively, you may ask your lawyer to make the file available to you on a regular basis to view at his or her office to keep current with developments in your case.

Your lawyer should be able to take you through the case step-by-step to explain the procedures and anticipated timeline. Ask the lawyer how often you can expect him or her to contact you about your case. If you know the general timeline of your case, it will help you understand how often to expect contact from the lawyer. For example, once your documents are filed with the court, it may be at least thirty days before the other parent is required to file any response. Set up a method of contact that is convenient for you and reasonable for your lawyer.

Keep this in mind—many problems that arise between a client and lawyer in family law cases could easily be resolved by clear communications between the client and his or her lawyer.

Understanding Custody and Visitation 2

Historically, from as far back as early Roman times, children were seen as the property of their parents. In the United States, fathers held the rights to control their children until the mid-1800s. But as the country became more industrialized, a shift took place and until the middle part of this century, courts usually held that a mother was the most appropriate custodian for a child, especially a young child. This was called the *tender years doctrine*.

Today, many fathers successfully seek custody of their children because the emphasis is now on who is the best caretaker for the child. This is one reason why it is very important that the person seeking custody of a child has a history of full participation in the child's life. In many cases, the mother has been the primary caretaker for the child, so when a custody contest arises, a court may still award custody to the mother. For example, in one national study conducted in the 1980s, mothers were awarded custody more than seventy percent of the time, and fathers just under ten percent; while the parents shared custody about fifteen percent of the time. Others, such as grandparents, were awarded custody in the remaining cases. Since more fathers today share in primary caretaking responsibilities for their child, those figures have changed.

For example, while fathers are still in the minority as sole caretakers of their children, they have increased in numbers as the residential parent for their children over the past fifteen years. U.S. Census data shows that in 1985, father-child families doubled from 896,000 households to 1.8 million; while mother-child families went from 6 million to 7.6 million during the same period (U.S. Bureau of Census data, Dec. 11, 1998). Comparable numbers were seen in cases of divorce, in which the number of fathers who had sole residential parenting responsibilities tripled from 1980 to 1998—going from 503,000 to 1.4 million households—while the mothers' number increased around twenty percent during that same period, rising from 4.6 to 5.7 million (U.S. Bureau of Census data, released Jan. 7, 1999). In addition, in a study funded by the U.S. Department of Health and Human Services, evidence of parental participation and payment of child support was examined using one of the two major national demographic surveys funded by the Bureau of the Census. This survey determined that twenty percent of custodial parents (1.3 million) have a joint custody arrangement. (U.S. Department of Health and Human Services, *Noncustodial Parent's Participation in Their Children's Lives: Evidence from the Survey of Income and Program Participation*, 1997.)

Courts do not look with favor upon a parent who tries to use custody as a bargaining tool to obtain a better property settlement or to avoid alimony. A parent who files for custody to try to get a greater share of a property settlement may not be successful in getting either one. It is better and fairer, to the child and to the parents, that custody be valuated on what is in the best interests of the child. This is exactly what courts try to do.

WHAT ARE CUSTODY AND VISITATION?

TRADITIONAL
CUSTODY AND
VISITATION

The issue of who has custody of a child is determined by the laws of each state. The term *custody* means the right and responsibility to make decisions on behalf of a child, including those related to the child's health, education, and discipline. Traditionally, custody of a child has been granted to one parent called the *custodial* parent (who is usually the mother) with the *noncustodial* parent (usually the father) having certain visitation rights.

JOINT CUSTODY   In the 1970s, the notion that both parents should have more active roles and responsibilities in their child's life led to the development of the concept of *joint custody*. There are two types of joint custody:

1. Joint *legal* custody, in which parents share the control and responsibility for raising their child. They each have the right to participate in major decisionmaking about their child and they each have access to important records concerning their child (such as school and health records). A joint legal custody arrangement may (but does not have to) include the alternating of physical custody of the child between the parents.

2. Joint *physical* custody, in which the child lives alternately with each parent according to a *parenting schedule*. Most often, the daily decisions are made by the parent with whom the child is currently living, but major decisions (like religion, education, medical care, discipline, choice of school or camp) are jointly made.

When both parents equally share the legal and physical custody of the child, it is sometimes called *shared parenting*. Because of the degree of contact required between the parents, this type of arrangement works best where both parents are able to communicate well and are committed to resolving their differences for the sake of raising the child in a caring, nurturing environment.

SPLIT CUSTODY   The term *split custody* covers situations where there is more than one child and each parent has sole custody of at least one child with the visitation rights in the other parent. For example, the son may live with the dad and visit his mom and sister, while the daughter may live with the mom and visit her dad and brother.

WHO CAN GET CUSTODY?

MARRIED
PERSONS

Unless a court orders otherwise, when parents are married, both parents have custody. Both parents have the same rights and responsibilities to make decisions for the child.

UNWED
PARENTS

When the parents were never married, the issue of custody and visitation is determined by law. Parental rights must be determined before a person can assert them. Therefore, the legal father of the child must be recognized by law in a *paternity* or *parentage* case. In many states, where both parents agree, parental rights may be established by filing a document, typically called an *affidavit of paternity* or *acknowledgement of parentage*. Once this form is filed, paternity is established and custody and support may then be determined.

A man who the mother claims is the father is called an *alleged father* or a *putative father* until paternity is established. If the alleged father does not agree that he is the legitimate father, the mother may file a paternity complaint against the alleged father to ask a court to determine paternity after scientific tests (usually DNA tests) are performed and evaluated. If the father wishes to legitimize his interest in his child, but the mother does not agree, the father can also file a paternity complaint, and the same tests can be made to legally determine the question of fatherhood. See the examples of the forms used to establish paternity in appendix B and a blank form in appendix C.

UNFIT PARENTS

When parents cannot or will not properly care for the child, all states provide a procedure for another person (or the State) to get custody. This may or may not lead to adoption of a child. When a parent is determined to be unfit, the court can terminate parental rights. A termination of all parental rights and obligations includes custody, visitation, and support. While states differ in the specific factors required to be proven to terminate a parent's rights, the grounds generally include child abuse, neglect, or abandonment. For example, a child is brought into the emergency room of a hospital by a parent. Due to the nature of the child's injuries, and other circumstances, the emergency room physician in good faith reports a belief that the child has been abused to the state's child welfare agency. To protect the child, the agency takes emergency temporary custody. An investigation confirms that child abuse did take place and one of the parents was the abuser. The state then files a case in court against the parent to protect the child and to determine the parents' fitness. If the court finds that the child has been abused by a parent, the court has the power to take the necessary action to protect the child, which may include placing the child in foster care or with a suitable relative, ordering the parent into counselling or to take a parenting class, and even terminating all parental rights of that parent.

PSYCHOLOGICAL
PARENT

If a third person has established a parental bond with the child because the parent has died, has disappeared, or is not interested in raising the child, this third person is sometimes referred to as a *psychological parent.* A foster parent, for example, may become the child's psychological parent.

There are two schools of thought in deciding custody between a parent and a nonparent. Most states presume that it is best for a child to be in the custody of a parent, so unless the parent is unfit or unwilling, the parent is the preferred custodian. Some courts today, however, will look at which person would provide the best environment for the child. If a child has lived with another family member or a third person and has become integrated into that home, a court may grant custody to this psychological parent where the child's interests are best served by staying in the custody of that psychological parent.

GRANDPARENTS

Every state has passed laws concerning grandparent visitation. Also, in recent years, grandparents have sought and won custody judgments over the objection of a parent. For example, in an Alaskan case reported in 1998, grandparents who had raised two boys for three years were able to keep custody against a challenge by the natural father who had remarried. The Alaska Supreme Court found that the grandparents took the place of the mother, and the children's stability outweighed the father's interest in custody. [See, *C.R.B. v. C.C. and B.C.,* 959 P.2d 375 (Alaska, 1998).] For more information, see *Grandparents' Rights,* by

Traci Truly, available through your local bookstore, or directly from Sphinx Publishing by calling 1-800-226-5291.

OTHER PERSONS   In some states, stepparents or other persons may be entitled to visitation with the child. For example, stepparents are specifically granted the right to seek visitation by statutes in California (Cal. Family Code Ann., § 3101) and Wisconsin (W.S.A. § 767.245). Virginia allows not only stepparents, but also blood relatives or family members to seek visitation under certain circumstances [V.C.A. § 16.1-241(a)].

TAXES AND CUSTODY

The tax laws administered by the Internal Revenue Service govern the issue of taxes and custody. Currently, the parent with custody in a sole custody arrangement is entitled to the dependency exemption for a child. For joint custody arrangements, the exemption goes to the parent who has physical custody for the greater part of the year. In sole custody or joint custody cases, the exemption can be transferred to the other parent by agreement, and by filing a form with the IRS. Because the revenue rules change periodically, check with your local IRS office for the proper form and filing requirements.

THE LAW OF CUSTODY AND VISITATION 3

Courts will usually be guided by what is in the "best interests of the child" in determining custody and visitation. Most states have laws which list the relevant factors to be considered in deciding what is in the best interests of the child. These factors will be discussed in more detail below. In some cases, most of the factors will weigh in favor of one parent. Then, it is easy for the court to decide. However, where both parents are "fit and proper" persons to have custody of their child, a court will look carefully at the relevant factors. The fact that a court might find it to be in the best interests of a child to place custody with one parent does not necessarily mean that the other parent is not also a fit and proper parent; nevertheless, it does mean that the court has weighed the relevant factors and found that the weight of those factors favored one parent more than the other.

THE BEST INTERESTS OF THE CHILD

The "best interests" of the child include considering all of the parents' and child's wishes and the living circumstances that impact on the child's well-being. Many states define "best interests" in their state statutes or codes by listing the factors that will be considered. (See appendix A for a listing of state statutes and codes.)

Where parents contest custody, a judge weighs the various "best interest" factors to decide the matter. In considering the issue of custody/visitation, courts are guided by the overriding principle that a child should be raised in a stable environment with a parent who can put the child's best interest ahead of their own when the two conflict.

Generally, the relevant topics and questions that are asked in the examination of the best interests of a child include:

LOVE AND
AFFECTION

The relationship that exists between the parents and their child is one of the most important factors in determining what is in the best interests of that child. Courts want to know how a parent and child interact with one another. When the child is happy or has a problem, to whom does the child go? What has the child said on this topic? In considering the child's opinion, courts consider the child's age and maturity, reason for their desire, existence of external pressure (to say or do one thing or another for one parent or against the other), and whether the child changes his or her mind (and if so, why?).

PARENTAL CARE

Parental care relates to which parent can more adequately undertake the upbringing and homemaking responsibilities for a child on a daily basis. Who spends more hours per day with the child? Who cooks the meals? If it is a young child, who bathes and dresses the child? Who stays home from work when the child is sick? Who takes responsibility for involvement in school, and who helps to complete homework assignments when needed? Who goes to the school conferences? Who attends school events? How does the child get to and from school activities? Who takes responsibility for involvement in after-school activities? Who is responsible for the child's religious education (if any)? Who makes the doctor and dentist appointments and who takes the child to these appointments? Who is responsible for setting up and maintaining child care arrangements?

OTHER
RELATIONSHIPS

A court will also look at the significant relationships in the child's life. Are there brothers or sisters who will be affected by the custody decision? Children often wish to stay together, and the impact of any separation on them will be reviewed carefully. Also, are there new relationships in the parents' lives that will affect the child?

ECONOMIC RESOURCES

Although courts do consider resources and economic issues, they are careful not to give too much consideration to the parent with the most assets in determining the best interests of a child. This is because both parents have a duty to support the child, so this factor can be equalized by child support, regardless of who has custody. This topic considers who pays for the child's food, clothing, medical care, or other basic needs. Who has greater earning capacity? Who has a greater likelihood of future income? Who carries (or has the ability to obtain) insurance for the child?

GUIDANCE AND DISCIPLINE

When analyzing the issue of guidance and discipline, the court with which parent provides the necessary correction for the child. The questions that are asked are such as: In what manner is the child corrected? Who disciplines the child? Under what circumstances is the child disciplined and how is the discipline done or handled? How do the parents view each other's choice of corrective methods? Does each parent have the ability to separate the child's needs from his or her own needs? How does each parent empathize with the child?

STABILITY AND PERMANENCE

Stability is one of the most important factors in determining best interests. Questions in this topic include: Who has more flexibility to adjust working hours if needed to care for the child? Who has access to extended family? Greater access to grandparents, family members, or friends who can provide care for the child is important in the issue of stability. In the area of permanence, the court examines the length of time the child has lived in a satisfactory environment and whether that should be continued. Who can provide continuity?

SECURITY

Courts are very concerned with the safety of a child's environment. In examining what is in the child's best interest, the court will examine each parent's past and present conduct as it relates to the child's security. Who can provide a safe environment? Has there been any verbal abuse? Does a parent have a substance abuse problem? Has a parent been arrested or convicted of a crime?

Domestic violence, whether directed at the child or witnessed by the child, is an important security issue. Have there been incidents of violence in the home? Were police called? Are there any threats of kidnaping? Has a parent ever failed to produce a child for visitation? Has a parent failed to appear for visitation? Was anyone notified? Has the parent ever interfered in visitation or failed to return the child at the scheduled time?

MORAL FITNESS

The consideration of moral fitness has been somewhat narrowed over the last several years, but the moral fitness of the parents as it relates to how they will function as parents remains important. Moral fitness sometimes overlaps with the topic of security. Covered in this category are questions of verbal and substance abuse, abuse of the child, and other illegal conduct. Also, offensive behaviors, such as a parent's questionable ethics or antisocial behavior, will be scrutinized to determine the impact on the child.

MENTAL AND PHYSICAL HEALTH

Physical or mental health problems that significantly interfere with the child's health and well being are relevant in determining what is in the best interests of a child. How does the parent respond if a child needs special care? In addition, courts will examine the parents' health. Does either parent smoke, or use drugs or alcohol? Do they have physical or mental ailments? How will these affect the child?

COOPERATION

The willingness of a parent to cooperate is extremely important to a court in deciding what is in the best interests of a child. Alienating a child from the other parent is usually viewed negatively in considering what is in the best interest of the child. Courts will also consider how conflicts have been resolved in the past. What are the parents willing to do to encourage a continuing relationship with each parent? Who is most likely to facilitate a good relationship for the child with both parents?

STATUTORY
CUSTODY
FACTORS

Many states' laws list the following relevant factors in deciding custody:

☞ The wishes of the child's parent or parents as to custody

☞ The wishes of the child as to his or her custodian

☞ The interaction and interrelationship of the child with his or her parent or parents, siblings, and any other significant person in the child's life

☞ The child's adjustment to home, school, and community

☞ The mental and physical health of all the parties

☞ Threats or violence against, or witnessed by, the child

☞ The ability of the parents to cooperate

☞ The residential circumstances of the parents

In addition, states may, through their individual laws or court opinions, consider other factors, such as:

☞ Interference with the other parent's relationship with the child

☞ Attempting to change the child's name

☞ Wealth of the parents, work history, or failure to pay child support

☞ Work patterns of parents

☞ Integration of child into parent's family unit

☞ Age, sex, and religious considerations of the parties

☞ Cohabitation or lifestyle issues

DESIRES OF THE
CHILD AND
PARENTS

The wishes of the parents are given considerable weight in determining custody. But these wishes are also weighed against whether they are in the best interest of the child. For example, a parent who wants custody to punish the other parent or because they "deserve" it, will not have their wishes given much weight.

Courts will also consider the wishes of the child. However, while younger children may be asked for their preference, their answers will be weighed against their age, growth, and development. For example, an eight year-old's desire to live with mom instead of dad because mom lets him stay up later on school nights will not be given much weight where other factors are equal. In most states, once the child reaches the age of twelve to fourteen, his or her preference as to the custodial parent will be given greater consideration.

In cases where there is more than one child, each child may express a different preference. While the law generally prefers to keep the children together, it does recognize that there are situations in which it is appropriate to separate the children. These cases may result in a form of *split custody*, where each parent has sole custody of at least one child, with visitation rights to the other. Split custody cases most often arise where one or more of the children are teenagers. For example, in a case where two brothers cannot get along, if the older one expresses a strong desire to live with his father, the court might order split custody, with the boys spending weekends together.

Keep in mind, though, that the preferences of parents and the child are not binding on the court. Generally, the weight to be given the parents' preferences, whether to consider a child's wishes, and what weight to give those wishes, are matters left to the discretion of a trial court judge. Sometimes, courts have said they give little weight to a younger child's desires because the child was not old enough to express a real preference.

ENVIRONMENT   One of the most important factors in deciding what is in the best interests of a child is the child's adjustment to home, school, and his or her environment. Courts are reluctant to disrupt a child's daily living activities involving school and friends. It is important to provide consistency in living conditions especially where young children are concerned.

Integration of the child into the home life of a parent is a critical factor in determining custody. This is one of the reasons why the status quo is so important. If, at the time of separation, one parent keeps the child in the home, the child can continue in the same school and with the same friends. A court will weigh this heavily. It favors the determination that a child has become a part of that home. The court will also be less inclined to disrupt the child's living circumstance.

Environmental concerns also involve the living conditions for a child. For example, in one case, photographs demonstrating serious sloppiness in a mother's housekeeping were considered by a court in deciding against joint custody. In another case, a father who was a doctor with a busy practice lost custody on appeal because the mother who did not work outside the home had a great deal more time to spend with the child. In this case, the father proposed to hire a babysitter when he was not present, but the court did not believe this was an acceptable alternative to the care of the other parent. The moral of this case is that no one is superman or superwoman, and the effort to create a healthy environment for a child is extremely important in determining the best interests of a child.

LOCATION

The proposed location of the child's home is important in considering custody or visitation. The parents can be restricted from moving to a distant location under the terms of a custody or visitation agreement or by court order. For example, a custodial parent may be restricted from moving to a location more than twenty-five miles from his or her present home. One (or both) parents may also be ordered to pay for transporting the child to and from one home to the other.

RELIGION

The parent with custody is usually the person who has control over the religious upbringing of a child. Because the First Amendment guarantees religious freedom, the particular religion will only be a factor if the religious practices cause physical, emotional, or mental harm to a child. For example, if the demands of a certain religion interfere with the child's educational activities, a court might consider the effects of that religion on the child.

ETHNIC, CULTURAL, MORAL, AND LIFESTYLE ISSUES

Ethnic, cultural, moral, and lifestyle issues can be raised in a custody proceeding, but they will only be relevant to the extent that they have an impact on the child. As the Supreme Court of Michigan explained:

> [moral fitness], like all the other statutory factors, relates to a person's fitness as a parent. To evaluate parental fitness, courts must look to the parent child relationship and the effect that

the conduct at issue will have on that relationship. Thus, the question...is not "who is the morally superior adult"; the question concerns the parties' relatives fitness to provide for their child, given the moral disposition of each party as demonstrated by individual conduct. We hold that in making that finding, questionable conduct is relevant...only if is a type of conduct that necessarily has a significant influence on how one will function as a parent.—*Fletcher v Fletcher*, 447 Mich. 871 (1994).

Years ago, a mother who lived with her new boyfriend (or a father who lived with his new girlfriend) might face a loss of custody. Today, that fact alone is usually not enough to establish a reason to deny custody. Instead, the court will look at the totality of the circumstances to determine whether and how the living arrangements affect the best interest of the child. Sexual activity outside the presence of the child is also often viewed to be irrelevant to the question of custody or visitation. For example, as the Supreme Court of Michigan has explained, in the *Fletcher* case quoted above, extramarital conduct of which the children are unaware does not affect the person's fitness as a parent.

Although lifestyle will rarely be the sole factor by which morality is judged, a parent's gay or lesbian lifestyle has sometimes been used to deny custody to a parent or to influence a decision about visitation. However, in many states, this question, like any issue of a parent's intimate relationship, will be examined for how it impacts the child's best interests. That is, if the child is not endangered or harmed by the relationship, the court will not likely see the relationship as a factor in its decisionmaking. But there are cases where the new boyfriend/girlfriend is given freedom by the parent to discipline the child, and courts have not looked positively on this aspect of such a relationship.

If the parents come from different cultural or ethnic backgrounds, a court will examine this difference strictly to determine what impact it would have on the child to live in each society.

RACE

The United States Supreme Court ruled in *Palmore v. Sidoti*, 466 U.S.429 (1984), that the race of the parent or child may not be a basis for deciding custody.

NAME CHANGE

Changing, or attempting to change, a child's name can be scrutinized by a court in determining custody. Some courts recognize that a change of a child's surname can contribute to a loss of relationship between the father and child. As one court has said: "A change of name imposed upon a child could represent to him a rejection by his father; or evidence that his father is deserving of rejection or contempt...or a statement by his mother and stepfather that his true identity is a shame and embarrassment to them and others. Such consequences could be enormously harmful to the child." *Mullins v. Mullins*, 490 N.E.2d 1375 (Ill.App.1986).

A mother, for example, who simply uses her new husband's name when registering a child for school or listing the child's name for activities, can be harming her case for custody. Some courts view such behavior, especially where there are other indications, as part of a scheme to deprive the father of his relationship with the child.

Other courts have allowed a child's application for a name change for more appropriate reasons. For example, where the reasons were that a change to the stepfather's surname would give the child the same last name as her stepbrothers who attended the same school, the child expressed a love for her stepfather, but did not want to disassociate herself from her father, and there was no misconduct by either the parents or the stepfather regarding the change, the court granted the name change even though the father opposed the change and had consistently paid child support.

MISCONDUCT BY THE PARENT

The impact of misconduct by a parent on a child is an important factor in determining custody or visitation. Many types of misconduct have been considered by courts in determining what is in the best interests of a child, such as: verbal abuse, drinking problems, lying about the parent's past alcohol abuse problems, a bad driving record, an arrest record, permitting a son to drink from the parent's beer, physical or sexual abuse of children, and other illegal or offensive behaviors. The list of misconduct is as long as the ways in which parents have engaged in negative or criminal behavior.

A parent who seeks custody or visitation should be aware that the failure to pay child support may be considered negatively on the question of custody or visitation.

Punishing a parent is not the goal of a court in determining custody or visitation. Nonetheless, substance or alcohol abuse is treated more seriously by today's courts. The problem will be considered and may operate to deprive a parent of custody or visitation unless the parent can show that he or she has sought and received treatment and has overcome the negative impact on their child.

Additional issues relating to kidnaping, domestic violence, child abuse, and interference with visitation are considered in chapter 6.

FACTORS IN DECIDING VISITATION

Ordinarily, unless there are compelling reasons otherwise, where one parent is granted custody, the other will be given visitation (although the terms used may vary from state-to-state). This is because the goal of a custody/visitation proceeding is to maintain as much of the child's relationship with each parent as possible.

In deciding whether to grant visitation, courts again look to what is in the best interests of the child. For example, a history of cruelty to a child may result in a denial or significant limitation of visitation. Other negative factors include substance abuse and the inability to properly care for a child. Even in these cases, however, courts are loathe to deny visitation entirely and may instead provide that visitation will take place under the supervision of a neutral third person. This permits the child to continue the relationship with the parent but is designed to minimize the child's exposure to the negative parental behavior.

In granting visitation, there is no set rule on how much visitation to grant. How often the visitation will occur, and under what circumstances, depends on the particular circumstances of the parents and child. Nonetheless, to avoid problems of enforcing "reasonable" visitation rights in working out a plan for visitation, it is usually best to specify the visitation details: length, frequency, location, notice of missed visitation, etc. (See the sample visitation language in chapter 4 and the sample agreements in appendix B.)

GEOGRAPHIC
LOCATION

A court may limit the geographical area where the visiting parent may take the child. This may happen when there is a real fear that the parent may take the child away from the court's jurisdiction. Of course, when one parent resides out of state, a court will normally not deny the visitation in the out of state location but may require that parent to pay an amount of money to the court to be held until the child is returned to the state.

GRANDPARENT
VISITATION

In the past, grandparents have not had any right to visit their grandchildren, but legislatures and courts began to increasingly recognize the importance of this relationship for the child. Today, the laws of every state provide for some level of grandparent visitation when it is in the best interests of the child to do so. (However, as this book goes to press, this type of grandparent visitation law is being challenged in the United States Supreme Court.) Some states also allow other third parties, such as aunts and uncles, to file for visitation under certain limited circumstances. (For more information, see *Grandparents' Rights*, by Traci Truly, available through your local bookstore, or directly from Sphinx Publishing by calling 1-800-226-5291.)

STEP-PARENT OR
NONPARENTS

In determining whether to grant visitation and how it should be exercised, courts look first to the language of their own statutes for guidance. For example, a stepparent who parented the child for a substantial period during the parent's second marriage may seek visitation when that second marriage ends because there is a long-term and substantial relationship with the child. If the state permits such a request, some visitation right may be granted so that the child can continue his or her relationship with this important parent-figure.

AGREEMENT TO GIVE UP VISITATION TO AVOID CHILD SUPPORT

One parent's agreement to give up visitation in exchange for an agreement by the other parent not to seek child support is void, and it will not be enforced in the courts. This is because a parent cannot excuse the other parent from the obligation to pay child support. (For more information, see the child support chapters in this book.)

Custody and Visitation Agreements 4

Children often suffer when they are the subject of protracted custody disputes. Lengthy proceedings are also emotionally and financially taxing to the parents. Where the parents can agree on custody, it reduces the toll that these proceedings take on the child and encourages the parents to cooperate in raising their child. Parents who agree on the terms of a custody arrangement are also more likely to abide by the custody order. The agreement can operate to reduce later conflict between the parents. Finally, expenses saved on the litigation costs can be used more productively towards family expenses.

While a court is not required to accept the parents' agreement concerning custody and visitation, it usually will if the agreement is reasonable and not contrary to the best interests of the child.

Without an agreement, it is up to the judge to make the ultimate decision about what is in the best interest of the child. The risk, of course, is that the judge's decision may be based on the preferences of the judge instead of the desires of the parents. For example, in a 1996 study on judicial attitudes in custody decisionmaking, it was determined that judges preferred an arrangement where the child spent the school year with one parent and had summer vacation with the other. Thus, leaving the decision of custody up to the preference of a judge may not reflect what you as the parents, who have the greatest investment in the future welfare of your child, believe to be in the best interests of your child.

WHAT ARE YOUR OPTIONS?

THINK ABOUT
YOUR REASONS

Now that you understand something about the laws governing custody and visitation, you can begin to think about your options. As a preliminary matter, you should ask and answer the question: "What do I want?"

Upon first reflection, you might answer, "To win sole custody, of course!" But, such a "win" will cause you increased financial, physical, and emotional responsibilities. You will not be able to just leave and go out anytime. Being a child's sole caretaker means that you make all the decisions—the easy ones, the hard ones, and the scary ones—by yourself. This includes arranging all the details for the child's care if you travel, or any time you simply need free time for yourself.

On the other hand, you might think, "Well, I want to have the best of it—to visit the child whenever I want and have few or no burdens of childraising." But, without actively participating in your child's life, you may become little more than another "playmate," or simply a source of money or entertainment—buying your child instead of parenting him or her. And, whether you have custody or visitation, you will still have a duty to support your child.

At some point, you must ultimately consider whether you could both parent your children even with all the negatives? And, if so, do you both want to do so?

CONSIDER THE
POSSIBILITIES

What would work best for you, individually, considering your finances, schedule, work or school habits, or needs? What is in your best interest? If you had sole custody, how would it work with your lifestyle? What if the other parent had sole custody? How would you fit into that picture? What if you both shared custody? What would this require? How could it work? Finally, and most importantly, begin to focus on what kind of arrangement would be in your child's best interest.

Talk to the Other Parent

Once you have really thought about these issues, talk to the other parent if possible. It may not be an easy thing to do at first because relationship issues may get in the way, but if both parents desire to continue their relationship with the child, it is important to talk about those relationships whenever possible.

Sometimes it helps to meet in a public place, like a park or a restaurant, to avoid "turf" issues. Agree to keep the topic of discussion focused on your child. This will help reduce your personal conflicts. Keep in mind that, just like separation is a process, reshaping your relationships with your child is also a process. Recognize that it may take several discussions or meetings before you start shaping a plan for the future care of your child.

Try to begin the first meeting by recognizing that both of you are good parents and both of you need to think about what would be best for your child. Agree that each of you will not simply show up and announce, "I want custody" or "I am entitled to support." Such ultimatums are likely to lead to immediate disagreement and don't leave much room for anything other than bargaining for a position.

Brainstorm the Alternatives

It is easier if you can start by discussing the various alternatives without taking positions. This should be a session of *brainstorming*, where you put all the possibilities down on paper without making any argument for or against any of them. Agree to both consider all of the options on the paper and set a time to meet again to discuss those options.

For example some possible options are:

- ☛ Sole custody to Mom; child visits Dad
- ☛ Sole custody to Dad; child visits Mom
- ☛ Joint legal custody; child primarily lives with Mom, but sometimes stays with Dad

☛ Joint legal custody; child primarily lives with Dad, but sometimes stays with Mom

☛ Joint legal and physical custody; child lives part time with Mom and part time with Dad

☛ Split custody (if more than one child); Child X lives with Mom and Child Y lives with Dad (or Child X lives with Dad and Child Y lives with Mom)

The various matters to consider include:

☛ What kind of custody you want

☛ The needs of your child (age, medical, school)

☛ Your own needs (age, health, work/school schedules)

☛ Who has the most resources and support (babysitters, daycare)

☛ Who will make major decisions and how

☛ Who will be responsible for the child's religious training

☛ How much education will you expect the child to receive

☛ The last name of the child

☛ What to do if you or the other parent moves

☛ How to resolve disagreements (mediation)

☛ What happens if one person violates the agreement

Use the Custody and Visitation Checklist on pages 50 and 51 to help you in formulating your agreement. In the relevant spaces, fill in the information and preferences for each topic.

At the next meeting, assess the options. If some are unacceptable to both of you, delete them. This begins to narrow down the acceptable choices. Now begin to examine the pros and cons of the choices that are left. Make any necessary changes to the choices.

For those choices that are unacceptable to one parent, examine whether there are modifications which would make a choice acceptable to both of you. You need to realize that it is unlikely that you both will be able to agree on all the necessary points at one sitting. Disagreements over issues are common, but they can be the subject of agreement if both parents are willing to compromise and place their child's best interest over all others. Keep in mind that each point you can agree upon is a sign of progress towards your final custody arrangement. Once you both agree to the major points, you can continue to work out the details of remaining points of disagreement. Finally, remember that both of you are the persons with the greatest investment in your child's future.

TRYOUT PERIOD

If you are able to come to some informal arrangement, it is suggested that you both try it out for a while to see how it works. Maybe a month or so will allow you to "work out the kinks" before you look to put your agreement into writing for your court case.

While in this tryout period, log the daily activities that you do with your child. Keep track in the log of how the arrangement worked—what parts of it went well, what parts need to be improved, and how they need to be improved. Document the days and times that need adjustment. If it is feasible, make these adjustments and try it out again for a short period.

Trying it out will hopefully reduce the stress on the child and on yourselves. Agree to meet after the tryout period to make any necessary changes to improve the arrangement.

YOUR AGREEMENT IS UNIQUE

No two families are exactly alike, so no two custody solutions need be exactly the same. While some issues are guided or directed by law, much room for flexibility exists in this area to permit parents to fashion the remainder of their relationship with their minor child in a way that fits their lifestyle. Despite the deterioration of your marriage or relationship, some level of mutual respect for one another as the parent of your child will go far to help a child become a complete adult. Because that is what child custody is all about—raising a physically, mentally, and behaviorally well-cared for child.

FORMULATING AN AGREEMENT

Custody and visitation agreements may be very short documents or very long and detailed depending on the parents' personalities and desires. Most agreements fall somewhere in between. It is also true that the less cooperation between the parents, the more detailed the agreement should be to avoid "interpretation" problems. Ideally, a custody/visitation agreement should be detailed enough to avoid complaints, but flexible enough to accommodate inevitable changes over the course of several years. Remember that once the agreement is included in a court judgment, it becomes binding until you return to court and get it modified unless you provide otherwise. For a sample completed custody and visitation agreement, see the Parenting Plan (form L) in appendix B. To create your own Parenting Plan, see forms 17 and 18 in appendix C.

AGREEMENT TO COOPERATE

An *agreement to cooperate* provision is a general statement of the intent of you and the other parent to cooperate for the benefit of your child. It is not a formal requirement that you or the other parent do something but serves as a reminder to both of you that your primary concern should be your child.

CUSTODY

The custody provision describes the custody arrangement, usually in the terms used in your state's law. Depending upon the state, there may be a distinction between *legal* (or decisionmaking) custody and *physical* custody (regarding where the child lives a majority of the time). Also, the terminology used may vary by state. For example, Florida law refers to *parental responsibility* and *primary residence*; whereas Texas law refers to *managing conservatorship*.

VISITATION

In the past, many agreements or court orders referred simply to *reasonable* visitation. Although this option is presented in the Parenting Plan forms in appendix C, to limit disagreements about what is *reasonable*. In working out your arrangement, you should consider including specific visitation information. Another option in the Parenting Plan forms in appendix C refers to visitation considering the *convenience* of all the parties. But, what exactly does *convenience* mean? Ask a few people and you will get a few different answers. That is why most agreements should provide a greater level of detail. Consider:

☛ When can the parent visit? Which days, holidays, or vacation times are best?

☛ What should the frequency of visitation be (every weekend, every other weekend)?

☛ How will you handle visitation for summer vacations, Christmas vacations, spring vacations, and holidays?

☛ What holidays and other special occasions are to be included? Typical days of importance include: New Year's eve and New Year's Day, Good Friday, Passover, Easter, Memorial Day weekend, July Fourth weekend, Rosh Hashanah, Yom Kippur, Thanksgiving, the child's and parents' birthdays, Mother's Day, Father's Day, school holidays, and any other days of significance within your family (e.g., anniversaries, grandparents' birthdays, etc.).

☛ What times should the child be picked up and returned?

☛ Who is responsible for bringing the child and returning the child from the visitation location, and who pays the transportation costs?

The possibilities are as varied as are the schedules and geographic factors of the parents. For example, parents who live around the corner from one another may share significant time with the child; but for a parent who lives in another city or state, visitation will need to be more limited.

A drafting tip: Put each of these visitation sections in its own paragraph, identified by a number or letter. That way, any disagreements will be easier to resolve because the issue can be narrowed to a specific, identifiable section of the visitation agreement.

EDUCATION   Your agreement should include provisions relating to your child's education. You may agree to send your child to public or private school. You may also cover the issues of a change of school or special classes.

Decisions regarding continuing education after high school may also be addressed.

NOTICES AND INFORMATION

There are various types of notices and information from schools, health care providers, and others that are normally provided, or available, to parents regarding their children. These include such things as report cards, test results, school field trip information and permission slips, reminders of doctor and dental appointments, and medical records. When one parent has custody, such information is typically sent, or made available, to that parent. You may agree that such information will be given by the parent who normally receives it to the other parent, or that each parent will have direct access to the information. You should consider:

☛ Who should be contacted if the child gets sick or has a serious illness or injury?

☛ Who should have access to the child's medical records?

☛ Who should have access to information about the child's progress at school?

CONTACTING THE OTHER PARENT

Obviously, it is extremely important that parents share information about how they can be contacted by each other. Your agreement may include a provision that you will each keep the other informed of any changes in address or telephone numbers.

TRAVEL

Many families include travel in their vacation plans, and the custody/visitation agreement should cover this issue also. Consider:

☛ May the parent with custody or the visiting parent take the child on trips?

☛ If so, for how long?

☛ During what periods of time?

☛ To what destinations? Out of state? Out of the country? To certain foreign countries, but not others?

☛ What type and amount of advance of notice must be given to the other parent?

☛ If the parent with custody takes the child on a trip, and it interferes with visitation, or if the visiting parent takes the child on a trip and it interferes with the other parent's time with the child, how will this be handled? (Make up time?)

CHANGES IN VISITATION SCHEDULE
Some degree of flexibility should be built into the visitation schedule because it is common that some changes will occasionally need to take place. Special events or emergencies can occur that may make a change desirable or necessary. Consider:

☛ If the visiting parent wants to change the time or day of visitation, how much notice should be given and how will it be communicated? (Phone call, email, etc.)

☛ How much advance notice should be given if additional visiting time is desired?

☛ How much advance notice should be given if the visiting parent will not be able to visit as scheduled?

☛ What happens if the visiting parent does not visit as agreed?

MOVING
Moving is a common occurrence in our highly mobile world. The laws and rules regarding moving vary from state to state. States have the power to regulate relocation, either by statute—as in Illinois, Massachusetts, and New Jersey—or through their inherent power over the parents. Some states, like Colorado and Florida, generally permit relocation if the planned move is in the best interests of the child; but others, like New York, require a parent to show exceptional circumstances to permit a move. More recently, more states are willing to look at all the circumstances presented by the proposed move to see whether it is in the best interests of the child. Most often, agreements address this issue and place a restriction on moving. In some states, any agreement (which is incorporated into the order or judgment) must contain a provision that the child shall not be removed from the state unless by agreement of the parties or with the approval of a judge. Thus, you must consider what happens if a parent wishes to move.

In evaluating a proposed relocation plan, you might consider:

☞ Is the move in the best interests of the child?

☞ What is the motive?

☞ Will the out-of-state custodial parent be likely to comply with the visitation order?

☞ Will this visitation be adequate to foster a continuing meaningful relationship between the children and the noncustodial parent?

☞ What is the cost of transportation? Who will pay it?

RESOLVING
DISPUTES

Sadly, violations of custody/visitation agreements are common. This partly stems from the acrimony that sometimes accompanies the entry of the original custody/visitation order, or a belief by the "wronged" party that their rights are being abridged. This party may feel justified in retaliatory violations to the point where violations become the defining behavior of the agreement.

There are many reasons for not going back to see a judge every time you and your spouse have a dispute regarding visitation. Going to court can be expensive and time-consuming; and it can take some time to get a hearing scheduled. Therefore, you may want to put a provision in your agreement to attempt to resolve problems through some type of *alternative dispute resolution*. Examples of alternative dispute resolution are seeing a counselor or going through *mediation*, which is where a trained, neutral third party tries to help you and the other parent work out a settlement. Although not every problem should be the subject of alternative dispute resolution, you can agree to use this much less expensive alternative to try to settle any disagreements that may arise.

The question of how to resolve these problems, and how the costs of alternative dispute resolution will be paid, may be addressed in the custody/visitation agreement. If alternative dispute resolution does not work or is not suitable for the problem, there are still court proceedings available to enforce or change the agreement if necessary.

VISITATION WITH FAMILY MEMBERS AND OTHERS

All states provide some rights of visitation to grandparents, and some states grant other persons visitation rights. If you agree that another family member (or anyone else) should have visitation with your child, it should be specifically stated in your agreement.

JOINT CUSTODY

Joint custody arrangements became popular in the 1970s. At the beginning, it was thought that this would be the solution to contested custody cases. But, in the years that followed, it became clear that joint custody is not the best alternative for every case because it requires both parents to be willing to compromise self-interest for the the best interest of the child.

Joint custody requires extensive contact and intensive communication between parents. It does not work well in situations where the parties have a lot of hostility or manipulate the child for their own ends. Because of this, some states have strict statutory guidelines which must be met for a joint custody order. Also, in some states, before a court can grant joint custody, the parties must have agreed, in writing, to the terms of the joint custody (sometimes called a *joint parenting agreement*).

JOINT CUSTODY FACTORS

If you are considering joint custody, you should evaluate:

☛ Whether you believe joint custody would be the best choice

☛ Whether you can communicate well with each other

☛ Whether you agree to share decisionmaking

☛ Whether you both live reasonably close to each other in order to avoid disrupting your child's school, home, and friends

☛ Whether both of your home environments make it easy to take your child back and forth

☛ Whether your work schedules and routines accommodate your child's needs

☛ How your child feels about joint custody

JOINT PARENTING AGREEMENTS

A joint parenting agreement is basically the same as a custody/visitation agreement except that it has some provisions which are unique to the joint custody situation. For example, a joint parenting agreement will have the same types of provisions that were discussed in the previous section of this chapter. The following are some comments on matters that should be included in a joint parenting agreement:

AGREEMENT TO COOPERATE

The *agreement to cooperate* provision discussed earlier in this chapter should also be included in any joint custody arrangement. In addition, it is common to see more than one paragraph which expresses a desire to work together for the benefit of the child.

PARENTING TIME

Even though the joint parenting agreement forges a high degree of cooperation, it is still important to set forth the time that each parent will be responsible for their child. Like an agreement for custody and visitation, the parents should set out provisions for where the child will be on holidays, significant days, and vacations to avoid a potential disagreement. The main difference is that you will replace the terms *custody* and *visitation* with another terms, such as *parenting time*. It is also important to address for what each parent is responsible (activities, issues, checkups, etc.) during the time that the child lives with them and during the transition times.

LOCATION OF PARENTS' RESIDENCES

For a joint parenting arrangement (where the child spends significant time with each parent) to really work, it is ideal if the parents live in close proximity to one another. It is common to agree to a geographic distance within which they will live while the child grows. A paragraph on this topic would set forth why this is important and exactly what the parties agree is the maximum distance.

MOVING

If a parent desires to move during the term of the agreement, the parties would have to renegotiate the terms of the joint custody agreement to where each saw the child frequently because close proximity is such a big part of the agreement. To do this, the parents could work out another joint parenting agreement or a sole custody/visitation arrangement and file the modification with the court for approval. (See chapter 7 on modification of custody and visitation orders.)

REMARRIAGE

The joint parenting agreement will be designed to be effective regardless of the remarriage of one of the parents. It is helpful, though, to place such a paragraph into your agreement in order to clarify that you both recognize this.

DISPUTE RESOLUTION

Recent studies show that when parties with joint parenting agreements work out their differences without having to turn to a court, they express a much greater overall satisfaction with the agreement and are more willing to follow it. Perhaps this is because, while we can't always get what we want, we can always listen to the other person and be heard ourselves. This is the function of mediation—keeping the lines of communication open. Remember, the parenting responsibility that you both have agreed to share will last throughout your child's youth.

What Is in the Best Interests of Your Child?
Checklist of Factors to Consider

TOPIC	MOTHER	FATHER

Time spent with a parent (before and after separation)
     Hours per day?
     How is time spent?
     How is substitute care arranged?		

Parental care
     Meals: purchase/preparation?
     Clothing purchase/dressing of child?
     School-related (conferences, transportation)?
     Child's outside activities?
     Medical & dental care?
     Child's special needs?
     Who works outside the home?
     Who can adjust work if child is sick or needy?		

Discipline
     Who is responsible?
     Kind of discipline used?		

Love and affection between parent and child
     How is love shown?
     Child more affectionate with?
     Child's preference?		

Guidance
     Who is more likely to provide?
     Who does child go to for help?
     Who does child tell of successes?
     Child's home and school performance while
         under guidance of parent?		

TOPIC	MOTHER	FATHER

Security
    Who can provide safe environment for child?
    Mental and physical health
    Abuse of child or other parent
    Substance abuse
    Arrest record
    Driving record
    General fitness of parent		

Stability
    Who can put child's needs ahead of their own?
    Who is more cooperative?
    Who has access to extended family support?
    How long has parent lived in residence?
    Past pattern of moves?
    Future intent to move?		

Permanence
    Who has greater earnings?
    Capacity for future earnings?
    Who provides insurance for child?
    Ages
    If there has been a trial period, how have parties handled:
        transportation
        visitation		

Other relationships that have an impact on the child
    with adults
    with other children		

THE CUSTODY OR VISITATION CASE 5

Now that you have considered your options, and possibly began working out an arrangement, you are ready to start the process of filing for custody or visitation. You may be filing for custody or visitation as part of your divorce case or as an independent case. The forms in appendix C will be helpful. The explanations in this chapter provide information on the custody/visitation portions of the case. Later chapters on child support will explain the support sections of your case.

This chapter is designed to make you an informed participant in the legal system in the area of child custody and visitation. But, if you are not able to communicate with the other parent, and you believe that the other parent will contest custody, you are well-advised to seek a consultation with a lawyer before you proceed in court. (The role of the lawyer was discussed in chapter 1.) Like any other resource, a legal professional can help you sort through your state's specific laws and nuances, so that you can proceed with the best information available.

PREPARATION FOR YOUR CASE

Once you have considered your options and, where appropriate, discussed them with the other parent, you are ready to begin preparing your case. Even if you and the other parent have agreed to all of the terms regarding custody and visitation, you will still need to gather certain information to put into the documents you must eventually file with the court. If you have not agreed, or believe you may not be able to agree, this information and the documents discussed below will be essential for you to prove your case.

In preparing to file your custody or visitation case, you must gather certain information about yourself, your child, and the other parent. Because the issues of custody and visitation are bound together with the issue of child support, much of the information and documents you will need are financial in nature. The financial information you will need to gather is discussed in detail in chapter 10. The sections below describe the non-financial areas in which you will need to collect information while preparing your case.

PARENTAL INFORMATION

In addition to the financial information discussed in chapter 10, you will need basic information about you and your spouse, such as:

☛ Your full name, birthdate, social security number, and current home and business addresses and phone numbers.

☛ The other parent's full name, birthdate, social security number, and current home and business addresses and phone numbers.

☛ Employment information for you and the other parent, especially information about employment hours and travel requirements. In a custody dispute, this may be important to show the relative time each of you has available to be with the child, especially at vital times such as when the child gets home from school and in the evening. In visitation, this may be important to setting up a visitation schedule. (You will also need financial information about employment, which will be discussed in detail in chapter 10.)

☛ Information about your and the other parent's health. If the other parent has a medical condition that may affect his or her ability to care for your child, obtain the name and office address of the other parent's doctor.

☛ Who else lives in each of your households. This may have a bearing on issues such as who else might be available to help care for your child, whether there is adequate space in your home, and how the child might get along with other household members.

INFORMATION ABOUT YOUR CHILD

The type of information you will need about your child will depend somewhat upon the issues that are raised in your case. The following information and questions should be considered. Some of what is listed below will be needed in your case, and some are things to consider simply for the benefit of your child. You will also need information about finances that relate to your child; however, as this relates more directly to child support, it is discussed in detail in chapter 10.

☛ The full name, age, date of birth, and social security number of each child.

☛ Information about any mental or physical condition or illness of the child. Does your child have handicaps or special requirements? What is the name and address of your child's doctor?

☛ School information about the child.

☛ With whom does your child now reside? For how long has this arrangement existed? What were the living arrangements prior to the separation of the parents?

☛ Are there any previous custody orders relating to your child? If so, you will need copies of them.

☛ Have you spoken to your child about custody? Have you spoken to the child about the other parent (or yourself) visiting with your child? How did the child respond to these questions? Did he or she express any preferences? What is your child's attitude? Consider why the child has this attitude.

☛ What are your plans for vacations?

Gathering and Saving the Documents

Gather copies of any documents which contain the above information to use later in your case. Keep the documents in a safe place and periodically update the documents with more current information. Also, keep up the daily log that you began writing during the custody and visitation "tryout" period. Even if there is no tryout period, a log will help you see what responsibilities you undertook to care for your child during the time you kept the log. Also, write down problems, issues, and unusual expenses, along with the date, time, place, and names of any persons who were present. When you are ready to take the next step of filing your case in court, you will find that much of the information you will need will be available at your fingertips.

Who can File

Only a person with the legal right to do so may file for custody. State law will determine who has such a right. In all states, either the child's mother or father can file for custody or visitation. If the parents are married to each other, the issues of custody and visitation will be addressed as part of a case for divorce (in some states this may be called a *dissolution of marriage*), legal separation, or annulment. If the parents are not married to each other, a separate lawsuit for custody or visitation may be filed.

If permitted by state law, certain persons who are not parents may also file for custody. This may include grandparents, aunts, uncles, or anyone else. In addition, all states have laws permitting some form of grandparent visitation, so a grandparent may file for visitation.

WHAT MUST YOU PROVE?

In a case seeking a determination of child custody or visitation, the petitioner must prove, by a *preponderance of the evidence* (meaning at least a fifty-one percent probability), that it is in the best interests of the child to follow the custody or visitation request as written in the petition.

WHERE TO FILE

Explaining where to file your case first requires a short explanation of the legal terms *jurisdiction* and *venue*. Jurisdiction means that a court has the power to hear a custody case. Venue refers to the actual physical location of the court which will decide the custody suit. For example, the State of California will have jurisdiction for parents who live with their child in San Diego, California; however, the courts of San Diego will be the proper venue within which to file the suit for custody.

You will file your documents with the clerk of the court. The clerk's office is responsible for accepting documents, collecting the fees for filing, and maintaining the files. Remember that there will usually be fees due, unless you can show that you qualify for exemption by virtue of your poverty status. Check with your clerk's office for exact information on filing fees and supporting documents required to be filed. Also, if you believe you qualify, check on how to file the necessary forms to avoid paying the filing fees. Also, ask how many copies of each form they require. Bring two extra copies so that they can be stamped with the filing date and the case number. One such copy may need to be delivered to the local sheriff's office for service, and you will want to keep a copy for yourself.

Determining where to file is made more difficult when both parents do not live in the same state. The Uniform Child Custody Jurisdiction Act (UCCJA), which is the law in all fifty states and the District of Columbia, gives guidance on where to file a custody case when the parties live in different states. This law is extremely important because it effectively eliminates the problems that arise when more than one court has jurisdiction, which can cause contradictory court orders that are impossible to enforce.

The UCCJA says that one of the following four situations must be present for a court to have jurisdiction over a custody case:

1. *Home state.* The court is in the *home state* of the child when the case is filed. The home state is the state where the child has lived for at least six months (or from birth if the child is less than six months old). The home state is still the child's home state even if the child is now being kept outside the state, as long as the parent or person claiming custody is still in the state. This has come to be called the *six-month* rule.

2. *Significant connection.* The court has a significant connection to the child and at least one parent (or party), and there is substantial evidence available to present to the court.

3. *Emergency circumstances.* The child is present in the state and some emergency condition exists, such as abandonment of the child, or a threat of abuse or neglect.

4. *No other state has jurisdiction.* No other state would fit in the first three categories, and it would be in the best interests of the child to have the custody or visitation question decided.

Thus, if you move to the State of Florida, and reside there with your child for at least six months before filing for custody, Florida would have jurisdiction under (1) above to hear the custody case.

For (2), the question is whether there is a *significant connection*. For example, in one case the parties were married and lived in Illinois. Upon their divorce, the mother moved to Virginia. Mom had the children for the summer in Virginia, while dad had the children during the winter in Illinois. Under the UCCJA, the Illinois courts retained jurisdiction. Custody was granted to the mother in Virginia as a result of alleged abuse by the father in Illinois. Illinois had a significant connection because the children would continue to visit the dad in Illinois, and there was ongoing court-ordered counseling of dad which would take place in Illinois.

As you might expect, there are many cases filed and fought over which court has the proper jurisdiction in cases where the parents reside in different states. These cases have produced a confusing body of law, and further discussion of this issue is beyond the scope of this book. If you get involved in a situation where this type of dispute arises, you need to get a lawyer.

WHAT TO FILE

PETITION

A custody or visitation case is commenced by filing a *petition* or *complaint* with the proper court. (To simplify matters, the term *petition* will be used in this book.) If a petition for divorce, legal separation, or annulment is filed, it will include the matters of custody and visitation. If the parents are not married to each other, or if a non-parent seeks custody or visitation, a petition for custody or visitation will be filed.

SUMMONS

In either situation, there will also be a form called a Summons, which will be delivered to (the legal term is *served on*) the other parent along with the petition in a manner required by the law of your state. The most common method is to have these papers personally delivered to the other parent by a sheriff's deputy.

ESTABLISHING
PATERNITY

Remember that in most states, a father who never married the mother must establish that he is the legal father of the child in order to be entitled to custody or visitation. This usually requires either that both parents sign and file a document (typically called an *acknowledgement of parentage* or an *acknowledgement of paternity*), or that the court is asked

59

to determine who is the child's father. Having the court determine this may be done either through a *paternity* or *parentage* court proceeding filed before the petition for custody or visitation is filed, or as a part of the petition for custody or visitation.

OTHER FORMS

There may be additional forms required by your court, so always check with the local court clerk's office for specific information. Many court clerks' offices now list some basic pleading forms on the Internet which are printable or downloadable. It may also help to request to see a few files that are pending. Go to your local clerk's office and ask to see these public files. You will usually be able to view the files at the office. You may also be able to make copies of documents. Ask the clerk for blank forms of documents that are court-generated. Some of the more common forms will be discussed later in this book.

THE PARTIES

Whoever files the petition is usually called the *petitioner* (if a petition is filed) or the *plaintiff* (if a complaint is filed). The person the petition is filed against is commonly called the *respondent* (in a petition) or the *defendant* (in a complaint).

FILING FEES AND OTHER COSTS

FILING FEES

There are filing fees for cases seeking to establish parentage, parenting time (custody/visitation), and child support. The clerk's office has a schedule of fees, and will be able to provide you with specific filing fee information for the type of case you are going to be filing. The clerk's office can also tell you the accepted methods of payment of the fees. For example, some courts may not accept personal checks. Fees will vary from state-to-state, and possibly even from county-to-county. For example, the fee for filing a custody case is $150 in Arizona, $160 in Texas, and $220 in Illinois.

OTHER COURT CLERK FEES

Some states also charge other miscellaneous fees, such as for the preparation and issuance of subpoenas, a judgment fee, a court reporter's fee, photocopying charges, and a fee to certify orders and judgments.

SERVICE FEES

There are also separate fees (and possibly mileage costs), typically charged by the sheriff's office, for the service of the complaint and summons, and the service of subpoenas or other notices.

IF YOU CAN'T AFFORD COURT FEES AND COSTS

If you do not have funds to pay filing and service fees, check with your clerk's office for a form to request a waiver or deferral of payment. Usually a waiver of the fees is available only to those with a very low income. Deferral of payment allows you to pay the fees in installments, or at a later time. You may also be able to request in your complaint or petition that the other party be ordered to pay some or all of these fees.

THE PETITION FOR CUSTODY OR VISITATION

The Petition to Establish Paternity, Custody and Time-Sharing, and for Child Support (form 1 in appendix C) is designed to cover most of the matters that may arise in a custody case. You may need to change the wording to comply with local custom, or eliminate portions that do not apply to your situation. Still, this form should give you a good start.

While all states' court systems may not have the same look to their documents, they cover the same basic information. For example, the court in the sample on the next page is called a *Circuit* Court. In another jurisdiction, this level of court might be called by a different name, such as a *Superior* Court, *Family* Court, *County*,Court or *District* Court. In order to find out how your court is designated, check with your local clerk or review a custody case file in the local clerk's office.

To organize and keep track of documents filed in court, all cases are assigned numbers which appear on the face of all documents filed in that case. The case number will be assigned by the clerk's office at the time you file your Petition. Therefore, you will leave the case number line blank on your Petition. The clerk will write or stamp the number on the face of the Petition when it is accepted for filing. Thereafter, you will type in the case number on all of the documents you file.

Notice that the sample below has the name of the court and its location, a place for the parties' names and a case number, and a title of the document. This portion of a legal form is called the *caption* or *case style*. Whatever the specific format, the caption to your case will include the same basic information to identify your case and the court.

IN THE CIRCUIT COURT FOR THE
TWELFTH JUDICIAL CIRCUIT
DIVORCE COUNTY, STATE OF BLISS

IN RE THE PETITION OF)
Jane Doe,)
          Petitioner,)
)
    v.)   No. _____
John Doe,)
          Respondent.)

PETITION FOR CUSTODY/VISITATION

The above example is titled a *Petition*; however, in some states, this document may be called a *Complaint*. Once again, check your local court rules before filling out the forms in order to determine exactly what you should title your initial document.

The Petition generally includes basic information about both parents (such as names and address) and the child (such as name, address, birthdate, age); and tells the court for what you are asking (establishing paternity, custody, visitation or child support). At a minimum, your Petition should include the following:

1. Your name and address.

2. The other parent's name and address.

3. The child's name, address, date of birth, and age.

4. The relationship of the parties to each other.

5. Information to show that the court has jurisdiction (this is usually information showing that a residency requirement has been met and that the child has a sufficient connection with the state).

6. A statement as to what you want the court to do (such as establish paternity, or grant custody, visitation, or child support).

A Petition may also include requests for additional remedies. For example, in a divorce action, the petitioner may also be seeking *alimony* (sometimes called *maintenance*), and a division of property. In a custody case where the parties never married, one of the paragraphs is going to allege that the male party is the father of the child. Whether there is a marriage or not, child support will also be a subject of the case. The petitioner will also be required to sign the petition and verify that, to the best of his or her knowledge, the facts within it are true.

The degree of formality with which this information is customarily presented may vary from court to court. For example, in some states, a Petition may begin with a statement in very simple English, such as:

> The Petitioner alleges as follows:

However, in another state it may be customary to use more traditionally formal language such as:

> Comes now Jane Doe, the Petitioner in the above entitled action, and for her Petition against John Doe, the Respondent, hereby alleges and avers as follows:

You may get by using the first version even if most of the lawyers in your area use the second version. However, you may run into difficulty having the court clerk accept your Petition. This is one reason it is important to research the format of the forms used in your court. Your research should include looking at the local court rules, checking for form and practice books at a law library, looking at files from other cases at the clerk's office, and asking if there are any standard forms that can be provided by the clerk. Try to match the local format and language as much as possible.

OTHER DOCUMENTS

Depending on your state, other forms may be required upon filing the petition. For example, some states require a form attesting that no other court has jurisdiction under the Uniform Child Custody Jurisdiction

Act, or require a financial information form be filed to determine child support issues. (See form 5 in appendix C.)

THE SUMMONS AND SERVICE

A summons is designed to notify a person that he or she is being sued. Because the Petition must accompany the summons, the respondent will also know why he or she is being sued. Although a sample Summons (form 2) is included in appendix C, every jurisdiction has its own summons form, so make sure you use the form which is right for the court in your area.

If the parents have agreed to the terms of custody, the respondent can waive service of the summons. Otherwise, the Summons and Petition must be *served on* (delivered to) the respondent.

Usually, the local sheriff will serve the summons, but you must find out how to arrange this. When you file your Petition, ask the clerk how service arrangements are made. In some states, the clerk will take a copy of the Petition and Summons from you and send it automatically. In other states, there is a box or a bin in which to leave your Summons and Petition. In still other states, it will be up to you to take a copy of the Petition and Summons to the sheriff's office. The sheriff's office is often either within or near the court building, so you can walk there once your documents are filed.

Unless you have been previously exempted from paying fees, there will be a fee due to the sheriff or other agency that will serve the documents on the respondent. Make sure you find out how much it costs (when you talk to the clerk about filing) and bring sufficient funds.

If the respondent lives in another state, get the address of the local sheriff in the county where the respondent lives, and sent the file-stamped Petition and Summons (along with a check for the correct amount) to the proper office and request that respondent be served there.

A summons may be served on the respondent in person to the locations that you put on the face of the summons (usually work or home). Make sure you put times when respondent is likely to be at the specified location (such as work hours), so that the sheriff will not waste time trying to find respondent.

When the respondent has been served, the sheriff will file what is usually called a *return of service, affidavit of service,* or a similarly-named document, which explains the details of how the Summons and Petition were served. As the petitioner, you should get a notice of this from the sheriff's office, but if some time passes and you don't hear from them, you can always check your court file at the clerk's office to see if the sheriff's return of service has been filed.

Once the respondent has been served, then he or she will have a few weeks to respond to the petition. The exact number of days depends on the jurisdiction, and will be listed in the notices section on the Summons form. Knowing the date of service means you can compute how long the respondent has to file an answer to the Petition. This will dictate your next move.

RESPONDENT NOT FOUND

If the sheriff tries but cannot find the respondent at the location you listed, the sheriff will indicate in the return of service document that the Summons could not be served. If you learn, or know, of another address at which the respondent may be found, you will have to prepare another Summons with the new location information. You will then have it issued by the clerk and pay the fees a second time to have it served.

If you do not know where the respondent is, the law permits a form of notice called *service by publication.* A notice of your pending lawsuit is published in a newspaper. This is considered giving notice to the world—including the respondent. The rules for service by publication are different in each state, so check your laws carefully to learn the requirements for this form of notice.

To serve notice by publication usually requires court approval, and therefore, the filing of a motion requesting permission to serve the respondent by publication. Generally, your motion must include information about what steps you took to search for the respondent. This is called a *due diligence* requirement.

Once the court grants you permission, find out which newspapers are approved to publish notice of lawsuits. Take your publication notice (often called a *notice of action*) to the newspaper, and pay the fee the newspaper charges to publish your notice. The notice will usually appear in the newspaper several times—the exact number of times and the timing being determined by the law of your state. When it first appears, the newspaper should provide you with a clipping. If not, get a copy of the newspaper and check to see that the notice has been accurately printed. Notify the newspaper immediately if there are any errors.

RESPONDING TO A PETITION FOR CUSTODY OR VISITATION

If both parents have worked out an agreement on custody/visitation (and any other issues in the Petition), the issue of the respondent's response will be resolved when the agreement is presented for court approval.

FILING A RESPONSE

If, however, the parents have not completely agreed to all the issues raised in the Petition, it is considered a contested case. Once the respondent is served with the Summons and Petition, he or she will have an opportunity to file a *response* (sometimes called an *answer*) to the petition. Like all documents filed in the case, the Response will have a caption and will answer each of the allegations in the Petition. (See form 4 in appendix C.)

If you are served with a Summons and Petition, you should not ignore them. If you fail to respond within the time limit set by your state (as stated in the Summons), the relief sought in the Petition may be granted, and you will not have had an opportunity to contest the allegations. In your Response, you may choose to raise new claims (for example, your own request for custody). Usually in your Response you may admit, deny, or state that you have insufficient information upon which to base an answer.

FAILURE TO RESPOND

If a respondent simply ignores the Petition instead, then upon the lapse of time within which the respondent had to file a Response (determined by your state's law), the petitioner can file a motion with the court to declare the respondent in *default*. Once the respondent is defaulted (either by court order or by a docket entry of the clerk), the court can act on the requests in your Petition.

MEDIATION

The delay and expense of contested court cases have led parties in many types of family law cases to try to settle their differences outside of court, through various types of *alternative dispute resolution* (ADR). In divorce, custody, visitation, and support cases, the type of ADR most commonly used is *mediation* (also be called *conciliation*). A third type of ADR, *binding arbitration*, is where a neutral third party resolves the issues in the case and the parties agree to be bound by that decision. Binding arbitration is commonly conducted in other types of civil cases, however, because a court has an independent duty to determine what is in the best interests of a child, an arbitration award cannot be binding in a case involving custody, visitation, or support.

WHAT IS MEDIATION?

In mediation, a person called a *mediator* facilitates confidential discussions and, over a period of sessions, helps shape a parenting plan which is acceptable to both parties. Mediation can be conducted by the parties even before a case is filed, or while the case is pending.

Mediation does seem to play a positive role in the later willingness of parents to abide by the terms of their custody judgment. For example, one 1994 study found that a higher rate of fathers complied with court orders when their custody cases were resolved through mediation rather than litigation.

More than forty states have programs to mediate contested custody, visitation, and child support. Of those, nearly half are mandatory mediation programs. For example, in Virginia, the court may refer the parties to a mandatory evaluation session in which a mediator will assess the case to determine whether it is appropriate to resolve the matter through mediation. In California, a mediation attempt is required if a custody dispute arises.

CHOOSING
MEDIATION

In determining whether voluntary mediation is right for you, consider whether both of you:

☛ Can deal fairly with each other

☛ Want to try mediation

☛ Agree to hear each other has to say

☛ Are willing to seek a resolution of your parenting or financial differences

If one party is hostile or has real concerns about full and fair disclosure of information, then mediation will not likely assist in settling your differences. Mediation is not usually recommended in cases involving domestic violence or child abuse. Some states do not permit mediation when there is an allegation of domestic violence between the parties. Oregon permits a waiver of mediation when a party files a motion with the court stating that mediation would cause "severe emotional distress."

FINDING A
MEDIATION
PROGRAM

In some states, court mediators work in the courthouse. In others, the courts certify mediators or contract with a bar association or nonprofit corporation to handle court-referred disputes. Mediators may be part of a court-referred program or may be a private agency or individual. Parties who choose voluntary mediation may jointly hire a mediator, who may be an attorney and who should have specific training in mediation techniques. There are national dispute resolution organizations like The Academy of Family Mediators, The Society of

Professionals in Dispute Resolution, and the American Bar Association which have adopted codes of professional conduct for mediators.

QUALIFICATIONS OF A MEDIATOR

Most states require court mediators to complete twenty to forty hours of training before they take cases. Some state courts have adopted qualification standards. For example, the Ohio Supreme Court requires certain qualifications for mediators employed or referred by the court for custody or visitation cases. These family mediators must have: a bachelor's degree or equivalent in education; at least two years of professional experience with families; completion of at least twelve hours of basic mediation training or equivalent experience as a mediator; and after satisfying the above requirements, completion of at least forty hours of specialized family or divorce mediation training in a program approved by the Ohio Supreme Court. Private mediators should have some training or experience in your type of case, but they need not be attorneys.

CHOOSING A MEDIATOR

If you are choosing a mediator (or your court referral permits you to choose), consider the following:

☛ Whether the mediator provides a free consultation before taking the case

☛ The mediator's fee and scope of services

☛ How mediation will be paid

☛ The number of sessions anticipated

☛ The mediator's background (training, education, cases mediated)

☛ Most importantly, you should feel comfortable with the mediator

Today most private mediators charge hourly fees which may range upwards of $150 per hour. Court-based mediation programs may charge a schedule of fees; a sliding fee scale based on the parties' ability to pay; or charge an administration fee with the parties paying the mediator directly. In cases where the parties cannot pay a mediator's fee, some courts have mediators available at no cost.

THE MEDIATION PROCESS

The mediator will facilitate the discussions, but it is the parties who will actually work out their parenting plan and financial support arrangements during the mediation process. Depending upon the complexity of the problems presented and the parties' ability to resolve their parenting or financial differences, the number of mediation sessions will vary.

The mediator should provide an overview of the mediation process before you begin. Within the sessions, the mediator will help the parties identify issues, collect information, evaluate options, and find acceptable solutions. Both parties must agree to voluntarily exchange information and documents and sign authorizations to obtain information from third parties (employers, insurers, banks, etc.) where necessary. Once the parties have come to an agreement, the mediator will draft a written agreement which can then be signed by both parties and filed with the court clerk.

Sometimes mediators will suggest that, after the agreement is reached, each party have it reviewed by an attorney of their choosing. An attorney may be useful in providing legal advice on the fairness of the proposed agreement, the potential enforcement issues raised, or the likelihood that a court will approve the agreement.

Because mediation is based on each party's concerns being heard and considered, participating in developing the agreement increases the likelihood of cooperation in carrying out the terms of the agreement in the future.

TEMPORARY CUSTODY OR VISITATION

Once the case has been filed, the court has jurisdiction to award temporary custody, visitation, and support. These temporary orders grant rights and responsibilities until the case is resolved. The person requesting the temporary order must do so by filing a Motion for Temporary Relief (form 13). Depending upon the state, this may be called a *motion for temporary custody and support*, or some similar name.

If the judge grants your request, you will usually need to prepare an Order for Temporary Relief (form 14) to reflect exactly what the judge orders. Forms 13 and 14 are designed to include the various matters that may be the subject of temporary orders. You may need to modify these forms to fit the requirements of your court or your circumstances.

Remember, in filing a motion for temporary relief with the court, you must also notify the respondent (unless he or she has been defaulted). However, you only needed to use a Summons form at the beginning of the case. Once the respondent has been served with the Summons and Petition, any subsequent notices or copies of court documents may be sent by mail or by other means allowed by the court rules of your state. (See form 6 in appendix C.)

THE CONTESTED CUSTODY CASE

When parents cannot agree on custody, the court must decide the issue for them. Since the judge doesn't know the parties or the child, this often results in an outcome that is less satisfactory to both parents than if they had compromised to reach an agreement. Because custody is so emotional, a contested custody case is pretty accurately called a "war." It is all to often an outlet for hostilities between the parents, and the child may be put squarely in the middle and be forced to take sides with one parent or the other.

> ***Note:*** If you are facing a contested custody case, it is wise to seek consultation with a lawyer before proceeding in court. Because of the emotions involved, it may also be useful to seek mental health assistance before you might actually need it, so that you can be better prepared for the road that lies ahead in a contested custody case. In a contested custody case, you need to realize that your conduct will come under scrutiny for review and consideration in the case. It has been said that during the pendency of a custody case, you will feel like you are living in a "fishbowl."

EDUCATIONAL PROGRAMS	In some states, parents are required to attend an educational program in order to learn how their legal battles will affect their child. It is becoming common to require at least a short program to help parents understand the impact of their custody quest and to help parents assist the child to cope with the emotional fallout from the case. Many courts have guidelines that they provide to parents as part of the process.
THE GUARDIAN AD LITEM	As in any litigation where the parties do not agree on what the outcome should be, the custody/visitation proceeding will be considered *adversarial*. The parties are the mother, the father, and (usually) their lawyers. In most states, there will also be another lawyer, called a *guardian ad litem*, who is a person appointed by the court to represent the child's interests.

In order to protect the child's interests independent of the parent's concerns, a growing number of states provide for the appointment of a guardian *ad litem*. The job of the guardian *ad litem* is to file any necessary papers with the court on the best interest of the child. The guardian *ad litem* will interview the child, siblings, and other family members; investigate the school and home situation; and advise the court as to what would be the best decision for the child. The job of the guardian *ad litem* is to argue for what he or she believes to be in the child's best interest, which may or may not be what the child wants. |
| THE JUDGE | The judge's role is to provide a fair forum in which the determination of custody/visitation can be made. As such, the judge's job is not to take sides, but instead to allow each party the opportunity to fully (but also fairly) present their case for consideration. However, judges do have their own views and perspective on what is considered common sense parenting. One big factor in the decision of the judge is the credibility of each parent. This is why it is essential to present your case to the judge in the best manner possible. Acts based in anger, frustration, and revenge may affect your credibility as a "fit and proper" parent.

Child custody/visitation cases are generally considered priority cases by the courts, and judges usually try to move the case along on a fasttrack as compared to other types of cases. |

DISCOVERY

Whether the case is settled by agreement or decided after a trial, both parties require knowledge of all the facts necessary to decide custody, visitation, and child support. Parties can exchange this information voluntarily. If not, there are court rules and procedures in every state which permit a party to obtain this information through a process called *discovery*. A court may enforce discovery by ordering compliance or by punishing the noncompliant party or person.

INTERROGATORIES

A common type of discovery are *interrogatories*. These are written questions which are sent to the other parent. Interrogatories must be answered under oath. The rules concerning interrogatories are governed by your state or local court rules. For example, the Los Angeles Superior Court Local Rules state that:

> (1) Interrogatories should be used sparingly and never to harass or impose undue burden or expense on adversaries; (2) Interrogatories should not be read by the recipient in an artificial manner designed to assure that answers are not truly responsive; and (3) Objections to interrogatories should be based on a good faith belief in their merit and not be made for the purpose of withholding relevant information. If an interrogatory is objectionable only in part, the unobjectionable portion should be answered.

The court rules will also govern the number and type of questions permitted to be asked. Some states may have standard, approved interrogatories for use in family law cases. Interrogatories usually include the following areas: sources of income, property, expenses, location of documents or assets, and the names and addresses of potential witnesses. (A blank set of family law interrogatories is included as form 8 in appendix C.)

REQUEST TO ADMIT FACTS

Another form of discovery is known as a *request to admit facts*, or a *request for admissions*. This is somewhat similar to interrogatories in that it consists of written statements sent to the other parent which must be responded to under oath. Unlike interrogatories, this form of discovery lists a fact and asks the other parent to admit, deny, or state why the proposed fact cannot be admitted or denied. A request to admit facts may be useful after the answers to the interrogatories have come in, and you determine that certain facts are not being disputed. This can save time (and attorney's fees) at trial by focusing on what is in dispute.

SUBPOENAS Another common form of discovery is a *subpoena*, which is an order directing the other party or another person to provide certain information, either verbally or by providing documents or other items. For example, a subpoena may be sent to the other parent's employer, bank, or stockbroker in order to obtain financial information. The form of a subpoena varies by state, and can often be obtained from the court clerk. (See form 7 in appendix C.)

DEPOSITIONS A *deposition* involves asking questions of a party or other person under oath, usually before a court reporter, and having the court reporter make a transcript of the questions and answers. This is a costly form of discovery because transcripts may run in the hundreds of dollars.

COURT PROCEDURES

The trial of a custody/visitation case is like any other civil case. Each party will have an opportunity to make a brief opening statement. The purpose of an opening statement is to provide an overview of the case.

YOUR COURT TESTIMONY Both parents have an opportunity to testify as to the nature of their relationship with their child and explain why they should have custody. Preparation for court will make your testimony much smoother. If possible, familiarize yourself with court procedures. For example, stop in and watch another case being heard. Watch how the judge and the attorneys handle the case.

Your testimony should cover the factors discussed in chapter 3. If you state's law lists specific factors (see appendix A), you should cover those items. In many states, which parent has been the child's primary caretaker is of special importance. For example, parents will provide testimony on who spends what amount of time with the child and what activities are undertaken during this period. Parents will testify to questions such as: Who takes the child to the doctor when he or she is sick? Who is the person that gets up in the middle of the night? Who changes the baby's diapers? Who takes the child back and forth to school activities? Who goes to the parent-teacher conferences? Who signs the child up for preschool activities? Who arranges to have the birthday parties?

Once the testimony establishes the history of the parental relationships with the child, the next issue which must be addressed is how the parents plan to undertake, maintain, or continue their relationship. So, the focus turns to the future envisioned by each parent.

In order to measure the parent's future plans, a court will examine how the parties have conducted themselves during the pending case. If a temporary order has been entered, the person with custody must show that he or she has been able to meet the conditions of the custody and visitation arrangement. For instance, has the custodial parent helped to make sure that visitation was provided? The parent with visitation must show how he or she has met the visitation requirements provided in the temporary order. These questions will help the court understand the history of the parents' conduct to be better able to assess wether the parties can place their child's needs and interests above their own in the future.

After you have said what you wanted to say, the other parent (or his or her attorney) will have an opportunity to ask you questions about what you have said. The judge may also ask you questions. In answering these questions, you should follow these basic rules:

- ☛ Remain calm.

- ☛ Be straightforward and speak clearly.

- ☛ Listen carefully to the question before answering.

☛ If you don't understand a question, say so.

☛ Do not volunteer extra information. Try to answer the question as simply as possible.

☛ Look at the judge when answering a question.

☛ If a question cannot be answered with a yes or no, say so; or explain that you must give two answers to a two-part question.

☛ Do not argue with the other parent's attorney or the judge.

OTHER
WITNESSES
In addition to your own testimony, you may request other witnesses to appear (either voluntarily or by subpoena) to testify on your behalf. The choice of your other witnesses is determined by the custody, visitation, or child support issues involved. These persons may include friends, family members, neighbors, and your child's teacher, physician, or psychologist.

Keep in mind that before you ask a person to testify on your behalf, you must determine just what that person would say because the last thing you want is a surprise from your own witness. You may be required to provide some basic information for the court about your witnesses, such as the witness' name and what information they have that is relevant to the issue for which they are testifying. Witnesses (unless they are qualified by the court as expert witnesses) must testify on matters within their own knowledge; so stories, rumors, or gossip (called *hearsay*) are usually not permitted testimony. However, a witness can testify to statements made to the witness by the other parent.

Write out the exact questions you plan to ask each witness. The questions should be short and should address a single point at a time. Allow the witness to answer one question before you pose another one.

For example, assume you have temporary custody and are seeking sole custody. Your child is in school, and you have determined it is important to introduce testimony about your child's school performance, the interactions you have had with the school, and the lack of interactions the other parent has had with the school. You may want your child's teacher to testify. A few questions you might ask the teacher include:

- ☛ Please state your name.

- ☛ What school do you teach at?

- ☛ What grade?

- ☛ Do you teach *{your child}*?

- ☛ For how long have you taught *{your child}*?

- ☛ How is *{your child}* doing in school?

- ☛ How is *{your child's}* attendance at school?

- ☛ Have you ever participated in parent-teacher conferences with *{the other parent}* and me?

- ☛ Has the notice of these conferences been sent to both parents?

- ☛ Has *{the other parent}* ever attended these conferences?

- ☛ To your knowledge, has *{the other parent}* ever attended any school-related function at which you were present?

Or, if your neighbor has observed significant interactions between you (or the other parent) and your child, you may determine that it is important to show the court the quality of those interactions. For example, if the other parent failed to show up for the child's last birthday party, and it was very devastating to the child, you might ask:

- ☛ Please state your name.

- ☛ What is your address?

- ☛ Where is that in relation to my house?

- ☛ How well do you know *{the child and parents}*?

- ☛ What kind of activities have you engaged in with our family over the past ___ years?

- ☛ Did you attend *{the child's}* birthday party on *{date}*?

- ☛ Was *{the other parent}* present?

- ☛ How did this affect *{the child}*?

Expert Witnesses. Experts may also testify. Two of the most common types of expert witnesses called to testify in custody cases are psychological and medical experts. Experts may be obtained by the parent or by an order of the court. Their role is to evaluate the parties on the best interest factors. Experts who are appointed by the court will report directly to the court after meeting with the parents and child and interviewing them as appropriate. The expert then prepares a report and may also testify as to the report's contents. The evaluation process can take a few months, and may be costly—hundreds, or even thousands of dollars.

ADMISSION OF DOCUMENTS

You may wish to put a document into evidence, such as a child's school report card, a medical report, a police report, or the other parent's pay records. A document is usually introduced through the testimony of a witness who can show that the document is authentic and describe the nature of the document. For example, the child's school report card for the previous year may be important proof of how the child is performing in school. To introduce the report card, you would typically use the procedure on the following page.

In most courtrooms, the judge will have one or more people to assist with the court's operation. This may include a clerk, a bailiff, and a court reporter. One of these people will have the duty of keeping track of paperwork, including documents and other exhibits offered by the parties. If there are no other court personnel present, then the judge will perform this function. In our example, when the teacher is testifying, you would begin by handing the report card to the appropriate person in the courtroom, and say "I would like this marked as an exhibit." That person will then mark the exhibit, usually by either placing a sticker on it, stamping it, or writing on it. Usually one party's exhibits are designated with letters (A, B, C, etc.) and the other party's exhibits are designated with numbers (1, 2, 3, etc.).

After the report card is marked, it will be handed back to you. You will then either hand the report card or a copy of the report card, to the other parent or his or her lawyer, so that they understand about what it is you will be asking the teacher. You would next have an exchange with the teacher similar to the following:

Question: Did you prepare any grade reports for my son Jimmy during the past school year?

Answer: Yes.

Question: I am showing you what has been marked as Petitioner's Exhibit A. Do you recognize this document?

Answer: Yes.

Question: What is this document?

Answer: It is my grade report for last year concerning Jimmy.

The other parent (or his or her attorney) has the right to ask the witness questions about the document and to raise any objections to it being used. The most common objections are that the document has not been shown to be authentic, and that the document is not relevant to the issues before the court. However, neither of these objections are likely with a teacher and that teacher's grade reports.

When the document is properly shown to have been true and correct, you may ask any relevant questions about your child's grades and refer to the grade report when asking the teacher further questions. Finally, ask the judge to have the grade report admitted into evidence ("Your honor, I move that Petitioner's Exhibit A be admitted into evidence.") At this point, the other party is entitled to raise any objections he or she might have to the document being admitted into evidence.

If there was more than one year or semester of grade reports that were relevant, you would go through the same process with each document, having each document assigned its own exhibit number.

THE OTHER PARENT'S PRESENTATION

After you have finished presenting all of your evidence, the other parent has an opportunity to present his or her evidence. During this phase of the hearing, the roles of you and the other parent are reversed. That is, you have the right to ask questions of the other parent and his or her witnesses (called *cross examination*), and to raise any objections you might have to the witnesses' testimony or the documents introduced. However, cross examination is a skill that not even all lawyers possess, and there are numerous rules of evidence you would need to know to make proper and effective objections. Both cross examination skills and the rules of evidence are beyond the scope of this book.

CLOSING
ARGUMENTS

When each side has completed presenting their evidence, each party has an opportunity to give a *closing argument*. This is where you summarize what you think the evidence shows and state your position as to what you want the judge to do (award you custody, child support, etc.). The judge will then announce his or her decision.

FINAL JUDGMENT

After the judge makes his or her decision, that decision needs to be put in writing in the form of an order. Depending upon your state and whether the order is temporary or permanent, this document may be called a *judgment, final judgment, decree, order,* or some similar name. In a case where the parties reach an agreement, instead of repeating all the terms of the agreement in the judgment, the judgment will usually just have a statement that it *incorporates* the agreement of the parties, thereby giving the agreement binding effect. In a contested case, the judge sets the rules of custody and visitation, which are spelled out in detail in the judgment. The Judgment (form 23) in appendix C is designed to cover most types of orders a judge might make. As with many of the other forms in this book, you may need to modify this form to comply with local requirements and your particular situation.

In either type of case, the judgment binds the parties until it is modified. A modification can take place either as the result of an agreement between the parties (which is approved by the judge), or by one party requesting a change by filing a motion, sometimes called a Petition to Modify Judgment (see form 25). After a hearing, if the judge agrees to modify the Judgment, he or she will sign an Order Modifying Judgment (see form 26).

KIDNAPPING, ABUSE, VISITATION PROBLEMS, AND OTHER EMERGENCIES **6**

Custody battles may take a long time to resolve and may produce emergencies during that period. A parent may take their child and hide to avoid losing their child or because they do not trust the legal system. A parent who is experiencing domestic violence may need a protective order. A parent may refuse to abide by the temporary custody or visitation orders, necessitating a return to court for enforcement assistance or a change in the order. The court's priority in such emergencies is to protect the child.

If you reasonably suspect criminal behavior on the part of the other parent, report it to authorities in order to get immediate intervention. Today, there are specialized techniques which can help determine whether abuse is present and what needs your child may have as a result of the abuse.

KIDNAPPING

WHO KIDNAPS A CHILD?

Every year in the United States, thousands of children are taken and hidden by parents or family members. This most often occurs when a parent is afraid of losing custody, or believes the child will be abused or not adequately cared for when with the other parent. While the intent to protect the child may seem noble, kidnapping is still a crime.

Sometimes the parent and the child go into hiding together. Other times, the child is hidden with a parent's relatives or friends, and if the parent is taken into court, he or she either denies knowing where the child is staying, or refuses to give such information. In either situation, this certainly creates a serious risk of harm to the child. As a result, today kidnapping is considered a form of child abuse. Fathers are reportedly more likely to take their child when there is no child custody order, while mothers are more likely to take their child after a child custody order has been entered.

The risk of kidnapping is higher when one or more of the following situations exist:

☞ There is considerable animosity between the parents

☞ A parent threatens to kidnap the child

☞ A parent lives, works, or is preparing to move, out of state

☞ There are allegations of physical or sexual abuse, and a parent feels the courts are slow in their reaction and fears for the child's life or welfare.

PREVENTING
KIDNAPPING

If you believe that a risk of kidnapping exists, you may try to minimize the chances by one or more of the following actions:

☞ Ask your local police or prosecutor to warn the other parent that kidnapping is a crime.

☞ If you already have a custody order, give a *certified* copy of that order to your school, day care center, and baby sitter (you can obtain a certified copy from the court clerk). Tell them not to release your child to anyone except on your direction.

☞ If the child is old enough, teach him or her how to contact you; including teaching the child your telephone number and how to use the telephone to call home.

☞ Keep identifying information about the other parent and the child, such as a current photograph, social security information, driver's license number, and financial account numbers.

☞ If the other parent lives out of state, file a certified copy of your custody order in that state to let the courts know of its existence. A certified copy can be obtained from the clerk of the court which issued the custody order. By filing a certified copy of your custody order with the clerk of the out-of-state parent's local court, both your state and the other parent's state will recognize and enforce the custody order pursuant to the Uniform Child Custody Jurisdiction Act. The court clerks maintain a registry of orders to facilitate communication and enforcement. You may file by mail. There may be a filing fee to register your custody order.

PREVENTIVE COURT ORDERS

Court orders may also assist in preventing kidnapping, by restricting visitation conditions or supervising visitation (see below) or by prohibiting a parent from taking the child on a trip outside the state without prior court approval. If the fear is that the parent with custody will take the child, the same restrictions can be placed on that parent.

Parents may also be required to post money with the court in the form of a bond (usually an insurance policy) as security for the return of a child. If the parent does kidnap the child, the proceeds can help pay for the search to find and return the child.

IF YOUR CHILD IS KIDNAPPED

Criminal penalties exist for kidnapping, and if your child is kidnapped you should call the police and report your child as missing.

If you have not yet obtained a custody order, you should file for custody. If you do have a custody order, the Uniform Child Custody Jurisdiction Act (UCCJA) is designed to prevent the other parent from taking children and crossing state lines to file for a new custody order. All fifty states have now adopted the UCCJA, and courts will recognize and enforce orders made in other states. In other words, your order will be recognized as binding even if the other parent tries to get a later order. Contempt penalties may also be entered in your court proceeding against the other parent.

You should also look for your child. The Parental Kidnapping Prevention Act (PKPA) is a federal law that permits the federal government to assist in locating parents who have taken their child in violation of a court order. This is done through the Federal Parent Locator Service, which will search computer files on address information for the kidnapping parent.

When your child is found, make sure you file your custody order with the clerk's office where the child is located and request that police help you in picking up your child.

DOMESTIC VIOLENCE AND CHILD ABUSE

Sadly, the numbers of parents who are accused during a custody battle of abusing their children has increased over the years. The issue usually arises in connection with an allegation of sexual abuse. Once this type of charge is made, the parties are not likely to settle the custody case, and the cost of litigation is high.

These cases often are lengthy, and sometimes are resolved only after complete psychological and home studies are completed on the parents and child to determine the truth and accuracy of the allegations. If the child has been abused, the child will need the appropriate protection, enforceable through court orders. If the child has not been abused, it is important to resume the child's relationship with both parents as soon as possible.

Even if the case is decided by a trial, the matter is not always over. If one party believes that the court decided wrongly in giving the other party custody or visitation, that parent may flee with the children or may send the child away to live with others for protection. The parents may continue the court battle, perhaps resulting in the parent who refuses to produce the child being held in contempt or even prosecuted for child abduction.

PROTECTIVE ORDERS

Every state provides for *protective orders* prohibiting domestic abuse. These orders are usually filed with the local police, and may permit police to arrest a parent upon a violation. Although these orders may be pursued by an attorney, many court clerk's offices have protective order packets available. These are written in simple, clear language; and can be filed and heard in court usually within a very short period of time. These orders may be "permanent," but they commonly last for some specified duration of time (e.g., two years) to protect the abused person (and the child) from specified types of behavior which may include, stalking, following, threatening, harassing, and physical violence.

PRIVACY OF
NAME AND
ADDRESS

Many states recognize that the victim of abuse is put at greater risk when having to disclose a new name or address. Therefore, petitions for protective orders, as well as petitions for divorce, custody, and support, may be filed without having to disclose this information. Check with your jurisdiction before putting this information in your petition.

VISITATION PROBLEMS

One common source of problems for parents in cases of sole custody is a parent's right to visitation. This is especially true in the many cases where the court order simply says the noncustodial parent is entitled to "reasonable" or "reasonable and liberal" visitation. When parents do not get along, the question then becomes, "W hat is the definition of reasonable?" And "Who decides what is reasonable?"

To help avoid disputes, it is very helpful for the order to be as specific as possible about visitation rights. The order should set forth the starting and ending days and times for visitation and allocate vacations, holidays, birthdays, and other special days or events. If telephone access is contemplated, this should also be addressed in the order. (See earlier chapters and the Parenting Plan forms in appendices B and C for suggested language.)

Sometimes, a parent's abuse of visitation will be sufficient to change the visitation, or even the custody order. For example, in a case where the custodial parent continually interferes with the visitation rights of the other parent, the parent who is denied reasonable visitation rights can go back to court and seek a change in the order to be more specific about when visitation will occur. Occasionally, where the custodial parent demonstrates a refusal to comply with any visitation order, judges have changed custody to the parent who has been denied visitation.

SUPERVISED
VISITATION

Some situations require *supervised* or *monitored* visitation orders. These cases might involve situations where a parent presents a danger to the child, where the child has been kidnapped previously, or where threats have been made to kidnap the child.

The person given the responsibility for supervising the visits may be a law enforcement officer, social worker, clergyman, relative, family friend, or any person (or agency) designated by the court or agreed upon by the parties.

While not yet available everywhere, *visitation centers* have been a growing phenomenon over the past decade. These centers provide a neutral, supervised location within which visitation may be monitored. The staff have training in custody issues and will protect the child if needed. In cases where there has been an incident of abuse or parental neglect, the family may be ordered to have visitation at one of these centers.

EXCHANGE OF
THE CHILD

Exchanging a child for visitation often requires some level of contact between the parents. When there is a high degree of anger or frustration between the parents, this contact can lead to a refusal to produce or return the child in a timely fashion. Or, it may lead to arguing in the presence of the child over other issues (often child support).

Some parents decide to make the exchange in a public place where there are witnesses. In other cases, visitation may begin and end at a neutral location such as a visitation agency in which the parent with custody drops the child and the visiting parents takes and returns the child to the center. In this way, parents can reduce their contacts with one another. The details of how the exchange will take place can also be included in the order or parenting plan.

MEDIATION AND
COURT ORDERS

If there is a problem with visitation, and the parties agree, the issue could be the subject of mediation in an effort to workout the differences to a mutually agreeable solution. Absent an agreement to mediate, the court may order mediation. However, if the parents cannot agree that they want to try mediation, it may be unlikely that court-ordered mediation would be successful.

CUSTODY/VISITATION: MODIFICATION, TERMINATION, AND APPEAL

7

MODIFICATION

A child custody agreement or order is intended to last as long as the child needs a caretaker. Parties can agree to a change of custody or visitation, but because the court has jurisdiction, it must be put in writing and filed in the proper court.

Courts generally agree that the less disruption in the child's schedule and environment, the better, so they are reluctant to change custody or visitation orders. Inevitably, however, circumstances change and sometimes these circumstances lead to a request by a parent to modify, or change, the custody or visitation order. This is why it is said that a child custody or visitation order is never truly final.

Sometimes the original order of custody or visitation is too uncertain. The parties may interpret it differently, which can lead to frequent disputes. In such a case, the court might modify the order to specify the details of the custody and visitation.

JURISDICTION: WHERE DO YOU GO?

To modify an order, a parent may return to the same court that entered the original order. It is not unusual for one parent to have moved, and that parent may seek a modification in their new home state.

THE UCCJA

The Uniform Child Custody Jurisdiction Act (UCCJA) applies not only to initial custody orders, but also to modifications between parties from different states. The goal of the UCCJA in modification issues is to reduce the chances that two states will enter conflicting orders.

TIME LIMITS

To limit the opportunity for parents to seek modification, some states prohibit parents from seeking changes to their custody and visitation orders before some specified period of time. In Illinois, for example, parties must wait two years before returning to a court seeking modification unless there are substantial changes in circumstances which show that the child's current environment endangers his or her well being.

WHAT DO YOU NEED TO SHOW?

A court will generally not revisit the facts which led to the initial order of custody or visitation. The parent seeking the change will have to present facts that show there has been a substantial change of circumstances since the order was issued, and that the requested change in custody or visitation will be in the best interests of the child.

Like most other determinations involving a child, there is no single standard by which it can be determined when enough circumstances have changed to make it *substantial*. The court will be guided by what is in the best interests of the child. The simplest way to think about it is to recognize that the measure of what is substantial will be looked at through the effect that the change in circumstances has on the child— not the effect on the parent. For example, winning the lottery will not amount to a sufficient change of circumstances to deprive the nonwinning parent of custody. If that nonwinning parent needs more funds to properly care for the child, the proper remedy would be to seek an increase in child support—not a modification of custody or visitation.

Among the most common reasons for seeking a change are:

☞ the same concerns that were raised and considered in the initial determination of custody or visitation;

☞ remarriage of one of the parents;

☛ allegations that the parent with custody has engaged in a pattern designed to disrupt the relationship between the child and the visiting parent; and

☛ allegations that one of the parents has not complied with the current provisions for custody or visitation. For instance, if the current order requires split custody, but that has not proven to work out for the family (especially for the children), a court may reconsider the order, and change it as necessary.

It is usually not enough to show that the visiting parent does not always exercise his or her visitation with the child, or that the child has been disappointed on holidays or special occasions; unless these occurrences have a substantial negative impact on the child.

REMARRIAGE   The remarriage of a parent alone is not enough to change custody or visitation. But it may be a factor which, when combined with other factors, results in the requested change. Often, with a remarriage comes a move into a new home. This may result in the merging of new family members, the increased expenses of the new family, or increased income. The change in homelife of the child may have an effect on the request to modify custody or visitation. For example, the attitude of the new stepparent, the treatment of the child in the new home, or the new environment or religious upbringing that the child may experience, are all factors that a court may examine. Also, the relocation often involved in a remarriage of the custodial parent may result in difficulty for the noncustodial parent to visit the child.

MOVING   Once a custody or visitation case has been filed in a court, a parent who wishes to move with the child to another state, or even to a distant point within the state, must have permission of the court to do so. A court will grant permission only if it is in the best interests of the child to do so. If the noncustodial parent is moving, special provisions for visitation will need to be made. The court can also order the parent who wishes to move to pay for transportation costs and to post a bond to the court to secure the return of the child.

TRAVEL

A parent must obtain the court's or the other parent's permission to even take the child out of state temporarily on a vacation. For example, some states now require the vacationing parent to provide the other parent with information on where the child can be reached during the vacation or other absence from the state and the dates of the proposed absence before the child can leave.

MISCONDUCT BY A PARENT

If the parent with custody engages in a pattern of disrupting the child's relationship with the visiting parent or otherwise interfering with visitation, this may result in a request for a transfer of custody. Similarly, if the visiting parent interferes with the custodial parent's relationship with the child, this can result in a denial or limitation of visitation.

Courts may first try to achieve the desired result of stopping the interference or alienation of the child through other methods such as warning the parent or holding the parent in contempt of court, but if there is a strong pattern of disrespect and even hatred shown, the court may change custody or visitation on the grounds that it is in the best interests of the child to do so.

ABANDONMENT

Sometimes a parent with custody will give the child to another person, such as the child's grandparent, to raise. A temporary arrangement will usually not result in any kind of custody change, but if the child is not returned to the parent within a reasonable amount of time, custody may be transferred to the visiting parent.

For example, if the parent with custody has a chance to get a job in another city, it may be okay to have the child finish the remaining few months of the school year with the grandparents. But, if the parent with custody is not looking for a place to live with the child and apparently intends to leave the child with the grandparents indefinitely, the visiting parent's request for a change of custody may be granted.

COURT ORDER REQUIRED

Even if the parties agree to a change of custody or visitation, it will only be binding once a court has approved it. The ultimate decision to grant a request for a change in custody or visitation rests with the judge.

Ordinarily, the court can change custody or visitation in the following situations:

☞ The parties have agreed to the change of custody

☞ The child has been integrated into the home of the visiting parent who is requesting the change with the permission of the parent with custody

☞ The child's present home environment is dangerous to his or her health and a change of environment is in the child's best interests

FILING FOR A CHANGE IN CUSTODY OR VISITATION

To notify the other parent, file a motion or petition with the court (see form 25). You will need to explain why the change is sought, which will be done either in the petition itself or in a separate affidavit depending upon the practice in your state. The parent filing the request must notify the other parent because, in the absence of an emergency, a change of custody or visitation will not be made without proper notice so that the other parent has an opportunity to be heard. Different courts require different levels of notice. Notice by publication may be permitted when the parent does not know, and cannot find out, where the other parent lives.

The court will hold a hearing, and if a parent objects to the request, a full trial may be held in which both parents may have to present witnesses and put on evidence. The parent who requests the change has the burden to prove how the circumstances have substantially changed since the child custody order was entered.

As can be seen, the request to change custody or modify visitation is a very serious matter, and is treated by the courts as seriously as the initial grant of custody or visitation.

TERMINATION

EMANCIPATION
OF THE CHILD

A child custody order terminates when the child reaches the age of majority (usually eighteen). Note that child support may continue after this time under certain circumstances. (See child support chapters.)

DEATH OF
PARENT

Although in some states, the power to make further custody orders ends with the death of a parent, in others, a court still has power to change the order.

REMARRIAGE

Remarriage of a parent is not a factor that will operate to terminate a child custody order.

APPEAL

WHO CAN
APPEAL?

Either party to the case may file *post-trial* proceedings seeking to change the decision in the case. Every state has a system of courts designed to hear appeals. No testimony is taken in the appellate process. The court decides the appeal based on the objections that are filed and the records and transcript of the trial court. If a serious mistake was made, the judgment can be overturned and the case sent back for a retrial.

WHAT CAN
AN APPEALS
COURT DO?

Although many appeals may be taken in family law cases, reversals are rare. This is because the appellate court will uphold the trial judge's decision unless there has been an abuse of discretion or a serious error in applying the law. This makes sense because it is the trial judge who has (perhaps) interviewed the child, listened to the parents, and heard the experts testify. An appeals court simply reads the arguments of the parties, reviews the record of the proceedings in the trial court, and decides if a significant error was made. Since the factors and guidelines are very broad, it is hard to prove an abuse of discretion in most cases.

CHILD SUPPORT 8

The laws of all states provide that every parent has a legal duty to support his or her child. This is true whether the parents are married or not, and whether the child lives with them or not.

Historically, judges examined each parent's ability to pay and the needs of the child in determining child support, but even so, many parents were not awarded child support. As late as the mid-1980s, over thirty percent of the more than eight million parents who had custody of their children were not awarded any child support at all.

It was estimated that by 1989 forty-two percent of the ten million mothers with children under age twenty-one whose fathers were living apart from the family did not have a child support order. Also, the dollar amount of the orders that were entered ranged from very low to unreasonably high. For example, in one court, child support orders in cases where there was a single child ranged from six percent to forty-one percent of the paying parent's adjusted income. The range was almost exactly the same when there were two children to be supported (five percent to forty percent).

Worse still, parents were not paying as required by their orders. For example, one study showed that in 1989, of the half-million women due child support, twenty-four percent received partial payment, and twenty-five percent received nothing.

The problems with child support awards came to the attention of the federal government because it was public subsidies that increasingly took over when parents did not pay. To make child support more fair and certain, the federal government now requires every state to adopt guidelines for use in determining child support.

In the Personal Responsibility and Work Opportunity Reconciliation Act of 1996, the federal government mandated sweeping changes to child support laws. States are now required to pass uniform interstate laws which provide for uniform rules, procedures, and forms for inter- state child support cases. For example, in 1998, all states were required to adopt the Uniform Interstate Family Support Act (UIFSA). These provisions are designed to help track parents who move across state lines. The federal law also requires states to establish central registries of child support orders, centralized collection and disbursement units, and expedited procedures for child support enforcement. Further, states must have registries of newly hired employees, have laws and procedures to make it easier to establish paternity, and strengthen penalties for failure to pay child support.

As a result of these federal initiatives, the government has cracked down on parents who do not pay support. The latest figures of the federal Office of Child Support Enforcement show that in fiscal year 1996, a record $12 billion was collected on behalf of children. This figure is more than a fifty percent increase from 1992.

THE BASICS

WHAT IS CHILD
SUPPORT?

The legal obligation to support a child includes the child's basic living needs such as housing, food, and clothing expenses. It also includes medical costs and other expenses such as education, after school activities, and vacation expenses.

Also, it must be noted that child support is not always limited to the payment of money. For example, part of a child support order in a divorce case may award the family home to the parent with custody until the child reaches the age of majority, with the noncustodial parent paying some or all of the mortgage, insurance, and property tax payments during that time. On the other hand, once child support has been ordered by a court, it must be paid in money. Gifts of clothing, and other items in lieu of money, will not be credited against the support amount due unless a court gives the parent prior permission to do so.

WHO CAN GET SUPPORT?
: Any parent (or person who has legal custody of a child) may be eligible to seek an order for child support from a parent.

HOW CAN YOU GET SUPPORT?
: Child support is typically raised as an issue in divorce proceedings, custody actions, and paternity (also called *parentage*) cases. In divorce cases, some states combine child support with support for a spouse into a *family support order*. A person seeking child support may also file an independent case to establish a child support order.

The parent (or other eligible person) may also file an application for child support enforcement services with a state agency. Every state has a child support enforcement program which is usually operated by the state's social services agency, the State Attorney General's Office, or some other agency. Persons who are receiving governmental financial assistance, such as Medicaid or Aid to Families with Dependent Children (AFDC) are eligible to receive state support enforcement services for free. Some states charge a small fee for persons who are not receiving state aid. See appendix A for the listing for your state's child support enforcement agency.

WHO PAYS?
: Both parents share responsibility to support their child whether they are married to each other or not. This is true even if the parent is a minor. In one Illinois case, for example, a father, who was fifteen years old at the time his child was born to his girlfriend, argued that because he was a child himself, he didn't have an adult's duty of child support. The court rejected this argument, finding that the child's right to support outweighed the father's rights as a minor. (*In re Parentage of J.S.,* 550 N.E.2d 257, 258 (Ill.App.1990).

If the parents have married, the support obligation exists before, during, and after the marriage. It is a joint obligation. In some cases, even the parent who has full custody may be ordered to pay child support to the other parent while the child visits because the decision of custody does not automatically answer the question of who should pay support.

How Support Is Determined

Child support is determined by examining both parents' ability to pay and measuring the child's support requirements. Because every state examines and weighs factors somewhat differently, the two most common methods for how support is determined are shown in this chapter. Later in this chapter, you will learn about various state's guidelines. You may also look in appendix A for a summary of your state's specific factors for determining child support.

When parents come to an agreement on child support, they often agree on a support amount above the basic guidelines of their state law. This is because the guidelines are minimum threshold amounts, and parents who have the ability often agree that providing their child with a comfortable standard of living requires a support amount above the guideline amounts.

Factors in Setting Child Support

The amount of support is based on a number of factors with the goal being to make reasonable provisions for the welfare of the child. Factors to be considered include: financial resources of the child and parents, the standard of living the child would have had if the marriage had not ended, the physical and emotional condition of the child, and the child's educational needs. State guidelines also factor these items into their payment schedules. If the parents were married, misconduct during the marriage (such as adultery) will generally ***not*** be considered in determining child support.

FINANCIAL
RESOURCES

To be enforceable, any child support order must take into account the ability of the parents to pay the amount needed. Financial resources means more than just income. Also considered will be the parent's assets (bank accounts, property) and the standard of living of the parent. State guidelines take into consideration the reasonable and necessary living expenses of a parent in determining a child support order.

NEEDS OF THE
CHILD

Perhaps the most overriding factor for determining child support is the needs of the child, and state guidelines factor in a basic level of need. While *needs* means more than just basic living requirements, it does not include unnecessary expenses. If the parents have been married, a court may look at the standard of living the child had prior to the divorce or separation of the parents. If so, the determination of child support will attempt to maintain that standard of living for the child.

HEALTH
INSURANCE

Health care is a required element of state guidelines. If the parents do not agree to provide health insurance, the court will order it paid regardless of which parent has custody.

For example, in any child support case in Louisiana, the court may order one of the parties to enroll or maintain an insurable child in a health benefits plan, policy, or program. In determining which parent should be required to enroll the child or to maintain such insurance on behalf of the child, the court considers each parent's individual, group, or employee's health insurance program; employment history; and personal income and other resources. The cost of health insurance premiums incurred on behalf of the child are added to the basic child support amount.

Other states provide for a health insurance coverage assignment, which means that a court order is entered which requires the noncustodial parent's employer (or other person providing health insurance to the noncustodial parent) to enroll the child in the parent's health insurance plan. The order also authorizes the employer of the noncustodial parent to deduct the cost of the health care premiums from the noncustodial parent's earnings.

States also provide for the award of extraordinary medical expenses where appropriate. In Kentucky, for example, this would include medical, surgical, dental, orthodontal, optometric, nursing, and hospital services.

EDUCATIONAL EXPENSES

The reasonable education expenses of a child may be agreed to, or the court may order a parent (or both) to pay for the education of a child. Some courts limit these expenses to public school education, but where the party has the ability to pay, a court may order payment for the cost of a private school and even a boarding school.

Although a college education may not be considered a *necessity* by some courts, where the parent has the ability to pay, the court may order the parent to support a child after high school—through technical school or college. This will often depend on the child's academic abilities and interests and may require the child to maintain a certain grade point average.

OTHER EXPENSES

Parents may also agree, or the court may order a parent, to pay for various other expenses for a child, such as summer camps and vacation costs. One common item in the "other" category is child care costs while a parent is completing an education or job hunting. Many state guidelines address this as an adjustment to the support obligation.

GUIDELINES

All states have guidelines that help to determine the basic amount of support for a child. There is no single guideline model used in each state, but the states generally set forth their basic principles in their guidelines. It is important to note that the guidelines in each state are required to be reviewed at least every four years, so they may change. If you are researching your state's guidelines, make sure you are using the most recent version of them. (See appendix A for your state's law citations and the section on "Finding the Law: Legal Research" in chapter 1 for how to find the law in your state.)

Parents may agree to child support that is outside the guidelines. Although adjustments can be, and often are, made to the guideline amounts, generally a court (or administrative agency if permitted) must make a written finding that the application of the guidelines would be unjust or inappropriate in a particular case.

Each state lists the main principles of their guidelines. For example, the following California statute explains in detailed fashion the objectives of the State's guidelines:

In implementing the statewide uniform guideline, courts shall adhere to the following principles:

(a) A parent's first and principal obligation is to support his or her minor children according to the parent's circumstances and station in life.

(b) Both parents are mutually responsible for the support of their children.

(c) The guideline takes into account each parent's actual income and level of responsibility for the children.

(d) Each parent should pay for the support of the children according to his or her ability.

(e) The guideline seeks to place the interests of children as the state's top priority.

(f) Children should share in the standard of living of both parents. Child support may therefore appropriately improve the standard of living of the custodial household to improve the lives of the children.

(g) Child support orders in cases in which both parents have high levels of responsibility for the children should reflect the increased costs of raising the children in two homes and should minimize significant disparities in the children's living standards in the two homes.

(h) The financial needs of the children should be met through private financial resources as much as possible.

(i) It is presumed that a parent having primary physical responsibility for the children contributes a significant portion of available resources for the support of the children.

(j) The guideline seeks to encourage fair and efficient settlements of conflicts between parents and seeks to minimize the need for litigation.

(k) The guideline is intended to be presumptively correct in all cases, and only under special circumstances should child support orders fall below the child support mandated by the guideline formula.

(l) Child support orders must ensure that children actually receive fair, timely, and sufficient support reflecting the state's high standard of living and high costs of raising children compared to other states.

Similarly, the Idaho guidelines state the same general principles but word them a bit differently:

(a) Both parents share legal responsibility for supporting their child. That legal responsibility should be divided in portion to their Guidelines income, whether they be separated, divorced, remarried, or never married.

(b) In any proceeding where child support is under consideration, child support shall be given priority over the needs of the parents or creditors in allocating family resources. Only after careful scrutiny should the court delay implementation of the Guidelines amount because of debt assumption.

(c) Support shall be determined without regard to the gender of the custodial parent.

(d) Rarely should the child support obligation be set at zero. If the monthly income of the paying parent is below $800 the Court should carefully review the incomes and living expenses to determine the maximum amount of support that can reasonably be ordered without denying a parent the means for self-support at a minimum subsistence level. There shall be a rebuttable presumption that a minimum amount of support is at least $50 per month per child.

All of the states' guidelines assist in identifying minimum amounts to be paid for child support and offer schedules of income and allowable expenses to calculate the presumed award amount. Even though the guidelines exist, each case is examined on its own merits because no two families have exactly the same obligations and needs. The makers of the guidelines recognize this and there are provisions for adjustments to the guideline amounts.

DEFINING INCOME

Income used to determine child support may be *gross income* or *net income*, depending on your state's guidelines. Gross income will be defined by the guidelines and will usually include money, property, or services from most sources, whether or not it is reported or taxed under federal law. If net income is used, the law will usually define what is included in gross income, and what deductions are allowed in computing the net income. Under either method, income from public assistance programs is usually exempted.

For example, Idaho's guidelines, which use the parents' gross incomes, define gross income as including income "from any source, and includes, but is not limited to, income from salaries, wages, commissions, bonuses, dividends, pensions, interest, trust income, annuities, social security benefits, workers' compensation benefits, unemployment insurance benefits, disability insurance benefits, alimony, maintenance, any veteran's benefits received, education grants, scholarships, other financial aid, and disability and retirement payments to or on behalf of a child." Idaho courts may consider when and for what duration the receipt of funds from gifts, prizes, net proceeds from property sales, severance pay, and judgments will be considered as available for child support. Unlike some states, benefits received by a parent from public assistance programs in Idaho are included as income (except in cases of extraordinary hardship).

Recognizing that parents sometimes try to quit their job to avoid paying support, a court may use the parent's earning capacity rather than actual earnings to determine support. Earning capacity is based on the parent's education, training and work experience, and the availability of work in or near the parent's community. For example: A noncustodial parent voluntarily quits a job paying $40,000 a year and works part-time for $12,000. The court may use the earning capacity of $40,000, not the actual gross income of $12,000, to determine the amount of child support.

Some state guidelines set out certain deductions from gross income to arrive at a net income figure from which the child support is determined. These deductions vary between states by type and amount, but standard deductions generally include:

- ☞ Taxes
- ☞ Social security deductions
- ☞ Health insurance
- ☞ Mandatory retirement contributions
- ☞ Prior child support

States may also permit subtractions from gross income for certain identified reasonable expenses. For example, in Wisconsin, gross income would be reduced by business expenses which the court determines are reasonably necessary for producing that income or operating the business.

COMBINED
INCOME
GUIDELINES

Many states guidelines determine child support by combining the income of the parents, then calculating the guideline percentage of income available for support from each parent. This model is often called the *Income Shares Model*. For example, the Indiana Child Support Guidelines use this model and explain that it is based "on the concept that the child should receive the same proportion of parental income that he or she would have received if the parents lived together."

Determining child support under this model generally involves five basic steps (although it may take several state worksheet pages to cover these steps):

1. Identify the gross and net income of each parent

2. Add the income of each parent together for a combined total income

3. Find the child support due for that total income amount on your state's guideline

4. Add or deduct the amounts that are permitted by your state

5. Determine the proportionate share due from each parent

States that use this model recognize that the parent who has caretaking responsibilities will pay the support directly for the child, while the other parent will pay a dollar figure for child support.

For example, to calculate child support for one child in Alabama:

1. Assume that the parent with custody has a gross income of $1,000 per month while the noncustodial parent has a gross income of $2,000 per month

2. The incomes are added: $3,000

3. Next, look to the Alabama child support schedule chart to determine the guideline amount:

Combined Gross Income	1 Child	2 Children	3 Children	4 Children	5 Children	6 Children
2900.00	426	660	826	931	1015	1085
2950.00	431	669	837	944	1029	1100
3000.00	437	677	848	956	1042	1114
3050.00	443	686	859	969	1056	1129

The guideline calls for a total child support sum of $437

4. Prorate the basic child support sum ($437) between the parents, based on their income: the noncustodial parent will pay two-thirds

of the total due, or $291. (For this example, we are assuming no special adjustments are needed.)

A similar result with the above example would be reached in Virginia:

1. Once again, the parents incomes would be added for a combined income of $3,000.

2. Look at the guidelines in the Virginia law to determine the child support due:

Combined Gross Income	1 Child	2 Children	3 Children	4 Children	5 Children	6 Children
2850.00	430	667	836	941	1027	1098
2900.00	435	675	846	953	1039	1112
2950.00	440	683	856	964	1052	1125
3000.00	445	691	866	975	1064	1138
3050.00	443	686	859	969	1056	1129

From the chart shown above, the amount would be $445.

3. Add any allowable adjustments. For our example, let's assume there is a $50 expense for child care and a $15 expense for extraordinary medical expenses. That would bring the total to $510.

4. Under Virginia's scheme, you would prorate the amount due between the custodial parent and noncustodial parent. The non-custodial parent would pay child support under the Virginia guidelines of $339.99 (this is 2/3 of $510.99).

PERCENTAGE INCOME GUIDELINES

Another type of guideline commonly in use is based on the percentage of income of the noncustodial parent. Some states use a flat percentage, while in other states the percentage depends on the level of income of the parent. As you will see below, although the method of determining the child support is different, the result, if we use the same example, is not too much different than the states above.

Determining child support under this model generally involves three steps:

1. Identify the gross and net income of the parent who does not have custody

2. On your state's guideline, find the percentage of income due for child support

3. Add or deduct the amounts that are permitted by your state

The percentage of income guidelines in Wisconsin are typical. Wisconsin law establishes that child support amounts are based on the belief that both parents are responsible for supporting their children, and both parents will support their child whether they live together or apart. Although this type of guideline looks only at the income of the parent without custody, the guidelines again assume that the parent who has caretaking responsibilities will pay his or her share of the support directly for the child, while the other parent will pay a dollar figure for child support. The Wisconsin guidelines are as follows:

For one child   Seventeen percent of gross income
For two children   Twenty-five percent of gross income
For three children   Twenty-nine percent of gross income
For four children   Thirty-one percent of gross income

So, as reflected in the following chart illustration, if a noncustodial parent's gross monthly income was $1,200, and there was one child, the support would be $204 (seventeen percent). If there were two children, the amount would increase to $300 or twenty-five percent of the gross income:

Noncustodial Parent's Gross Income	1 Child	2 Children	3 Children	4 Children
	17%	25%	29%	31%
1,200.00	204	300	348	372
2,000.00	340	500	580	620

To compare the guideline amounts with those in our combined income guideline states, look at the earlier example of the noncustodial parent's income of $2,000. In Wisconsin, the chart above shows that the guideline percentage for one child is seventeen percent. Calculating seventeen percent of $2,000 is $340. Notice how this is very close to both examples above (Alabama and Virginia) using the combined income guidelines. The point is that, while states have different methods of reaching the basic support levels, they often lead to similar support amounts.

ADJUSTMENTS Many states permit add-on amounts or special adjustments. These may increase or decrease the basic support obligation. While each state has its own adjustment definitions, most include:

☛ Extraordinary medical, psychological, dental, or educational expenses

☛ Independent income or assets of child

☛ Child support, alimony, or spousal maintenance previously ordered

☛ Age or special needs of child

☛ Split or shared custody arrangements

☛ Which parent takes the IRS dependency exemption

States may also add other bases for adjusting child support orders. For example, in addition to the above-factors, the Florida guidelines state that a court may adjust child support based upon:

☛ The payment of support for a parent which regularly has been paid and for which there is a demonstrated need.

☛ Seasonal variations in one or both parents' incomes or expenses.

☛ The greater needs of older children.

☛ Special needs, such as costs that may be associated with the disability of a child, that have traditionally been met within the family budget even though the fulfilling of those needs will cause the support to exceed the proposed guidelines.

☛ The particular shared parental arrangement, such as where the children spend a substantial amount of their time with the secondary residential parent thereby reducing the financial expenditures incurred by the primary residential parent, or the refusal of the secondary residential parent to become involved in the activities of the child, or giving due consideration to the primary residential parent's homemaking services. If a child has visitation with a noncustodial parent for what the court determines is a significant amount of time, the court may reduce the amount of support paid by the noncustodial parent during the time of visitation.

☛ When application of the child support guidelines requires a person to pay another person more than fifty-five percent of his or her gross income for a child support obligation for current support resulting from a single support order.

☛ Any other adjustment which is needed to achieve an equitable result, such as a reasonable and necessary existing expense or debt.

Courts must state the reasons for a departure from the guideline amounts. In California, for example, if the support order differs from the guidelines, a court must explain in writing or on the record, the following information:

1. the amount of support that would have been ordered under the guideline formula;

2. the reasons the amount of support ordered differs from the guideline formula amount; and

3. the reasons the amount of support ordered is consistent with the best interests of the children.

PRE-EXISTING CHILD SUPPORT ORDER

One of the most common scenarios that affect the support guidelines is where a parent has been divorced before and has a previous court order to pay child support. Even though there is a second family, it does not mean that the paying parent's responsibility to the first family ends. However, the amount of support in the second case can be affected because that parent has the responsibility for supporting other children from the first case. In these situations, the guidelines may factor in, as a deduction from income, the amount of the first child support order.

Example. A man was divorced from his first wife in 1990 and is subject to a court order to pay monthly child support of $350 for a child from that marriage. He is now going through a divorce from his second wife, with whom he has a child. His guideline income is $3,000 per month. The guidelines would subtract the first child support ordered amount from his income ($3,000 - $350 = $2,650), then determine the support for the second child by applying the guidelines to the new income figure of $2,650.

SHARED OR
JOINT CUSTODY

State guidelines deal with joint, or shared, custody arrangements in a number of ways. In some cases where the parents share nearly equal parenting time, each parent's pro rata share of support offsets the other's, so that they do not exchange support. Instead, each parent essentially pays all costs when the child is with him or her. In other cases, custody may be shared, but one parent spends more physical time with the child. In such cases, prorating the total amount due for child support and factoring in the parenting time will once again yield a sum to be paid for support.

Some states include tables in their guidelines for adjusting the guideline amounts based on the percentage of shared parenting time. For example, if both parents were required to spend seventeen percent of their income on their child and Parent A had an income of $2,000 per month and Parent B had an income of $1,500 per month, their initial child support due would be:

Parent A $2,000 x 17% = $340

Parent B $1,500 x 17% = $255

But if Parent A spends forty-four percent (or 160 days) of the time with the child and Parent B spends the remaining fifty-six percent (or 205 days), the state guideline schedule on the following page prorates the amount of child support due:

Reduction of support based upon forty-one to fifty-nine percent of time spent with child:

Percent of time with child	Percent of original child support amount
43	56.71
44	53.38
45	50.05
46	46.72
47	43.39
48	40.06
49	36.73
50	33.40
51	30.07
52	26.74
53	23.41
54	20.08
55	16.75
56	13.42

Now, apply the percentages from the table:

Parent A owes 53.3% of the original total ($340 x .5338% = $181.49)

Parent B owes 13.42% of the original total ($255 x .1342 = $ 34.22)

Final calculations would show that $147.27 ($181.49 - $34.22) was due Parent B from Parent A. This works out to a percentage due of 7.36%.

The above is just one example of how state guidelines approach the shared parenting arrangement. Your state may treat this issue differently in its guidelines.

SPLIT CUSTODY
States also attempt to apply their guidelines to cases in which the parents have more than one child and have sole custody of some, but not all of their children. In such a case, for example, if Parent A has custody of one of the three children under state percentage of income guidelines, then Parent A might pay twenty-five percent of his or her

income as child support (for the other two children). Parent B would owe the guideline seventeen percent for the one child in Parent A's custody.

If we assume their incomes are:

Parent A: $3,000 x 25% = $750 (2 children)

Parent B: $1,500 x. 17% = $255 (1 child)

Parent A owes Parent B the sum of $495 ($750 - $255 = $495) in child support.

VISITATION ADJUSTMENT

Visitation arrangements may result in an adjustment to a child support order. For example, some states prorate support based on time spent with each parent. In Nebraska, the guidelines permit a reduction of fifty percent for visitation periods of four weeks or more. In addition, a court may adjust support due if visitation requires long-distance transportation costs.

TAX CONSEQUENCES

Under current federal tax law, child support payments are neither deductible for the paying parent nor taxable to the receiving parent.

Ordinarily, the tax law presumes that the parent with custody is entitled to take the tax exemption for their child (see the section on "Taxes and Custody" in chapter 2). So, if the paying parent who does not have custody desires to take the deduction, the parent with custody must sign a form (currently called Form 8332), or a similar statement, agreeing not to claim the child's exemption. That agreement may cover one year, a number of years (for example, alternate years), or for all future years. Note that in some states, the actual federal and state income tax benefits of the parent who claims the Federal Child Dependency Exemption will be considered in making a child support award.

Because the revenue rules do change periodically, check with your local I.R.S. office for the proper form and filing requirements.

BANKRUPTCY

Filing for bankruptcy will not relieve a party from paying child support, because child support is not dischargeable in bankruptcy [see 11 United States Code, Section 523(a)(5)].

CHILD SUPPORT AGREEMENTS 9

Like custody decisions, when parents can cooperate, decisions concerning child support can work to the benefit of all parties, especially your child. So, a court will consider the terms of an agreement concerning support. Where it is just and reasonable under your state's laws and the circumstances, the judge will award the agreed upon amount. The amount and terms of your support agreement will then be included in your custody or visitation judgment.

If the judge determines, however, that the amount agreed upon is not fair or reasonable based on the laws of your state or the circumstances, your agreement will not be binding on the court. The judge may then choose to make an award of child support that is different from that upon which you have agreed. The primary consideration will be whether your agreement is in the child's best interests.

For example, an agreement that in essence says "If you don't ask for visitation, I won't ask for child support" is unacceptable to the courts in all states and will not be approved. No court would consider such an arrangement to be in a child's best interest, and parties will not be permitted to use their agreement to prevent a court from making a reasonable child support order. This holds true for any other order that serves the best interests of the child.

QUESTIONS TO CONSIDER

In agreeing on a child support amount, the parents should consider a number of factors, including:

☛ What your state's guidelines require

☛ Additional quality of life or standard of living issues

☛ Each parent's financial resources

☛ The needs of the child

☛ Who will be responsible for health care expenses

☛ What educational expenses will be paid

☛ Other expenses

☛ Who takes the tax exemption

☛ When and how will payments be made

☛ Will there be security (trust, life insurance) for the payments?

☛ What happens if the paying parent dies?

☛ If there is more than one child, what effect does it have on the payments if a child dies, becomes age eighteen, marries, or joins the military?

USE THE APPROPRIATE GUIDELINE

In the previous chapter, you generally learned about the child support guidelines in effect in every state. The guidelines that cover your case will be found either in your state's statutes, administrative rules, or court opinions. You can find the appropriate guidelines for your state by checking the listing for your state in appendix A to obtain the legal citation. You can obtain the exact guidelines from your legal resource library. Many states also list their guidelines on the Internet, but be aware that these are not necessarily the most current version. You can also contact your local child support enforcement agency for information on obtaining your state's guidelines.

Working through your state's guidelines may feel a bit like doing your taxes. Many states provide specific worksheets and forms to assist in the process. These are available through your local clerk's offices or your local child support enforcement agency. With your state's guidelines as a basis, you can formulate an amount of child support to put into your agreement on custody and visitation.

DETERMINE YOUR BASIC GUIDELINE AMOUNT

CHILD SUPPORT CALCULATION METHODS

The guidelines of all the states are based upon the income of one or both of the parents. Some states use the *combined income* of the parents, and other states just look at the income of the parent who will be paying support (often referred to as the *payor* or the *obligor*). States also differ in how they determine what income is used to calculate support. Therefore, in calculating what amount of support to expect in your case, you will first need to determine two things:

1. Does your state use the combined income method or the percentage of the payor's income method?

2. Does your state look at gross income or net income?

To help you calculate child support, you will find a Combined Income Child Support Worksheet on page 124, and a Percentage of Income Child Support Worksheet on page 125. To decide which of these worksheets to use, you will need to read your state's guidelines (refer to appendix A) to find out which method is used. If combined income is used, you will begin by determining the amount of monthly income that both parents have. If your state uses a percentage of the paying parent's income, you will begin by determining the income of the parent without custody.

GROSS INCOME | Your state's guidelines will probably begin with a definition of *income* or *gross income*, which will basically be income from various sources, without any deduction for taxes, social security, etc. For example, your state might include the following in its definition:

☛ Salary, wages, interest, and dividends

☛ Commissions, allowances, overtime, and tips

☛ Business income

☛ Disability benefits

☛ Workers' or unemployment compensation

☛ Pension or retirement payments

☛ Social security benefits

☛ Maintenance, alimony, or spousal support

Next, you will need to read your state's guidelines to determine whether *gross income* or *net income* is used. If your state uses the gross income method, the income from the sources listed will be the basis for calculating the support amount.

NET INCOME | If your state uses net income, you will need to deduct from gross income the permitted deductions that are set forth in the guidelines. Typically, this will include federal, state, and local income taxes; FICA, medicare, or self-employment taxes; mandatory union dues and retirement payments; health insurance (but not for the child, as this will be considered separately later in the calculation); maintenance, alimony, or spousal support paid; and child support for other children.

COMBINED INCOME | In combined income states, you next add the final income amounts for each parent to get their combined income. In a percentage state, you only calculate the guideline amount from the paying parent (so do not combine incomes in those states.)

ADJUSTMENTS TO INCOME | Regardless of whether your state uses gross or net income, check your state's guidelines to determine whether there are any unusual expenses that can be deducted.

APPLY
GUIDELINES

Once you have the income calculated, look to your state's guidelines to determine the amount of support to be paid at that income level. On the guideline schedule for your state (usually this is a chart of some kind), you will find the amount due for the income amount and the number of children for whom support is to be paid.

Combined Income Method. In combined income states, the chart will usually give you what is considered the minimum monthly amount required to raise that number of children. You then determine the proportionate share due from each parent. For example, suppose the father will be paying support, and his income is sixty percent of the parties' combined income. If the state guideline chart indicates $960 is the total monthly child support needed for the parties' combined income, the father would pay sixty percent of the $960, or $576 per month.

Percentage of Income Method. In percentage of income states, the chart will typically state a percentage of income based on the number of children for whom support is to be paid. For example, the chart may indicate that the child support amount is twenty percent of the payor's income for one child, thirty-one percent for two children, etc.

DETERMINE YOUR CHILD SUPPORT AMOUNT

ABOVE THE
GUIDELINE
AMOUNT

Now that you have determined what minimum guideline amount would be acceptable in your state, you and the other parent should consider what additional amounts, if any, you believe would be best applied to your child's support.

For example, every year the federal government publishes an annual estimate of how much it costs for both parents who live together to raise a child. Using these figures, researchers have shown that on average, it costs around $6,000 every year to raise a child when the family income is around $35,000. When the family income is between $35,000 and $58,000, expenditures for raising a child increase to about $8,400. The figures increase in households with more than one child.

Overall, housing accounts for the biggest share of the expense—about thirty-five percent of the total, followed by food (fifteen to twenty percent) and then transportation (fifteen percent).

One researcher compared these expenditures to child support payments and found that the guideline amounts represented only about twenty to thirty percent of raising a child. (See Mark Lino, "Do Child Support Awards Cover the Cost of Raising Children?" *Family Economics and Nutrition Review*, p. 29 (Winter, 1998). This researcher's conclusion was that overall, the guideline amounts were not adequate to raise a child.

Some states have raised their guideline amounts. You can compare your state's current guideline amounts to the annual United States Department of Agriculture annual expenditure amounts or simply compute the cost of raising your own child on a monthly basis. Check to see how it compares to the minimum guideline amount for a truer picture of how much you expend on child related costs.

BELOW THE GUIDELINE AMOUNT

If exceptional circumstances exist, you may determine that an amount lower than the guidelines is appropriate. State factors vary, and you will probably need to explain to a judge or hearing officer why you have agreed to support below the guideline amount.

Example. Hawaii permits a court or hearing officer to enter an order lower than the guideline amount where the parents' income is so high that application of the guidelines would result in an award higher than a child's reasonable needs.

Example. In California, a court will approve the parties' agreement for child support that is below the guidelines only if all four of the following conditions are met:

1. They are fully informed of their rights concerning child support

2. The order is being agreed to without coercion or duress

3. The agreement is in the best interests of the children involved

4. The needs of the children will be adequately met by the stipulated amount

WRITING YOUR AGREEMENT

Once you have worked through the relevant issues and determined that your agreement meets, exceeds, or is permitted to be less than the guideline amounts, begin writing. Forms are found in appendix C.

Make sure your written agreement covers:

☛ How much the payment will be

☛ The duration of the child support order

☛ When and how child support will be paid

☛ Who is responsible for health care coverage

☛ Any special conditions of support

☛ Who will take the tax credit or exemption

The agreement should indicate that you both are fully aware of your obligations under your state's guidelines. For example, you might state that:

> Child support will be set in accordance with the State of _____ *{your home state}* guidelines.

DURATION OF THE ORDER

The length of the child support order depends on the agreement of the parties or the terms ordered by the court. Many orders expire when the child reaches eighteen (the age of majority), but parents may agree that they will support a child after he or she reaches the age of majority (eighteen). This usually arises when the parents are in agreement that the child should go on to college. Sometimes, there will be an agreement to support the child until he or she becomes self-supporting. Unless some kind of agreement is made beyond the period of time that a child reaches the age of majority, usually the court will not order such support. Sometimes, though, there is a state law which requires the parents to support their child longer. For example, Maryland permits an order of support for an adult child where the child is "exceptional," such as where the child had emotional problems.

An example of the duration of a support agreement follows:

> We further agree that child support shall be paid until our child reaches the age of eighteen (18) [or nineteen (19) if still in high school], dies, marries, or joins the military. We also agree that we will review our child's progress and encourage our child to go on to college or technical school as their interests and abilities permit, and we agree to contribute sums towards our child's education beyond high school to the extent our financial situation reasonably permits.

PAYMENTS

Although historically, the child support order required the payments be made directly to the other parent, this has proven to be problematic in many cases. So, courts now often require that payments be made through the court clerk's office or some other government agency. In fact, some jurisdictions mandate that, unless the parties agree otherwise (and the court approves), the payments must be made to the court or some other agency.

A court may also order that support be paid directly to a designated court officer as trustee for the person entitled to the payments. This permits the court to maintain the record of payments made and dates of payment. To be effective, of course, the parent entitled to payments must be sure to notify the court if they move.

An agreement should include when and how child support shall be paid. For example the parents might agree that:

> Child support shall be paid by the Respondent on the fifteenth of every month to the Clerk of the Circuit Court for Columbia County, beginning on July 15, 2000.

INCOME WITHHOLDING

Automatic withholding of child support from the paying parent's income is one of the simplest ways to pay child support. If the paying parent is employed the child support is withheld when the employer makes out the payroll and sent to the support collection agency designated in a court order. The funds are then dispersed by the agency according to state and federal laws.

Income withholding is not limited to salary and wages. For example, Nebraska's income withholding law permits the withholding of nearly any kind of income, including: salaries or wages, unemployment and workers' compensation, investment funds, and retirement plans.

ELECTRONIC FUNDS TRANSFER

While some parents pay their child support directly by check, many states now offer an automatic payment option, known as *electronic funds transfer* (EFT). EFT automatically deducts the child support from your checking or savings account. This saves time preparing payments, saves money on postage and check fees, and ensures that your payments cannot get lost or delayed in the mail.

In some states, automated options exist for receiving the child support. If you are entitled to child support that is paid to you through a support collection agency, you may be able to use a direct deposit method for your child support payments. Using direct deposit provides quicker access to the support funds, and your check cannot be delayed in the mail, lost, or stolen. In these states, all that is needed is for you to have a checking or savings account, and the clerk of the court or the child support agency will electronically deposit your funds into your account.

SCHEDULE OF PAYMENTS

Many states permit payments to be in dollar amounts or as a percentage of income. Some states allow using a combination of both. In Wisconsin, for example, child support payments may be ordered as a dollar amount ($100 per month), as a percentage of income (twenty-five percent of income), or as a combination (seventeen percent of income but not less than $100 monthly).

Check your state's guidelines for the appropriate method of stating the child support payment.

HEALTH CARE

It should be clear in any agreement which parent is responsible for providing health care coverage for the child. Parents might agree that:

> It is agreed that the Respondent can obtain suitable health care coverage through an employer at the most reasonable cost. Therefore, the parents agree that health care coverage shall be provided by the Respondent. For out of pocket health care costs above those covered by insurance, the parents agree to prorate the expenses according to the state guideline percentage of support income which is currently sixty percent (60%) for Father and forty percent (40%) for Mother. These payments shall be made within thirty (30) days of the billing or insurance notice of payment due whichever comes last.

LIFE INSURANCE

As security for future support, parents may agree to maintain life insurance on themselves, naming their child the beneficiary. Parents might agree that:

> It is agreed that during the existence of the child support order both parents will obtain and maintain suitable life insurance coverage in the amount of $250,000. Both parents further agree that the child will be named the beneficiary of such policies. Each parent will provide the other with a copy of the policy and annual proof of payment of the premiums.

TAX EXEMPTION

Parents should cover this issue in any agreement. For example, parents might agree that:

> For income tax purposes, Mother can claim the child as an income tax exemption in odd numbered years beginning with the year 2001, and Father can claim the child as an income tax exemption in even numbered years beginning with the year 2000. Both parents agree to cooperate in the timely signing and filing of any required or necessary revenue forms to accomplish this purpose.

COMBINED INCOME CHILD SUPPORT WORKSHEET

	Mother	Father	Combined
1. Total Monthly GROSS Income:	_____	_____	

Less Monthly Deductions (if your state uses gross income method, ignore deductions and carry line 1 amounts to line 2):

	Mother	Father	Combined
Taxes	_____	_____	
FICA (social security)	_____	_____	
Health Insurance	_____	_____	
Mandatory Retirement	_____	_____	
Prior Child Support Order	_____	_____	
Total Deductions:	_____	_____	

2. Monthly NET/GROSS Income (subtract Total Deductions from line 1 amounts; if your state uses the gross income method, these will be the same amounts as on line 1): _____ _____

3. Monthly COMBINED Income (add line 2 incomes): _____ (Combined)

4. Each parent's percentage (divide each parent's line 2 amount by the line 3 combined income amount: _____ _____

5. Monthly Support Guideline Amount (from your state's guidelines: _____ (Combined)

6. Each parent's share (multiply line 5 by each parent's line 5 percentage): _____ _____

Note: You may have other additions or deductions to income as permitted by your state.

PERCENTAGE OF INCOME CHILD SUPPORT WORKSHEET

Noncustodial Parent

1. Total Monthly GROSS Income: _____

   Less Monthly Deductions (if your state uses
   the gross income method, ignore deductions
   and carry line 1 amount to line 2):

       Taxes   _____

       FICA (social security)   _____

       Health Insurance   _____

       Mandatory Retirement   _____

       Prior Child Support Order   _____

   Total Deductions: _____   _____

2. Monthly NET/GROSS Income (subtract Total
   Deductions from the line 1 amount; if your state
   uses the gross income method, this will be
   the same amount as on line 1):   _____

3. Monthly Child Support Amount (find the
   percentage due according to your state guidelines,
   and multiply line 2 by that percentage: _____

Note: You may have other additions or deductions to income permitted by your state.

THE CHILD SUPPORT CASE 10

You may be filing for child support as part of your divorce case (or legal separation or annulment case), as part of an independent custody case, or as an independent case for child support alone. If you have worked out an agreement, you can include that agreement in your divorce settlement agreement and judgment; in your child custody/visitation agreement and order; or as an agreement and order in your independent child support case.

If you have no agreement, you will need to proceed with the legal process to have a judge issue a support order. This chapter will discuss the various steps in going through the legal process. To get support, you must know where the other parent lives or works. This will allow you to properly notify the other parent that you are seeking child support and to easily obtain necessary income information about the other parent in order to get an appropriate child support amount determined. Basically, you will need to supply the judge with information about your financial situation, the other parent's financial situation, and your child's financial needs.

If you are seeking a child support order for the first time, you may also need to established paternity (see page 132 for more information about establishing paternity).

GATHERING FINANCIAL INFORMATION

Every state requires that both parties disclose certain financial information to properly determine the amount of child support. Although the financial information relates directly to the determination of child support, states may also require such information to be provided in connection with filing a petition for custody or visitation. This will often be in the form of financial affidavit (such as form 11 in appendix C).

Therefore, in addition to the information you gathered about the other parent and your child in preparing your case (see chapter 5), you should obtain financial information (as discussed below) about yourself and the other parent.

EMPLOYMENT   To obtain a complete picture of the earning capacity of a parent, courts consider the employment pattern of a parent for some period of time prior to the filing of the petition—usually three to five years. Financial employment information should include:

☛ The name and address of the parent's employer(s) for the past three years

☛ The type and hours of employment

☛ The parent's gross and net salary or wages per month, and upon what the deductions are based

☛ Whether there are any other employment benefits (e.g., commissions, bonuses, or profit sharing, stock purchase, insurance, or retirement plans)

OTHER INCOME SOURCES   To properly measure the expenses of a parent and the available resources, many states consider whether there are other adults in the parent's household who are available to contribute to living expenses. Also, child support received under a prior court order may be considered, and in some states, child support paid by a parent for a prior child will be deducted as an adjustment to income. Some states also consider the child's available resources and the source of that income. Information to gather includes:

☛ Child support received form other relationships

☛ Income of other adults in the parent's home

☛ Available cash (e.g., bank deposits, stocks, bonds, cash value of life insurance policies)

☛ The child's income

MONTHLY
EXPENSE
INFORMATION

Child support guidelines are premised on a recognition that a parent has certain living and personal expenses. This information is required to establish whether there is a basis for an increase or decrease in the support amount called for by the application of the guidelines. The following are standard categories of expenses found in the various states' child support worksheets, which are required to be completed in every state:

☛ Housing (rent, mortgage payments, property taxes, homeowner's insurance, utilities (electric, gas, water, sewer, garbage collection, telephone, cable television, etc.)

☛ Food and supplies (paper, tobacco, pets, groceries, meals eaten out)

☛ Child expenses (clothing, school tuition and expenses, tutoring, health allowances, recreation, daycare, and babysitting)

☛ Transportation costs (car payments, insurance, license fees, gas, oil, routine maintenance, parking, and public transportation)

☛ Health care (insurance premiums, uninsured medical, dental, orthodontic, and optical expenses)

☛ Parent's personal expenses (clothing, personal care, recreation, education, gifts, and other insurance costs)

FILING FOR CHILD SUPPORT

A parent (or eligible custodian for a child) may file for child support in their local courts, on their own, or through an attorney. Some states allow certain child support orders to be established administratively by a state agency designated by law to do so.

All states have a state-run child support enforcement program. These programs may provide the following services: location of absent parents, establishment of paternity, establishment and modification of support orders, enforcement of support orders, establishment and modification of medical support orders, and the collection and distribution of support payments. In Virginia and Washington, for example, the state's child support enforcement agency can also arrange child support orders. This is beneficial because it is faster than going to court.

While these services are available to all families, regardless of their financial status, many of the clients are aid-dependent families, and the child support payments collected go toward reimbursement of the assistance benefits paid to the families. To request child support services, an individual may apply through their local child support agency. (See your state's listing in appendix A.)

In many cases, unless the parent receives public assistance, there will be a fee for filing a petition. Some states do not charge for administrative filings, others permit the fee to be paid over time. States also permit a parent to request a waiver of fees by filing a special request explaining why you cannot pay the fees and costs of maintaining the case. You can obtain filing fee information from your local court clerk's office or child support agency. If you believe you are eligible for a deferral or waiver of the filing fees, these agencies will also have the necessary forms.

If you are filing an independent case for child support, you will need the same basic information as you would in preparing for a custody case. This is because custody will necessarily be decided at the time of ordering the child support. (See chapter 4.) Some states have child support worksheets to follow in preparing for your child support case. (See form 12 in appendix C, as well as pages 124 and 125, for sample worksheets.)

When you have completed the necessary worksheets and court or agency required forms, you may file them and arrange for service on the other parent. This is the same procedure as you would use in a custody filing (see chapter 4).

FINDING AND NOTIFYING A PARENT

In order to obtain an order for support, the child's parent must be notified and has a right to appear in court and answer the petition. Notifying the parent requires information on where the parent lives or works. If you do not know the current address or employer for the other parent, the easiest way to find a person is through their social security number, although names and addresses of friends and relatives, past employers, banks, utility companies, clubs, and organizations may also have helpful information.

If you have sought assistance from your local child support enforcement agency, it may also have resources that can assist in finding the other parent. State child support enforcement agencies have State Parent Locator Service (SPLS) facilities that can help find the absent parent. The SPLS will use the parent's social security number to check records of other agencies within your state, such as the motor vehicle registration agencies, unemployment insurance, income tax, and prison or jail facilities in an effort to find the absent parent. They can also request information from utility companies, schools, employers, and post offices, and more.

The most difficult child support cases are those in which the parent who has been ordered to pay child support lives in one state, and the child and the custodial parent live in another. All states provide methods to get child support in these cases. Federal law requires the state enforcement agencies to cooperate with each other in handling requests for assistance under the recently passed Uniform Interstate Family Support Act (UIFSA). All states have adopted UIFSA laws substantially similar to the Federal model, and rely heavily on them for pursuing enforcement in other states. UIFSA provides extended powers to states to reach beyond their own state lines for the establishment of support orders. All states have a Central Registry to receive incoming interstate child support cases, to review them to make sure that the information given is complete, to distribute them to the right local office, and to reply to status inquiries from child support offices in other states.

If the absent parent has moved out of state, the state can ask the Federal Parent Locator Service (FPLS) for assistance. The FPLS will search the records of the Internal Revenue Service (IRS), Social Security Administration, Department of Veterans Affairs, and State unemployment agencies, among others, to search for current address or employment information on the absent parent.

Most child support enforcement agencies have a very high demand for their services and they have to set priorities among the cases they receive. Interstate cases can take several months to complete. In fact, it can take nine months or longer for a custodial parent to receive support from an out-of-state parent.

Once the parent is located and notified, if a hearing is necessary, it may take some time to get a court date.

Establishing Paternity (if Necessary)

It has been predicted that more than half of the children born in the year 2000 will be born outside of marriage. Paternity is legal fatherhood. It legally establishes that a particular male is the father of a child. States must have procedures which allow paternity to be established up to at least the child's eighteenth birthday.

If the parties are not married, it is important that paternity be established as soon as possible, in order to preserve both parent's rights to the child. Once paternity is established, the father gains certain rights to his child, and the child also gains certain rights. Among these may be the right to inherit from the father, the right to medical and life insurance benefits, and the right to certain federal benefits, such as social security and veteran's benefits.

Under welfare reform laws enacted in 1996, it will be easier and faster to establish paternity. The father may acknowledge that he is the child's father in order for a child support order to be entered. When the child is born in a hospital, the father can acknowledge paternity right there. Many fathers voluntarily acknowledge paternity.

If the father does not voluntarily acknowledge paternity, the issue must be proven in court. Each state provides for the requirements to establish that the person is the parent of the child.

All states provide for some presumptions of paternity. For example, if a child is born during a marriage, that child is presumed to be the child of the husband and wife. If the husband believes that he is not the father, he can challenge this presumption. Genetic (DNA) testing can be done to determine the question.

Most states require that paternity be established by a "preponderance of the evidence," meaning that paternity (or lack of paternity) is "more likely than not." Putting this standard in terms of numbers, it means that there has to be a fifty-one percent weight to the evidence to find paternity. Some states insist on a higher "clear and convincing" standard, which is a tougher standard to meet than proof by a preponderance of the evidence.

Whatever the burden of proof on a person asserting or denying paternity, recent developments in DNA testing may make these distinctions irrelevant. The father, mother, and child can be required to submit to genetic tests. The results are highly accurate. With proper testing, most cases are decided on scientific evidence that is nearly always accurate.

COURT PROCEDURES

Once the parent has been notified, and if necessary, paternity has been established, the next issue is how much support should be awarded. Answering this question requires the court to consider the financial information forms required to be filed in child support cases and may require testimony from the parents and others, sometimes experts, regarding the contested income and expenses presented.

SEEKING A TEMPORARY ORDER OF SUPPORT

The court (or administrative agency, if permitted in your state) in which you file the application or petition for child support can enter a temporary order of child support. Whether support will be granted temporarily depends on the needs of the parent seeking that support during the time the case is pending. There will also be consideration given to whether the other parent has the ability to pay the support.

Requesting a temporary order of child support is made by a formal request to the court. The papers filed should indicate the financial needs of the child or children. (See forms 13 and 14 in appendix C.)

SECURITY FOR PAYMENT

Where the parties have not agreed on a support amount, a court may order security for payment of a child support order. This usually takes form in the establishment or maintenance of a life insurance policy or the creation of a trust for the children. Some states mandate that this be done.

Also, the court may order that the parent who pays support obtain a life insurance policy on him or herself to protect the payment plan. In some states, a child support order may automatically create a lien on the paying parent's property. For example, the court could order a lien against the real estate of the parent who owes support, so that if support remained unpaid, the property could be sold to pay the lien.

A court can also order a parent to obtain required health care coverage through a special order called a *qualified medical child support order* which requires that the employer's group health care plan provide coverage for a child. The employer can charge the parent for any premiums to carry out this order.

If the paying parent has a pension or retirement plan at work, the court can also order, in what is called a "qualified domestic relations order," the employer to add the child on as a payee of the plan as security for the child support order.

A court may also protect the best interests of the child by setting aside a part of either jointly-held or individually-held property of the parents in a separate trust or fund to pay for the support, education and welfare of a minor child or dependent child. This usually means that either the parent is ordered to hold property *in trust* or actually set up a trust account for the child.

RESPONDING TO A PETITION FOR CHILD SUPPORT

ANSWERING THE PETITION

Every state has statutes of limitations which govern the period within which a case may be filed. For example, a state may require that a child support case must be filed before the child reaches the age of eighteen. Therefore, check to be sure that the petition covers an eligible child.

Next, to pay child support, you must be found to be the father of the child in question. Paternity may be raised as a defense against a request for child support.

If you are the parent of the child, and you seek to have custody, you may wish to contest child support and file a *counterclaim* for custody and request child support of your own.

Or you may wish to challenge the child support amount requested on the basis that it is the product of incorrect income information, adjustments, or expense items. States' guideline amounts may be adjusted upward or downward based on a number of factors.

Failure to obtain the agreed upon (or ordered) visitation is not a defense to avoid paying child support.

Finally, if you agree that child support is due your child, you will answer the petition and provide your own financial affidavit to the court for review so that a complete picture of the child's needs and the parent's resources can then be evaluated and a proper child support award can be determined.

DEFAULT All states require the defendant (who may also be called a respondent) to respond within a certain time limit to the notice of the child support petition. If the defendant fails to respond, he or she can be "defaulted" which means that the case proceeds without them.

In such cases, courts rely heavily on the presumptions of the guideline amounts but will permit the parent who filed the petition to introduce evidence of additional need, and the support amount may accordingly be higher than the guidelines.

ENFORCEMENT OF THE CHILD SUPPORT ORDER

11

Obtaining the child support order is the first step to collecting support. Enforcing the order, however, is perhaps the biggest challenge facing parents today. Because each state had its own enforcement laws and procedures, the federal government stepped in and provided new enforcement options. Laws passed since 1975, have served to streamline enforcement and to make enforcement uniform for parents who live in different states. Also, new penalties have been added.

Some parents attempt to collect support owed to them by filing their own enforcement documents—others hire an attorney. Still others hire one of the myriad private agencies that may, for a fee, attempt to collect child support. Finally, some parents turn to the local public child support enforcement agency for assistance. Each of these methods has benefits and drawbacks. Doing it yourself may be time-consuming and frustrating (but is fairly inexpensive). Paying attorneys or agencies is more costly (but they do the "legwork"). Going through a public agency may be the least expensive of all, but probably takes more time, and may not be as successful as focused private efforts to collect support.

NEW METHODS   States are implementing strict child support enforcement techniques. For example, in Illinois in 1997, child support collections reached a record $295.8 million. Parents owing child support have been targeted not just by the state public aid agency, but by other state agencies and private firms in Illinois. The Illinois Departments of Revenue and Professional Regulation plus ten private agencies in Illinois now use their powers and resources to collect child support.

Some states have begun holding press conferences and developing press releases identifying the state's worst "deadbeat parents." For example, Kentucky has named its eight worst offenders as collectively owing over a quarter million dollars to their children.

One of the newest methods that is creating a lot of attention to the problem of parents who refuse to support their children is the posting of "Wanted" posters on the internet naming the top "deadbeat" parents who owe large amounts of child support. This has gotten some action from parents. For example, when Connecticut posted its fourth "poster" on the internet, three of the parents turned themselves in to begin a payment plan. These three parents allegedly owed a combined total of more than $110,000! Massachusetts reported that seven of the ten deadbeat dads featured on their state's "wanted" poster released in March of 1999 have been located. Also, in Massachusetts more than $1.3 million has been collected in overdue child support since the first "Most Wanted" poster was created in April, 1992.

On the federal level, the U.S. Postal Service is working with states to display in post offices "Wanted Lists" of parents who owe child support. Each state can provide their list to the Postal Service, and the list will be displayed in post offices within that state.

CONTEMPT   Historically, a citation for contempt of court was the most commonly used enforcement method for parents who had the ability to pay, but refused to do so. Once a court found the parent in contempt of court, the parent might be sent to jail for non-payment of child support or permitted to get out of jail by paying the contempt (or a scheduled) amount. Today, this power is combined with a number of the other options described below, such as license suspension.

To avoid being held in contempt for failure to pay support, you must show that you either did not have notice of the order, could not pay the order, or that your failure to pay was not willful.

For example, diverting income to support a new girlfriend or boyfriend will not be excused. Quitting a job or intentionally taking a lower-paying job will also not be an excuse for nonpayment.

DENIAL OR
LOSS OF
LICENSE

Part of child support enforcement reforms that have gone into effect permit states to suspend or deny applications for driver's licenses or professional licenses. This is a very effective tool in enforcing a child support order. For example, Nebraska's law permits the state to suspend the driver's, recreational, and professional licenses of parents who owe more than three months support. To avoid suspension, the parent must be in compliance with a payment plan for the past due support.

In Mississippi, the license suspension law applies to all regulated occupations and professions, from barbers to social workers to physicians, and extends to those seeking business and liquor licenses as well as driver's licenses and hunting or fishing licenses. Mississippi has a database that links the license information to those who are at least two months behind in their payments. Once notified, if the delinquent parent fails to work out a payment plan, the licensing agency suspends the license. A suspended license may be reinstated if the delinquent parent subsequently pays or agrees to a payment plan.

This sanction is very effective. In Connecticut, for example, in less than a year's time, the threat of losing a license has led to $12 million dollars in payments of past due child support.

LOSS OF TAX
REFUND

Federal and state tax refunds can be intercepted and used to collect overdue child support (as well as spousal support). Today, even lottery winnings of a parent may be subject to interception for overdue child support. By 1995, the federal government estimated that over $1 billion refunds had been intercepted for 1.2 million families. The average refund amount intercepted was $847. The federal government is very aggressive in this program. By 1996, refunds intercepted were up sixty-six percent since 1992.

Tax refund interception is possible today because most states now have computer database systems which record child support due and payments for that state. This is another reason why it is useful to have payments made through a state agency. Once a year, the states report the names of parents who owe overdue child support to the Internal Revenue Service and their state's taxation department.

There are threshold amounts which must be overdue for eligibility for the tax refund intercept program. Currently, for example, in Wisconsin, the past due amount must be $500 for the federal program, but only $150 for the state refund intercept program. Be aware that there may be a small processing fee taken out of the refund. In Wisconsin, for example, the fee will not be more than $25, and no fee is due if no refund is intercepted.

To protect against inevitable mistakes, before any refunds are intercepted, a notice will be sent to the paying parent's last known address explaining the program and how they can appeal. If the intercepted amount is more than the amount owed at the time the tax refund is received, the extra sum will be refunded to the taxpayer parent.

There are a number of limitations on tax intercept efforts. For example, no matter how much overdue support is owed, the most that can be intercepted is the amount of the refund. And, only the overdue amount submitted will be intercepted.

Also, to minimize repayment of an amount intercepted, amounts intercepted from a federal joint tax return will be held for up to six months before it is passed on to the parent owed the support. Even this does not guarantee that money received will not be recalled by the IRS or the state department of revenue, because tax returns can be amended for up to six years. For more information about your state's tax refund interception program, contact your state's child support agency (see the listing for your state in appendix A).

CONSUMER CREDIT BUREAU REPORTING

If a parent owes a considerable amount of past due child support, he or she can be reported to the consumer credit bureaus that track credit records. Having a child support debt on a credit record can mean not being able to get a mortgage, car loan, or new credit card. It may also have an effect on being able to rent an apartment, and obtain employment or a job promotion.

LIENS AND SEIZURE OF PROPERTY

A state may permit liens against any real property of the payor parent in that state. In some states, all child support judgments are automatic liens on the parent's real property, such as his or her house. The lien keeps that parent who owes child support from selling or refinancing the property until all the past due child support is paid.

A parent may seek to seize and sell the property of a parent who owes a substantial amount of past due child support. If the parent who owes past due support has bank accounts or investments, those assets are sometimes taken to pay back child support through a process called *garnishment*.

PARENTS WHO LIVE IN ANOTHER STATE

Over thirty percent of child support cases tracked by the federal government involved parents who owe child support and live or work in a different state than their children. In a pilot program, the federal Office of Child Support Enforcement showed that over sixty thousand delinquent parents had been located in a short period of time under a matching program conducted by certain states. This led to new federal laws which establish a Federal Case Registry and National Directory of New Hires to track delinquent parents across state lines. Employers are required to report all new hires to state agencies, which then report new hire information to the National Directory. This program is very effective. In the first six months of operation, the National Directory found over ninety thousand delinquent parents.

In Idaho, one of the top ten "deadbeat" parents was arrested in June of 1999 as a result of the New Hire Registry. This parent left Massachusetts and moved several times to evade investigators, allegedly owing more than $45,000 in back child support. Eventually, he moved to Idaho where he got a job with a state university. A routine reporting of new hire data collected from Idaho employers and sent to the national directory in Washington, DC, matched information against the Federal Case Registry, a database that holds child support cases from all fifty states. The "deadbeat" parent was arrested on fugitive from justice charges, and was held to answer to why he did not pay child support.

CRIMINAL PROSECUTION

The threat of criminal prosecution and the use of law enforcement's resources has become a real phenomenon in the stepped up effort to collect past due child support. For example, Connecticut estimated it has a deadbeat parent problem valued at $705.7 million dollars. In in one weekend in 1989, sheriffs in Connecticut tracked down and arrested more than fifty child support delinquents who allegedly owed more than $669,000.

On the state level, delinquent parents can be prosecuted criminally. On the federal level, the Justice Department is now investigating and prosecuting cases where parents cross state lines to avoid payment (the federal government estimates that billions of dollars in child support is owed to children whose parents have crossed state lines and failed to pay).

CHILD SUPPORT: 12
MODIFICATION, TERMINATION, AND APPEAL

MODIFICATION

While an existing child support order is always subject to modification, it is important to recognize that modifications are not automatic. Each parent may seek either an upward or downward modification. However, to do so requires the parent seeking the modification to return to a court (or administrative agency if permitted by your state) and obtain a new child support order.

In order to obtain some stability, most states require some period of time to pass (two or three years is common), or that the person seeking the modification show a substantial change in circumstances that warrants a review of the child support order. For example, in Washington, a child support order must be at least thirty-five months old before a party may request a modification.

In Virginia, reasons for requesting a review include: if there is a change in the gross income or employment status of either parent, if an order needs to be amended because medical support is not a part of the current support order, if extraordinary medical expenses for the child occurs, and if a change in the family's size occurs.

SUBSTANTIAL CHANGE IN CIRCUMSTANCES

In most states, it will be considered a substantial or significant change in circumstances if the guidelines have changed significantly. That is, if the guidelines amount at the time the order was entered is substantially different than the amount that would be due under the current guidelines.

In Arizona and Florida, for example, the law requires the person seeking the modification to show that an estimation of his or her current circumstances would result in a variance of fifteen percent or more from the existing amount. In Florida, the fifteen percent must equal at least a $50 difference. In Vermont, the change required for a modification of child support must be a "real, substantial and unanticipated change in circumstances," and must result in a change of at least ten percent between the current order and the amount calculated under the child support guidelines (not a ten percent change in income).

Some states, such as Arizona, permit a simplified proceeding. To show this variation, a parent is required to provide the court with a document proving the variance. The document will then be served upon the other parent. If no hearing is requested by the other parent, a court can simply review the request and enter the change in the order. If the matter is contested, there will be a hearing on the issue of the variance.

In Texas, only a court can modify child support—it can not be done by agreement of the parties. Grounds for a modification include either a material and substantial change in the circumstances of a child or the parent, or the passage of at least three years since the last child support order and the previously ordered monthly payment differs by either twenty percent or $100 from the amount called for by the current child support guidelines.

In most states, obtaining a modification requires acquiring a *certified copy* of the current support order (check with your court clerk), completing the necessary petition or form application for a modification, paying a filing fee (unless waived), and filing the forms with the child support agency or a court.

PAST-DUE SUPPORT
Modification of past due child support is not permitted by federal law. Modification can only be for future payments, so if a significant change in circumstances prevents payment of support, you must file your documents seeking a downward modification (or suspension) of support as soon as possible.

REMARRIAGE
The second marriage of a parent will not have an impact on a child support order, but new obligations to children will often result in that parent seeking modification of the order. The traditional view was that your child should not have support reduced because you decide to take on the obligations for a new family; however, many state guidelines now factor in obligations for such subsequent children.

CHANGE OF JOB
The change in employment of a parent may be considered for a modification of future child support. However, if unemployment or under employment results from an intentional choice or willfulness of the parent, the court may refuse to grant such a request.

CHANGE OF CUSTODY
A change in the parenting of a child will often be grounds for modification of a child support order. Keep in mind, however, that this is not automatic. The child support order will not be changeable until your petition to modify it is filed with the appropriate agency or clerk of the court.

TERMINATION

Just like some circumstances can cause a modification, certain events can trigger a termination of child support.

ADOPTION
The adoption of the child by the new spouse of the custodial parent usually operates to terminate a child support order. However, this will not usually relieve the paying parent of the obligation for any past due support.

EMANCIPATION
Age of majority. The general rule is still that a child support obligation ends when a child attains the age of majority (eighteen). However,

many states have laws which authorize a court to continue child support for a limited period of time past the age of majority (usually until age nineteen), as long as the child is enrolled as a full-time high school student. A few states have statutes which authorize the court to continue child support until the child graduates from college, and there have been cases where a court ordered the payment of graduate school; however, these situations are not common. Also, as stated previously in this book, the parties may agree to pay for the child's support for higher educational purposes or for some other reason until a specified event or date.

Child's marriage. A child's marriage operates as an emancipation event. So even if the child is still considered a minor under the law, the child support order will terminate upon marriage.

Child's military service. A child enlisting in the military is usually seen as an emancipation event, even if the child is still a minor under the law. A child entering the military service operates to terminate a child support order in most states.

If there is more than one child covered by a support order, the emancipation of one child will proportionately reduce the order in most states. The reduction occurs automatically. However, in some states, the order is not reduced unless the parent responsible for payment seeks a reduction.

DEATH OF PAYING PARENT
In all states, the death of a parent will not excuse any past due child support, and increasingly, the death of a parent will not terminate the child support order. Parties may agree to terminate support in the event of the death of a parent, upon payment of a lump sum such as through the purchase of a life insurance policy naming the child as beneficiary. Even if the order does not terminate, the death of the party owing support will usually be grounds for seeking a modification of the order. For example, out of the deceased parent's estate, the amount calculated to be due for support may be determined and converted into a lump

sum payment. If the deceased parent owes past due child support, a claim can also be made against that parent's estate.

APPEAL

If child support is contested, either parent can file a request for an appellate court to review a trial court's child custody order. Like appeals of custody decisions (see chapter 7), rarely does an appellate court reverse a child support decision. This is because if the child support amount is within the guidelines, the trial court has the discretion to make an award that is just and equitable. These terms are very broad, and a reviewing court would have to find that the trial court abused its discretion in entering the support order.

Appendix A
State Laws

The following section contains a state-by-state summary of the applicable laws relating to custody and child support, as well as the state agency to contact for information and assistance. While every effort has been made to provide up-to-date information, the information in this appendix can change at any time. Refer back to the section on "Finding the Law: Legal Research" in chapter 1 for more information about researching the law for your state.

Explanation of Terms

The following is an explanation of what information may be found under each of the headings in this appendix:

The Law: The first listing you will find is titled "The Law." This directs you to the title of the book where the laws for that state may be found. An abbreviation for the law, which is used in the following sections, is also given. The symbol "§" means "section." For some states, information is also given to try to help you find the specific volume or volumes you will need. For example, a direction to "ignore volume numbers" means that the books will give both a volume number and a section or chapter number on the cover. Use the section or chapter number, not the volume number. If the section number is followed by "et seq.," it means that the reference begins there and continues in several following sections in sequence.

Custody: This section tells you where to look for the general laws pertaining to child custody for your state, and gives a summary of what factors are considered.

Child Support: This section tells you where to look for the general laws pertaining to child support for your state, and gives a summary of what factors are considered.

Agency: This section gives the name and location of the central office of the child support agency in your state. There is most likely a local office, which you can locate by looking for the agency listed in your telephone directory, under the government listings.

ALABAMA

The Law: Code of Alabama Title 30. "C.A." Ignore volume numbers.

Custody: C.A. § 30-3-1. Upon granting a divorce, the court may give the custody and education of the children of the marriage to either father or mother, as may seem right and proper, having regard to the moral character and prudence of the parents and the age and sex of the children. In granting custody, the court will consider the children's safety and well-being.

Child Support: Alabama Rules of Judicial Administration 32. The basic child support obligation is determined by using the schedule of obligations. Child support is determined by adding the basic child support obligation, work-related child care costs, and health insurance costs. Child support is divided between the parents in proportion to their adjusted gross incomes. The obligation of each parent is computed by multiplying the total child support obligation by each parent's percentage share of their combined adjusted gross income. The custodial parent is presumed to spend his or her share directly on the child.

Agency: Department of Human Resources, Division of Child Support, 50 Ripley Street, Montgomery, AL 36130; (334) 242-9300; (in state only: 1-800-284-4347).

ALASKA

The Law: Alaska Statutes, Title 25. "A.S." Ignore volume numbers; look for "title" numbers. Supplement is in the front of each volume.

Custody: A.S. § 25.24.150. In an action for divorce or for legal separation, the court may make, modify, or vacate an order for the custody of or visitation with the minor child that may seem necessary or proper, including an order that provides for visitation by a grandparent or other person if that is in the best interests of the child. In awarding custody the court may consider only those facts that directly affect the well-being of the child. In determining the best interests of the child, the court shall consider: (1) the physical, emotional, mental, religious, and social needs of the child; (2) the capability and desire of each parent to meet these needs; (3) the child's preference if the child is of sufficient age and capacity to form a preference; (4) the love and affection existing between the child and each parent; (5) the length of time the child has lived in a stable, satisfactory environment and the desirability of maintaining continuity; (6) the desire and ability of each parent to allow an open and loving frequent relationship between the child and the other parent; (7) any evidence of domestic violence, child abuse, or child neglect in the proposed custodial household or a history of violence between the parents; (8) any evidence that substance abuse by either parent or other members of the household directly affects the emotional or physical well-being of the child; and (9) any other factors that the court considers pertinent.

Child Support: Alaska Civil Rule 90.3. This state uses a "net percentage of income" standard. In sole custody cases, the percentage by which the non-custodial parent's adjusted income must be multiplied in order to calculate the child support award is: 20% (1 child); 27% (2 children); 33% (3 children); and an extra 3% for each additional child. The court may allow the payor parent to reduce child support payments up to 50% for any period in which that parent has extended visitation of over 27 consecutive days. The order must specify the amount of the reduction which is allowable if the extended visitation is exercised. In cases of shared physical custody, child support is determined by calculating the annual amount (based on the percentages) each parent would pay to the other parent assuming the other parent had primary custody. The parent with the larger figure is the payor parent and the support due is equal to the difference between the two figures multiplied by 1.5. Child support is to be paid in 12 equal monthly installments unless shared custody is based on the payor parent having physical custody for periods of 30 consecutive days or more. In that case, the total annual award will be paid in equal installments over those months in which the payor parent does not have physical custody. There are exceptions to the guideline amounts, such as especially large family size, significant income of a child, divided custody, health or other extraordinary expenses, or unusually low expenses.

Agency: Child Support Enforcement Division, 550 West 7th Avenue, Suite 310, Anchorage, AK 99501; (907) 269-6900; (in state only: 1-800-478-3300).

ARIZONA

The Law: Arizona Revised Statutes Annotated. "A.R.S." Ignore volume numbers; look for "section" numbers.

Custody: A.R.S. § 25-403. The court shall determine joint or sole custody, either originally or upon petition for modification, in accordance with the best interests of the child. Joint custody is permitted if both parents agree and submit a written parenting plan and the court finds such an agreement is in the best interests of the child. The parenting plan must include: each parent's rights and responsibilities for the personal care of the child and for decisions in areas such as education, health care and religious training; a schedule of the physical residence of the child, including holidays and school vacations; a procedure by which disputes may be mediated or resolved; periodic review of the plan by the parents; and a statement that the parties understand that joint custody does not necessarily mean equal parenting time.

The court may order joint legal custody without ordering joint physical custody. The court must consider all relevant factors, including: (1) the wishes of the child's parent or parents as to custody; (2) the wishes of the child as to the custodian; (3) the interaction and interrelationship of the child with the child's parent or parents, the child's siblings and any other person who may significantly affect the child's best interest; (4) the child's adjustment to home, school and community; (5) the mental and physical health of all individuals involved; (6) which parent is more likely to allow the child frequent and meaningful continuing contact with the other parent; (7) which parent has provided primary care of the child; (8) the nature and extent of coercion or duress used by a parent in obtaining an agreement regarding custody; and (9) whether a parent has complied with Chapter 3, Article 5 (the domestic relations education section). Domestic violence or drug abuse will be considered as contrary to the best interests of the child. A.R.S. §§ 25-401 to 25-414.

No motion to modify a custody order may be made earlier than one year after its date, unless the court permits it to be made on the basis of affidavits that there is reason to believe the child's present environment may seriously endanger the child's physical, mental, moral or emotional health (such as evidence of domestic violence, spousal or child abuse) Six months after a joint custody order is entered, a parent may petition the court for modification of the order based on the failure of the other parent to comply with the provisions of the order.

Child Support: Supreme Court Administrative Order 96-29. This is a "combined adjusted gross income state." Gross income includes income from any source less public assistance benefits, certain self-employment expenses and payments under prior orders for child support and spousal maintenance. The adjusted gross income for each parent is added together to produced the combined adjusted gross income. The state schedule will show the amount of support due for this income level. Expenses for health insurance will be added and child care, education, older child and other extraordinary expenses may be added to this support amount. Next, each parent's percentage share is determined by dividing the parent's adjusted gross income by the combined adjusted income. The result is that parent's share of the combined adjusted gross income. A visitation credit may be awarded to the parent without custody. The parent without custody will be ordered to pay a certain amount while the parent with custody will be presumed to spend their proportionate share directly on the child. Upon written findings, a court may deviate from the guidelines where application of the guidelines is inappropriate or unjust for the particular case.

Modification is permitted upon a showing of a substantial and continuing change of circumstances, such as a 15% difference between the amount ordered and the guidelines. The Rule sets out the procedure and forms required. Approved forms are available from the Clerk of the Superior Court.

Agency: Division of Child Support Enforcement, 343 North Central Avenue, Phoenix, AZ 85012; (602) 252-4045; (in state only: 1-800-882-4151).

ARKANSAS

The Law: Arkansas Code of 1987 Annotated, Title 9, Chapter 13, Section 9-13-101 (A.C.A. § 9-13-101). Look for "title" or "chapter" numbers.

Custody: A.C.A. § 9-13-101. In a divorce, the award of custody of the children of the marriage must be made without regard to the sex of the parent, but solely in accordance with the welfare and best interests of the children. When in the best interests of a child, custody must be awarded in such a way so as to assure the frequent and continuing contact of the child with both parents. The court may consider, among other facts, which parent is more likely to allow the child or children frequent and continuing contact with the noncustodial parent. In cases of domestic violence, a court will consider its effect upon the best interests of the child, whether or not the child was physically injured or personally witnessed the abuse.

Child Support: Arkansas Administrative Order of the Supreme Court No. 10. The guidelines provide a chart of support due based on number of children and income level. Income means any form of payment including wages, salaries, commissions, bonuses, workers' compensation, disability, pension, and interest, less deductions for taxes, social security (FICA), medicare, and railroad retirement; medical insurance paid for dependent children, and presently paid support for other dependents by Court order. Visitation credit for extended visitation periods is permitted. Deviation from the guidelines is permitted if the evidence shows that the needs of the dependents require a different level of support.

Agency: Office of Child Support Enforcement, P.O. Box 8133, Little Rock, AR 72203; (501) 682-8398; (1-800-247-4549).

CALIFORNIA

The Law: West's Annotated California Codes, Family Code. (There is also a set called Deering's California Codes Annotated, which will contain the same section numbers.)

Custody: Fam. Code § 3020. The health, safety, and welfare of children will be the primary concern in determining the best interest of children in any orders regarding the custody or visitation of children. Unless the contact would not be in the best interest of the child (e.g., child abuse or domestic violence), children should have frequent and continuing contact with both parents after the parents have separated or dissolved their marriage, or ended their relationship. Factors include: (1) child's preference (if child is old enough); and (2) desire and ability of each parent to allow a relationship with other parent. Fam. Code §§ 3040-3044.

Child Support: Fam. Code §§ 4050–4076. The amount of child support to be paid by parents is based on the amount of time each parent spends with the child and their net income. Net income is calculated by taking a person's total income and subtracting certain expenses, such as federal and state income taxes, health insurance premiums, state disability insurance, and Social Security taxes. A court may permit other expense deductions. The percentage of income payable is: 25% (1 child), 40% (2 children) and 50% (3 children) which will then be adjusted according to the amount of time each parent spends with the child(ren). A court may also add in certain expense adjustments to child support, such as child care, medical bills not paid by insurance, travel expenses for visitation with the other parent, or a child's special education needs.

Modifications are permitted upon a significant change in circumstance or 24 month period, and may be permitted based on guideline application which shows that the order should be increased or decreased by at least $50 or 30 percent.

Agency: Office of Child Support Enforcement, Department of Social Services, 744 P Street, Mail Stop 17-29, Sacramento, CA 95814; (916) 654-1532; (1-800-952-5253).

COLORADO

The Law: West's Colorado Revised Statutes Annotated, Title 14, Article 10, Section 14-10-124 (C.R.S.A. § 14-10-124).

Custody: C.R.S.A. § 14-10-124(1.5). Both parties may submit a parenting plan or plans for the court's approval that address both parenting time and the allocation of decision-making responsibilities. If no parenting plan is submitted or if the court does not approve it, the court can formulate its own parenting plan. Parental responsibilities will be determined in accordance with the best interests of the child giving paramount consideration to the physical, mental, and emotional conditions and needs of the child as follows: (1) the wishes of the child's parents as to parenting time; (2) the wishes of the child if he or she is sufficiently mature to express reasoned and independent preferences as to the parenting time schedule; (3) the interaction and interrelationship of the child with his or her parents, his or her siblings, and any other person who may significantly affect the child's best interests; (4) the child's adjustment to his or her home, school, and community; (5) the mental and physical health of all individuals involved, except that a disability alone shall not be a basis to deny or restrict parenting time; (6) the ability of the parties to encourage the sharing of love, affection, and contact between the child and the other party; (7) whether the past pattern of involvement of the parties with the child reflects a system of values, time commitment, and mutual support; (8) the physical proximity of the parties to each other as this relates to the practical considerations of parenting time; (9) whether there is credible evidence that one of the parties has been a perpetrator of child abuse or neglect or spouse abuse; and (10) the ability of each party to place the needs of the child ahead of his or her own needs.

Child Support: C.R.S.A. § 14-10-115. Child support is determined using the schedule of basic child support obligations in the guideline. Child support will be divided between the parents in proportion to their adjusted gross incomes. "Adjusted gross income" means gross income less existing child support orders, alimony or maintenance actually paid by a parent. Except in cases of shared physical custody or split custody, child support is determined by adding each parent's obligations for basic child support amount, work-related child care costs, extraordinary medical expenses, and extraordinary adjustments to the guideline schedule. The custodial parent is presumed to spend his or her child support directly on the children. The noncustodial parent will owe his or her total child support to the custodial parent minus any payments ordered to be made directly for the child such as extraordinary medical expenses, or extraordinary adjustments to the schedule. In shared custody cases, each parent's share of the adjusted basic child support obligation is multiplied by the percentage of time the children spend with the other parent to determine the basic child support obligation owed to the other parent. The parent owing the greater amount of child support shall owe the difference between the two amounts as a child support to the other parent. This figure can also be adjusted by certain expenses or direct payment sums.

Agency: Division of Child Support Enforcement, 1575 Sherman Street, 2ndFloor, Denver, CO 80203-1714; (303) 866-5994 (no toll-free number).

CONNECTICUT

The Law: Connecticut General Statutes Annotated, Title 46b, Section 46b-56 (C.G.S.A. § 46b-56). Ignore "chapter" numbers; look for "title" numbers.

Custody: C.G.S.A. § 46b-56. The court may assign the custody of any child to the parents jointly, to either parent or to a third party, according to its best judgment upon the facts of the case and subject to such conditions and limitations as it deems equitable. The court may also make any order granting the right of visitation of any child to a third party (e.g., grandparents). In making or modifying any order with respect to custody or visitation, the court shall be guided by the best interests of the child, giving consideration to the wishes of the child if the child is of sufficient age and capable of forming an intelligent preference. In making the initial order the court may take into consideration the causes for dissolution of the marriage or legal separation if such causes are relevant in a determination of the best interests of the child and consider whether the party satisfactorily completed participation in a parenting education program. A parent not granted custody of a minor child shall not be denied the right of access to the academic, medical, hospital or other health records of such minor child unless otherwise ordered by the court for good cause shown.

Child Support: C.G.S.A. § 46b-215a-2. Child support is determined using the combined net income of both parents and applying it to the guideline schedule then adding the cost of the child's health insurance premiums. Calculate each parent's share of the combined net income, and multiply the result for each parent by the total obligation due. The custodial parent's amount due is presumed spent directly on the children. The noncustodial parent's total child support obligation is the basic child support amount reduced by the amount paid by that parent for health insurance premiums for the children. Shared custody arrangements may produce a different amount.

Agency: Department of Social Services, Bureau of Child Support Enforcement, 25 Sigourney Street, Hartford, CT 06106-5033; (860) 424-5251; 1-800-228-5437 (for problems) or 1-800-647-8872 (for information) or 1-800-698-0572 (for payments).

DELAWARE

The Law: Delaware Code Annotated, Title 13, Section 722 (13 D.C.A. § 722). Ignore volume numbers; look for "title" numbers.

Custody: 13 D.C.A. § 722. The court must determine the legal custody and residential arrangements for a child in accordance with the best interests of the child, including: (1) the wishes of the child's parent or parents as to his or her custody and residential arrangements; (2) the wishes of the child as to his or her custodian(s) and residential arrangements; (3) the interaction and interrelationship of the child with his or her parents, grandparents, siblings, persons cohabiting in the relationship of husband and wife with a parent of the child, any other residents of the household or persons who may significantly affect the child's best interests; (4) the child's adjustment to his or her home, school and community; (5) the mental and physical health of all individuals involved; (6) past and present compliance by both parents with their rights and responsibilities to their child; and (7) any evidence of domestic violence.

Child Support: Delaware Family Court Civil Rules. This state is a "combined net income" state which permits a deduction for self support of a parent. From gross income is deducted withholding for taxes, FICA, medical insurances, retirement, union dues and other permitted expenses. From the net income amount is also deducted a parent's self-support allowance, because each parent is entitled to keep a minimum amount of income for their own needs. The remaining sum is the net income available for child support. The primary support obligation is then determined by application to the guidelines for the correct number of children to be supported.

In determining the amount of support due to one to whom the duty of support has been found to be owing, the Court, among other things, shall consider: the health, relative economic condition, financial circumstance, income, including the wages, and earning capacity of the parties, including the children; the manner of living to which the parties have been accustomed when they were living under the same roof; the general equities inherent in the situation.

Agency: Division of Child Support Enforcement, Delaware Health and Social Services, 1901 North Dupont Hwy, P.O. Box 904, New Castle, DE 19720; (302) 577-4863 or 577-4800 (no toll-free number).

DISTRICT OF COLUMBIA

The Law: District of Columbia Code, Title 16, Section 16-911 (D.C.C. § 16-911).

Custody: D.C.C. § 16-911(a)(5). A court may award joint or sole custody according to the best interest of the child. Joint custody is presumed to be in the best interest of the child or children, unless abuse or neglect is present or where parental kidnapping has occurred. In determining the best interest of the child, the court shall consider all relevant factors, including: (1) the wishes of the child as to his or her custodian, where practicable; (2) the wishes of the child's parent or parents as to the child's custody; (3) the interaction and interrelationship of the child with his or her parent or parents, his or her siblings, and any other person who may emotionally or psychologically affect the child's best interest; (4) the child's adjustment to his or her home, school, and community; (5) the mental and physical health of all individuals involved; (6) the capacity of the parents to communicate and reach shared decisions affecting the child's welfare; (7) the willingness of the parents to share custody; the prior involvement of each parent in the child's life; (8) the potential disruption of the child's social and school life; (9) the geographical proximity of the parental homes as this relates to the practical considerations of the child's or children's residential schedule; (10) the demands of parental employment; (11) the age and number of children; (12) the sincerity of each parent's request; and (13) the parent's ability to financially support a custody arrangement.

Parties may agree to custody unless clear and convincing evidence indicates that such arrangement is not in the best interest of the minor child or children. Parenting plans can include: the residence of the child or children; the financial support based on the needs of the child or children and the actual resources of the parent; visitation; holidays, birthdays, and vacation visitation; transportation of the child or children between the residences; education; religious training, if any; access to the child's or children's educational, medical, psychiatric, and dental care records; except in emergencies, the responsibility for medical, psychiatric, and dental treatment decisions; communication between the child and the parents; and resolving conflict such as a recognized family counseling or mediation service before application to the court to resolve a conflict.

Child Support:	D.C.C. § 16-916.1. Parties may agree on a support amount as long as they are aware of the guideline amounts which are: 20% (1 child), 26% (2 children), 30% (3 children) and 32% (4 or more children). These guideline amounts are increased or decreased depending on the parent's gross income and the age of the child. Currently, the guidelines have 5 income levels with a different percentage applied at each level. The court may order at any time, that maintenance or support payments be made to the clerk of the court for remittance to the person entitled to receive the payments.
Agency:	Office of Paternity and Child Support Enforcement, Department of Human Services, 800 9th Street, SW, 2nd Floor, Washington, DC 20024-2485; (202) 645-7500 (no toll-free number).

FLORIDA

The Law:	Florida Statutes, Chapter 61, Section 61-13 (F.S. § 61-13). A new set is published every odd-numbered year, with hard-cover supplements every even-numbered year. Ignore volume numbers; look for "chapter" numbers. [There is also a set called "West's Florida Statutes Annotated," which includes supplements in the back of each volume.]
Custody:	F.S. § 61-13(a)(b). Custody is determined in accordance with the best interests of the child to encourage frequent and continuing contact with both parents after the parents separate or the marriage of the parties is dissolved and to encourage parents to share the rights and responsibilities, and joys, of childrearing unless the court finds that shared parental responsibility would be detrimental to the child (such as conviction of certain felonies, domestic violence) in which case it may order sole parental responsibility and make arrangements for visitation as will best protect the child or abused spouse from further harm.

For shared parental responsibility, the court may consider the expressed desires of the parents and may grant to one party the ultimate responsibility over specific aspects of the child's welfare or may divide those responsibilities between the parties based on the best interests of the child. Areas of responsibility may include primary residence, education, medical, and dental care, and any other responsibilities that the court finds unique to a particular family. The best interests of the child shall include an evaluation of all factors affecting the welfare and interests of the child, including, but not limited to: (1) the parent who is more likely to allow the child frequent and continuing contact with the nonresidential parent; (2) the love, affection, and other emotional ties existing between the parents and the child; (3) the capacity and disposition of the parents to provide the child with food, clothing, medical care, or other remedial care recognized and permitted under the laws of Florida in lieu of medical care, and other material needs; (4) the length of time the child has lived in a stable, satisfactory environment and the desirability of maintaining continuity; (5) the permanence, as a family unit, of the existing or proposed custodial home; (6) the moral fitness of the parents; (7) the mental and physical health of the parents; (8) the home, school, and community record of the child; (9) the reasonable preference of the child, if the court deems the child to be of sufficient intelligence, understanding, and experience to express a preference; (10) the willingness and ability of each parent to facilitate and encourage close and continuing parent-child relationship between the child and the other parent; (11) evidence that any party has knowingly provided false information to the court regarding a domestic violence proceeding; (12) evidence of domestic violence or child abuse; and (13) any other fact considered by the court to be relevant.

Child Support: F.S. § 61-13(a). The court initially entering a support order has jurisdiction to modify the amount and terms and conditions of the child support payments when the modification is found necessary by the court in the best interests of the child, when the child reaches majority, or when there is a substantial change in the circumstances of the parties. Support orders must contain provisions for health insurance for the minor child when the insurance is reasonably available. The court shall apportion the cost of coverage, and any noncovered medical, dental, and prescription medication expenses of the child, to both parties by adding the cost to the basic obligation determined pursuant to § 61.30(6). The court may order that payment of uncovered medical, dental, and prescription medication expenses of the minor child be made directly to the payee on a percentage basis.

If both parties request and the court finds that it is in the best interest of the child, support payments need not be directed through the county depository. The court shall provide a copy of the order to the depository. If there is a default in payments, any party may subsequently file an affidavit with the depository alleging a default in payment of child support and stating that the party wishes to require that payments be made through the depository. The party shall provide copies of the affidavit to the court and to each other party. Fifteen days after receipt of the affidavit, the depository shall notify both parties that future payments shall be paid through the depository.

Agency: Child Support Enforcement Program, Department of Revenue, P.O. Box 8030, Tallahassee, FL; 32314-8030; (850) 922-9590 (no toll-free number).

GEORGIA

The Law:
Official Code of Georgia Annotated, Title 19, Chapter 9, Section 1 (C.G.A. § 19-9-1). Ignore volume numbers; look for "title" and "chapter" numbers. [This is not the same set as the "Georgia Code," which is a separate and outdated set of books with a completely different numbering system.]

Custody:
C.G.A. § 19-9-1. In divorce or custody cases, parents who are not in default may be awarded custody, but in domestic violence cases, the court will look into all the circumstances of the parties, including improvement of the health of a party seeking a change in custody provisions, and, after hearing both parties, may place the children, if necessary, in possession of guardians appointed by the judge of the probate court. Children 14 and over have the controlling right to select the parent with whom he or she desires to live unless the parent so selected is determined not to be a fit and proper person to have the custody of the child. The court may issue an order granting temporary custody to the selected parent for a trial period not to exceed six months regarding the custody of a child who has reached the age of 14 years where the judge hearing the case determines such a temporary order is appropriate.

Child Support:
C.G.A. § 19-6-15. Child support is based on a percentage of gross income (100% of wages, interest, dividends, rental income, self-employment, and all other income, except need-based public assistance). The amount is determined by multiplying the gross income by a percentage based on the number of children. The percentages are stated in ranges: 17-23% (1 child), 23-28% (2 children), 25-32% (3 children), 29-35% (4 children), and 31-37% (5 or more children). Deviation is permitted upon written findings explaining why, under the guidelines, the child support would be unjust or inappropriate (such as ages of the children; extraordinary medical costs; educational costs; day-care costs; shared physical custody arrangements, including extended visitation; a party's other support obligations to another household). Support continues until the child reaches the age of majority, dies, marries, or becomes emancipated (can be extended to age 20 if the child is attending secondary school). Permits jury trials in contested cases.

Agency:
Child Support Administration, P.O. Box 38450, Atlanta, GA 30334-0450; (404) 657- 3851; (1-800-227-7993 for 706 & 912 area codes only or from area codes 404 & 770, dial your area code + 657-2780).

HAWAII

The Law:
Hawaii Revised Statutes, Title 571, Section 571-46 (H.R.S. § 571-46). Ignore volume numbers; look for "title" numbers.

Custody:
Hawaii Rev. Stat. § 571-46. In cases for divorce, separation, annulment, separate maintenance, or a custody proceeding courts may make an order for the custody of the minor child as may seem necessary or proper. In awarding custody, the court shall be guided by the following standards, considerations, and procedures: custody should be awarded to either parent or to both parents (or to third persons) according to the best interests of the child; if a child is of sufficient age and capacity to reason, so as to form an intelligent preference, the child's wishes as to custody shall be considered and be given due weight by the court. Reasonable visitation rights shall be awarded to parents, grandparents, and any person interested in the welfare of the child in the discretion of the court, unless it is shown that rights of visitation are detrimental to the best interests of the child. There is a presumption that it is not in the best interest of the child to be placed in the custody of a

perpetrator of family violence. In such cases, a court may prohibit overnight visitation or order that visitation be supervised at the expense of the perpetrator parent or the exchange of a child occur in a protected setting; order the perpetrator of family violence to attend and complete intervention or counseling programs or abstain from alcohol or controlled substances during the visitation periods; pay a fee to defray the costs of supervised visitation or require a bond be posted as security for the return and safety of the child.

A custody award shall be subject to modification or change whenever the best interests of the child require or justify the modification or change.

Child Support: Hawaii Child Support Guidelines. In low income cases, a simplified form of the guidelines may be used which is based on gross income which generally includes all income except public assistance. In higher income cases, the guidelines provide that parents are entitled to keep sufficient income for their most basic needs and to facilitate continued employment, but until the basic needs of the child(ren) are met, parents may not retain any more income than required to provide the bare necessities for the parent's own self-support. When income is sufficient to cover the basic needs of the parents and the child(ren), the child(ren) shall share in the parents' additional income. The total child support due includes this basic living amount plus a percentage of gross income of the parents less certain expenses paid directly by a parent for the child (such as medical insurance). The non-custodial parent must pay to the custodial parent the total amount of his or her obligation unless there are exceptional circumstances. The custodial parent is presumed to pay for the child's expenses directly. The guidelines provide special calculations for shared physical custody, split custody or extended visitation.

Agency: Child Support Enforcement Agency, Department of Attorney General, 680 Iwilei Street, Suite 490, Honolulu, HI 96817; (808) 587-3698 (no toll-free number).

IDAHO

The Law: Idaho Code, Title 32, Section 717 (I.C. § 32-717). Ignore volume number.

Custody: I.C. § 32-717. In an action for divorce the court may, before and after judgment, give such direction for the custody, care, and education of the children of the marriage as may seem necessary or proper in the best interests of the children. The court shall consider all relevant factors which may include: the wishes of the child's parent or parents as to his or her custody; the wishes of the child as to his or her custodian; the interaction and interrelationship of the child with his or her parent or parents, and his or her siblings; the child's adjustment to his or her home, school, and community; the mental and physical health and integrity of all individuals involved; the need to promote continuity and stability in the life of the child; and whether or not domestic violence occured in the presence of the child.

In any case where the child is actually residing with a grandparent in a stable relationship, the court may recognize the grandparent as having the same standing as a parent for evaluating what custody arrangements are in the best interests of the child.

Child Support: Idaho Rules of Civil Procedure, Rule 6(c)(6). The guidelines apply to children under the 18 years of age or children pursuing high school education up to the age of 19. The guidelines are based on the gross income of the parents (decreasing for higher income levels) less permitted adjustments (such as alimony, maintenance, and other child support paid). Health care expenses and work-related child care expenses may be added to the amount due. The total amount of child support would be divided between the parents as a proportion of their guideline incomes according to a schedule based on number of children and a sliding amount due per income bracket (For example, the schedule provides that for 1 child, 17% of the parents' combined guideline income of $10,000 is due plus, 15% of the next $20,000 and 13% of the next $20,000 and 10% of the next $20,000 etc.,). Adjustment to the guidelines are made in cases of shared physical custody (defined as more than 35% of the overnights in a year with each parent). For extended visits, the guidelines may also provide up to a 50% reduction of support for the duration of the actual physical custody in the visiting parent.

A substantial and material change of circumstances will support a motion for modification of child support obligations.

Agency: Bureau of Child Support Services, Department of Health and Welfare, 450 West State Street, 5th Floor, Boise, ID 83720 - 5005; (208) 334-5710; (1-800-356-9868).

ILLINOIS

The Law: West's Illinois Compiled Statutes Annotated, Chapter 750, Article 5, Section 602 (750 ILCS 5/602).

Custody: 750 ILCS 5/602. In a proceeding for dissolution of marriage, legal separation, declaration of invalidity of marriage, a proceeding for child support following dissolution of the marriage the court shall consider the best interests of the child, including: the wishes of the child and parents as to custody; the interaction and interrelationship of child with parents and siblings; the child's adjustment to home,school and community; the mental and physical health of all parties; domestic violence; willingness and ability of each parent to facilitate and encourage a close and continuing relationship between the other parent and child. Only that conduct which affects the parent's relationship to the child will be considered. Joint custody may be ordered pursuant to a joint parenting agreement or upon order of court if it is in the best interests of the child. A joint parenting agreement will specify each parent's powers, rights and responsibilities for the child's personal care, and for major decisions such as education, health care and religion. The agreement must also provide a method for resolving disputes and provide for periodic review. If sole custody is ordered, the other parent is entitled to reasonable visitation absent the presence of a serious risk of harm to the child.

Unless by agreement, requests for modification may be made no earlier than 2 years after the last order unless there is evidence of a serious risk of endangerment or changed circumstances.

Child Support: 750 ILCS 5/505. The court may order either or both parents owing a duty of support to a child of the marriage to pay an amount reasonable and necessary for his support, without regard to marital misconduct. The duty of support owed to a minor child includes the obligation to provide for the reasonable and necessary physical, mental and emotional health needs of the child. The guidelines are based on a percentage of the noncustodial parent's income: 20% (1 child), 25% (2 children), 32% (3 children), 40% (4 children), 45% (5 children) and 50% (6 or more children).

Departures from the guidelines may be based on: the financial resources and needs of the child; the financial resources and needs of the custodial parent; the standard of living the child would have enjoyed had the marriage not been dissolved; the physical and emotional condition of the child, and his educational needs; and the financial resources and needs of the non-custodial parent.

An order for support must include a date on which child support terminates. The date can be no earlier than the child turns 18 or is otherwise emancipated. The termination date does not apply to any unpaid support owed.

Each payment due under a support order is considered an enforceable judgment against the person obligated to pay. A lien arises by operation of law against the real and personal property of the noncustodial parent for each installment of overdue support owed by the noncustodial parent.

Agency:
Child Support Enforcement Division, Illinois Department of Public Aid, 509 South Sixth Street, Marriott Building P. O. Box 19405, Springfield, IL 62701-1825; (217) 524-4602; (1-800-447-4278 in Illinois only).

INDIANA

The Law:
Burns Indiana Code Annotated, Title 31, Article 17, Chapter 2, Section 8 (Burns Ind. Code Ann. § 31-17-2-8). *West's Annotated Indiana Code. "A.I.C." Look for "title" numbers.

Custody:
Burns Ind. Code Ann. § 31-17-2-8. The court shall enter a custody order in accordance with the best interests of the child. In determining the best interests of the child, there is no presumption favoring either parent. The court shall consider all relevant factors, including: the age and sex of the child; the wishes of the child's parent or parents; the wishes of the child, with more consideration given to the child's wishes if the child is at least fourteen (14) years of age; the interaction and interrelationship of the child with: the child's parent or parents; the child's sibling; and any other person who may significantly affect the child's best interests; the child's adjustment to the child's home, school and community; the mental and physical health of all individuals involved; evidence of a pattern of domestic violence by either parent. A court may also award custody to a non-parent caretaker, called a *de facto custodian*, upon consideration of additional best interest factors.

Child Support:
Indiana C.S.G. (Sup.Ct. Order). The guidelines state that the gross income of both parents is added together after certain adjustments are made, and a percentage share of income for each parent is determined from which certain work-related child care expense may be deducted.. Then applying the support tables, the total cost of supporting a child or children is determined. Work-related child care expenses and health insurance premiums for the child(ren) are then added to the basic child support obligation. The child support obligation is then prorated between the parents, based on their proportionate share of the adjusted income. If a judge believes that in a particular case application of the Guideline amount would be unreasonable, unjust, or inappropriate, a finding must be made that sets forth the reason for deviating from the guidelines (such as union dues owed, support for an elderly parent, purchase of school clothes, extraordinary medical expenses, the children spend substantially more time with the noncustodial parent than in the average case, certain visitation expenses).

Agency:
Child Support Office, 402 West Washington Street, Room W360, Indianapolis, IN 46204; (317) 233-5437; (1-800-622-4932).

IOWA

The Law: Iowa Code Annotated, Section 598.41 (I.C.A. § 598.41). Ignore volume numbers; look for "section" numbers.

Custody: I.C.A. § 598.41. The court, insofar as is reasonable and in the best interest of the child, shall order custody, including liberal visitation rights where appropriate, which will assure the child the opportunity for the maximum continuing physical and emotional contact with both parents after the parents have separated or dissolved the marriage. Joint legal custody is preferred, and the parties may agree as to custody. Joint legal custody does not require joint physical care, but permits equal participation in decisions affecting the child's legal status, medical care, education, extracurricular activities, and religious instruction. A court can also grant joint legal custody on the request of a single parent, however in such cases a court may require the parties to participate in custody mediation to determine whether joint custody is in the best interest of the child. The presence of domestic violence results in a presumption against custody.

Child Support: Iowa Child Support Guidelines. The guidelines schedules are based on net income of the noncustodial parent (gross income less deductions such as taxes withheld, social security deductions, mandatory pension deductions, union dues; health insurance premiums deducted from wages, prior child and spouse support paid pursuant to court or administrative order, and certain child care expenses). Parties may enter into an agreement for child support and medical support if the amount is in substantial compliance with the guidelines. If not, the court must determine whether it is justified and appropriate, and, if so, include the stated reasons for the variance in the order. The guidelines amount may be adjusted upward or downward if the court finds it is necessary to do so to provide for the needs of the children and to do justice between the parties under the special circumstances of the case.

Agency: Bureau of Collections, Department of Human Services, Hoover Building - 5th Floor, Des Moines, IA 50319; (515) 281-5580 (no toll-free number).

KANSAS

The Law: Kansas Statutes Annotated, Section 60-1610 (K.S.A. § 60-1610). You may find these either as "Vernon's Kansas Statutes Annotated," or "Kansas Statutes Annotated, Official." Both sets have very poor indexing systems.

Custody: K.S.A. § 60-1610. By law, joint custody is preferred, although equal residency time is not necessary. A court can also order sole custody, divided custody or custody in a relative or third person based on certain factors. A written custody or residency agreement is presumed to be in the best interests of the child, but a court may order differently upon specific findings of fact that the agreement is not in the best interests of the child. The court shall consider: the length of time that the child has been under the actual care and control of any person other than a parent and the circumstances relating thereto; the desires of the child's parents as to custody or residency; the desires of the child as to the child's custody or residency; the interaction and interrelationship of the child with parents, siblings and any other person who may significantly affect the child's best interests; the child's adjustment to the child's home, school and community; the willingness and ability of each parent to respect and appreciate the bond between the child and the other parent and to allow for a continuing relationship between the child and the other parent; and evidence of spousal abuse.

To seek a change in an order within three years of the date of the last order, a material change in circumstances must be shown. This is not required if more than three years has passed since the date of the last order.

Child Support: Kansas Administrative Order No. 128. A court may order child support and education expenses to be paid by either or both parents for any child up to 18 years of age (19 if still in high school) unless the parents agree in writing which is approved by the court, to pay support beyond the time the child reaches 18 years of age. In determining the amount, the court will consider all relevant factors, without regard to marital misconduct, including the financial resources and needs of both parents, the financial resources and needs of the child and the physical and emotional condition of the child. Until a child reaches 18 years of age, the court may set apart any portion of property of either the husband or wife, or both, for the support of the child. The schedules are based on the parents' combined income, the number of children in the family, and the ages of the children. The guideline schedules allow for certain deductions from gross income and special schedules apply to shared and divided custody cases. Every order requiring payment of child support shall require that the support be paid through the clerk of the district court or the court trustee except for good cause shown. The court may make a modification of child support retroactive to a date at least one month after the date that the motion to modify was filed with the court.

Agency: Child Support Enforcement Program, Department of Social & Rehabilitation Services, P.O. Box 497, Topeka, KS 66601 Street Address: 300 S.W. Oakley Street, Biddle Building Topeka, KS 66606; (913) 296-3237 (1-800-432-0152 for withholding, 1-800-570-6743 for collections or 1-800-432-3913 for reporting fraud).

KENTUCKY

The Law: Kentucky Revised Statutes, Chapter 403, Section 270 (K.R.S. § 403.270). Ignore volume numbers; look for "chapter" numbers. These are in a binder, with updates found in the beginning of each volume in a section marked "Current Service."

Custody: K.R.S. § 403.270. Custody, including joint custody, is ordered in accordance with the best interests of the child and equal consideration shall be given to each parent and to any primary caregiver as defined by the statute. The court shall consider all relevant factors including: the wishes of the child, parents and caregiver; the interaction and interrelationship of the child with his parents, siblings, and any other person who may significantly affect the child's best interests; the child's adjustment to his home, school, and community; the mental and physical health of all individuals involved; evidence of domestic violence; the extent to which the child has been cared for, nurtured, and supported by any primary caregiver; the circumstances under which the child was placed or allowed to remain in the custody of such person. For nonmarried parents, see KRS § 405.020.

The court shall not consider conduct of a proposed custodian that does not affect his relationship to the child. If domestic violence and abuse is alleged, the court shall determine the extent to which the domestic violence and abuse has affected the child and the child's relationship to both parents.

Child Support: K.R.S.§§ 403-210 to 403-213. To determine the amount of child support, Kentucky uses a worksheet, based on the guidelines. The worksheet uses the income of both parents and considers other factors such as medical insurance, maintenance payments, child care, and prior child support owed. Deviations from the guidelines are permitted upon a court's finding that the guidelines would be unjust or inappropriate (such as where there are extraordinary medical expenses). Modifications are permitted under § 403.213 every 2-3 years or where, for example, the obligation reflects at least a 15% change in the order.

Agency: Division of Child Support Enforcement, Cabinet for Families and Children, P. O. Box 2150, Frankfort, KY 40602; (502) 564-2285.

LOUISIANA

The Law: West's Louisiana Statutes Annotated Civil Code, Article 131. The books containing the laws of Louisiana are one of the more complicated sets of any state. There are several sets of books divided into subjects. All sets have the title of either "Louisiana Statutes Annotated," or "West's LSA," which is followed by the area of law such as Revised Statutes, Civil Code, Civil Procedure, etc. The divorce laws were completely rewritten in 1990 and may be found in a separate soft-cover volume titled "West's Louisiana Statutes Annotated, Civil Code." Look for a subheading titled "Ch.1. The Divorce Action."

Custody: La.Civil Code Ann., Art. 131, 132, and 134. The best interest of the child is of paramount consideration and joint custody is preferred.

Custody will be based on the following factors: (1) the child's love, affection and emotional ties with each parent; (2) capacity and disposition of the parties to give love, affection, guidance, education, and religious guidance; (3) capacity and disposition of the parties to give the child food, clothing, medical care, etc., (4) length of time the child has been in a stable, satisfactory environment, and the desirability for continuity; (5) permanence as a family unit of the existing or proposed home; (6) moral fitness of the parties; (7) mental and physical health of the parties; (8) home, school and community record of the child; (9) preference of the child, if old enough; (10) willingness of each party to facilitate a relationship between the child and the other spouse; (11) distance between parties residences; and (12) history of care and responsibility for child by each party.

Child Support: La. Rev. Stat. Ann. §§ 9:315 to 9:315.14. The guidelines are based on the combined gross income of the parents less preexisting orders for child or spousal support. A court may deviate from the guidelines if their application would not be in the best interest of the child or would be inequitable to the parties (such as for certain extraordinary medical expenses or extraordinary community debt of the parties). Parties may agree to support, but a court may require proof of income. Calculation of support is based on the proportionate percentage of the combined amount of adjusted gross income. Next, the basic child support obligation amount is determined from the schedule in R.S. 9:315.14 by using the combined adjusted gross income of the parties and the number of children. Finally, the amount due is adjusted to include health insurance and certain child care costs, education or transportation costs. Each parent's share of child support is then determined by multiplying his or her percentage share of combined adjusted gross income times the total child support obligation. The party without legal custody owes his or her total child support obligation as a money judgment of child support to the custodial parent, minus any court-ordered direct payments made on behalf of the child for work-related net child care costs, health insurance premiums, extraordinary medical expenses, or extraordinary expenses provided as adjustments to the schedule. There are special considerations in cases of joint custody.

Agency: Support Enforcement Services, Office of Family Support, P.O. Box 94065, Baton Rouge, LA 70804-4065; (504) 342-4780; (1-800-256-4650 in Louisiana only).

MAINE

The Law:
Title 19-A, Maine Revised Statutes Annotated, Section 1653 (19-A M.R.S.A. § 1653). Ignore volume numbers; look for "title" numbers.

Custody:
19-A M.R.S.A. § 1653. Encouraging mediated resolutions of disputes between parents is in the best interest of minor children. An agreement for shared parental rights and responsibilities will be granted unless there is substantial evidence that it should not be ordered. The court may award reasonable rights of contact with a child to a third person. The order must include: allocated parental rights and responsibilities, shared parental rights and responsibilities (and shared or primary residential care) or sole parental rights and responsibilities, according to the best interest of the child.

Consideration of the best interest of the child includes: the age of the child; the relationship of the child with the child's parents and any other persons who may significantly affect the child's welfare; the preference of the child, if old enough to express a meaningful preference; the duration and adequacy of the child's current living arrangements and the desirability of maintaining continuity; the stability of any proposed living arrangements for the child; the motivation of the parties involved and their capacities to give the child love, affection and guidance; the child's adjustment to the child's present home, school and community; the capacity of each parent to allow and encourage frequent and continuing contact between the child and the other parent, including physical access; the capacity of each parent to cooperate or to learn to cooperate in child care; methods for assisting parental cooperation and resolving disputes and each parent's willingness to use those methods; the effect on the child if one parent has sole authority over the child's upbringing; the existence of domestic abuse between the parents, in the past or currently, and how that abuse affects: the child emotionally and the safety of the child; the existence of any history of child abuse by a parent; all other factors having a reasonable bearing on the physical and psychological well-being of the child. Special conditions will be applied in cases of domestic violence.

Child Support:
19 M.R.S.A. §§ 2001-2010. Child support will be provided until the child turns 18 (19 if the child is in secondary school), gets married, or joins the armed services. The order may include automatic adjustments to the amount of money paid for the support of a child when the child attains 12 or 18 years of age; or when the child graduates, withdraws or is expelled from secondary school, attains 19 years of age or is otherwise emancipated. The basic support amount is determined by adding together the annual gross income of both parties, and referring to the child support table for the amount based on the number of children to be supported. To this will be added child care costs and extraordinary medical expenses. Then, the total support obligation is divided between the parties in proportion based on their respective gross incomes. The parent not providing primary residential care will pay their share of support to the parent providing primary residential care; it is presumed that the parent providing residential care will pay their share directly for the child's support. There are special calculations for shared custody.

Agency:
Division of Support Enforcement and Recovery, Bureau of Family Independence, Department of Human Services, State House Station, 11 Whitten Road, Augusta, ME 04333; (207) 287-2886; (1-800-371-3101 in Maine only).

MARYLAND

The Law: Annotated Code of Maryland, Family Code, Section 5 (A.C.M., Family Code § 5). *Annotated Code of Maryland- Family Law. "A.C.M." Be sure you have the volume marked "Family Law."

Custody: A.C.M., Fam.Code § 5-203. A court may order joint or sole custody. The parents of a minor child are both responsible for the child's support, care, nurture, welfare, and education and have the same powers and duties in relation to the child. If one or both parents of a minor child is an unemancipated minor, the parents of that minor parent are also responsible for any child support for a grandchild that is a recipient of temporary cash assistance to the extent that the minor parent has insufficient financial resources to fulfill the child support responsibility of the minor parent.

Child Support: A.C.M, Fam. Code § 12-201-204. The guidelines are based on a percentage of both parents combined actual income less adjustments for child support obligations and alimony actually paid, and the cost of health insurance for the child(ren). Basic child support is determined by applying the combined adjusted actual income to a schedule of amounts based on the number of children to be supported. Adjustments are made to account for child care expenses, extraordinary medical expenses, and the cost of special or private education and transportation between the homes of the parents. For sole physical custody cases, the total child support amount is divided between the parents according to their percentage share of the combined income. The amount owed by the custodial parent is presumed to be spent on the child. The amount owed by the non-custodial parent becomes the child support order. In a shared physical custody arrangement, additional adjustments are made to the support obligation amount to reflect the extra expenses incurred in such an arrangement and to account for the percentage of time the child spends overnight with each parent. The respective child support obligation amounts owed by each parent are offset against each other and the parent owing the greater amount would owe the difference to the other parent as child support.

Deviation from the guidelines is permitted if the court determines that application of the guidelines in a particular case would be inappropriate (such as contributions to other children).

Agency: Child Support Enforcement Administration, Department of Human Resources , 311 West Saratoga Street, Baltimore, MD 21201; (410) 767-7619; (1-800-332-6347 in Maryland only).

MASSACHUSETTS

The Law: Annotated Laws of Massachusetts, Chapter 208, Section 31 (A.L.M., Ch. 208, § 31).

Custody: A.L.M., Ch. 208, § 31. In a custody case, the rights of the parents shall, in the absence of misconduct, be held to be equal, and the happiness and welfare of the children shall determine their custody. When considering the happiness and welfare of the child, the court shall consider whether or not the child's present or past living conditions adversely affect his physical, mental, moral or emotional health. During the pendency of a custody case, absent emergency conditions, abuse or neglect, the parents shall have temporary shared legal custody of any minor child of the marriage; but the judge may enter an order for temporary sole legal custody for one parent if shared custody would not be in the best interest of the child. A parenting plan for shared legal or physical custody, should include: the child's education; the child's health care; procedures for resolving disputes between the parties with respect to child-raising decisions and duties; and the periods of time during which each party will have the child reside or visit with him, including holidays and vacations, or the procedure by which such periods of time shall be determined. Where the parents have reached an agreement providing for the custody of the children, the court may enter an order in accordance with such agreement, unless specific findings are made by the court indicating that such an order would not be in the best interests of the children.

Child Support: Mass. Child Support Guidelines. The guidelines are based on gross income. Added adjustments are made based on health care expenses and age of the child. The guidelines use a sliding percentage of income basis (plus or minus 2%) based on number of children. Special calculations apply to shared or split custody and extended visitation cases.

A modification may be allowed if there is at least a 20% difference between a support order and one calculated under the guidelines.

Agency: Child Support Enforcement Division, Department of Revenue, 141 Portland Street, Cambridge, MA 02139-1937; (1-800-332-2733).

MICHIGAN

The Law: Michigan Statutes Annotated ("M.S.A."), or Michigan Compiled Laws Annotated ("M.C.L.A."). Michigan has two separate sets of laws, each by a different publisher. Each set has a cross-reference index to the other set. Ignore volume and "chapter" numbers; look for "section" numbers. Michigan Compiled Laws Annotated, Section 25.312 (M.C.L.A. § 25.312); Michigan Statutes Annotated, Section 722.23 (M.S.A. § 722.23).

Custody: M.C.L.A. § 25.312(3, 5); M.S.A. § 722.23. In custody cases, the best interests of the child control. The court will consider: whether parents provide the child with love, affection, and guidance and continuation of the education of the child in its religion or creed, if any, the ability and willingness of the parents to provide the child with food, clothing, medical care or other care and other material needs; the length of time the child has lived in a stable, satisfactory environment, and the desirability of maintaining continuity; the permanence as a family unit, of the existing or proposed custodial home or homes; the moral fitness of the parties involved; the mental and physical health of the parties involved; the home, school, and community record of the child; the reasonable preference of the child, if the court deems the child to be of sufficient age to express preference; the willingness and ability of each of the parents to facilitate and encourage a close and continuing parent-child relationship between the child and the other parent; domestic violence; and any other relevant factor.

Visitation is called *parenting time*, and there is a presumption that it is in the best interest of a child to have a strong relationship with both parents. M.S.A. § 25.312(7a); M.C.L.A. § 722.27a. Grandparent or other third party may only get custody if: (1) child's biological parents were never married, and (2) the parent with custody dies or is missing and the other parent has not been granted custody, and (3) the person seeking custody is related within the 5th degree by marriage, blood, or adoption (grandparent or great-grandparent qualifies). M.S.A. § 25.312(6c); M.C.L.A. §§ 722.26c.

Child Support: Michigan Child Support Guidelines. The guidelines are based on the net income of each party which is then adjusted for the presence of other children in the home or prior support orders. Then the custodial parent's income is compared to the noncustodial parent's income on a table based on number of children to determine the guideline amount due.

Agency: Office of Child Support, Department of Social Services, P.O. Box 30478, Lansing, MI 48909-7978. Street Address: 7109 W. Saginaw Hwy., Lansing, MI 48909-7978; (517) 373-7570 (no toll-free number).

Note: Copies of the Michigan Child Support Guidelines are available for $5.00, prepaid to the State of Michigan at: Department of Management and Budget, Office Services Division, Publications Section, P.O. Box 30026, Lansing, Michigan 48909.

MINNESOTA

The Law: Minnesota Statutes Annotated, Section 518.17 (M.S.A. § 518.17). Ignore volume numbers; look for "section" numbers.

Custody: M.S.A. § 518.17. The best interests of the child means all relevant factors to be considered and evaluated by the court including: the wishes of the child's parent or parents as to custody; the reasonable preference of the child, if the court deems the child to be of sufficient age to express preference; the child's primary caretaker; the intimacy of the relationship between each parent and the child; the interaction and interrelationship of the child with a parent or parents, siblings, and any other person who may significantly affect the child's best interests; the child's adjustment to home, school, and community; the length of time the child has lived in a stable, satisfactory environment and the desirability of maintaining continuity; the permanence, as a family unit, of the existing or proposed custodial home; the mental and physical health of all individuals involved; the capacity and disposition of the parties to give the child love, affection, and guidance, and to continue educating and raising the child in the child's culture and religion or creed, if any; the child's cultural background; the effect on the child of the actions of an abuser, if related to domestic abuse, that has occurred between the parents or between a parent and another individual, whether or not the individual alleged to have committed domestic abuse is or ever was a family or household member of the parent; and except in cases in which a finding of domestic abuse has been made, the disposition of each parent to encourage and permit frequent and continuing contact by the other parent with the child. The court shall not consider conduct of a proposed custodian that does not affect the custodian's relationship to the child. The court must make detailed findings on each of the factors and explain how the factors led to its conclusions and to the determination of the best interests of the child.

Joint custody is presumed to be in the child's best interest. Where either joint legal or joint physical custody is sought, the court shall consider: the ability of parents to cooperate in the rearing of their children; methods for resolving disputes regarding any major decision concerning the life of the child, and the parents' willingness to use those methods; whether it would be detrimental to the child if one parent were to have sole authority over the child's upbringing; and whether domestic abuse has occurred between the parents.

Child Support: M.S.A. § 518.551 et seq. The court may order either or both parents owing a duty of support to a child of the marriage to pay an amount reasonable or necessary for the child's support, without regard to marital misconduct. The court will approve a child support agreement of the parties, unless the stipulation does not meet the guidelines, but the court may deviate from the guidelines if both parties agree and the court makes written findings that it is in the best interests of the child. Child support is determined by multiplying the obligor's net income by the percentage indicated by the guidelines schedule. Work-related and education-related child care costs paid will be allocated to each parent in proportion to each parent's net income. Reductions from the support order may be made when the child spends 30 days or more with the noncustodial parent.

169

Agency: Office of Child Support Enforcement, Department of Human Services 444 Lafayette Road, 4th floor, St. Paul, MN 55155-3846; (612) 215-1714 (no toll-free number).

MISSISSIPPI

The Law: Mississippi Code Annotated 1972, Title 93, Section 93-5-24 (M.C.A. § 93-5-24).

Custody: M.C.A. § 93-5-24. Custody may be awarded as follows according to the best interests of the child: physical and legal custody to both parents jointly; physical custody to both parents jointly with legal custody to either parent; legal custody to both parents jointly with physical custody to either parent; or physical and legal custody to either parent. In certain cases, a court can order physical and legal custody to any other person deemed by the court to be suitable and able to provide adequate and proper care and guidance for the child. The court may require the parents to submit to the court a plan for the implementation of the custody order. There is a presumption that joint custody is in the best interests of a child where both parents have agreed to an award of joint custody. Any order for joint custody may be modified or terminated upon the petition of both parents or upon the petition of one parent showing that a material change in circumstances has occurred.

Child Support: M.C.A. §§ 43-19-101 et seq. The guidelines are based on a percentage of adjusted gross income of the noncustodial parent. Adjusted gross income equals gross income less deductions for taxes, social security, certain retirement contributions, and prior court ordered amounts of child support. The percentages are 14% (1 child), 20% (2 children), 22% (3 children), 24% (4 children), and 26% (5 or more children).

Agency: Division of Child Support Enforcement, Department of Human Services, P.O. Box 352, Jackson, MS 39205; (601) 359-4861; (1-800-434-5437; or in Hines, Rankin, and Madison Counties, dial 1-800-354-6039).

MISSOURI

The Law: Vernon's Annotated Missouri Statutes, Chapter 452, Section 452,375 (A.M.S. § 452.375). Ignore volume numbers; look for "section" numbers.

Custody: A.M.S. § 452.375. The court shall determine custody in accordance with the best interests of the child. The court shall consider all relevant factors including: the wishes of the child's parents as to custody and the proposed parenting plan submitted by both parties; the needs of the child for a frequent, continuing and meaningful relationship with both parents and the ability and willingness of parents to actively perform their functions as mother and father for the needs of the child; the interaction and interrelationship of the child with parents, siblings, and any other person who may significantly affect the child's best interests; which parent is more likely to allow the child frequent, continuing and meaningful contact with the other parent; the child's adjustment to the child's home, school, and community; the mental and physical health of all individuals involved, including any history of abuse or violence of any individuals involved; the intention of either parent to relocate the principal residence of the child; and the wishes of a child as to the child's custodian.

The court will determine the custody arrangement which will best assure both parents participate in such decisions and have frequent, continuing and meaningful contact with their children so long as it is in the best interests of the child. If the parties have not agreed, the court will consider joint custody prior to sole legal custody. Any judgment providing for custody shall include a specific written parenting plan either submitted by the parties or determined by the court. In cases of domestic violence the court shall make specific findings of fact to show that the custody or visitation arrangement ordered by the court best protects the child and the parent or other family or household member who is the victim of domestic violence from any further harm.

Child Support: Mo. Sup. Ct. Rule 88.01, Civil Procedure Form 14. The guidelines are based on gross income for each parent less deductions for prior support orders. The total percentage due of combined income of each parent is then determined from the support chart. Work-related child care, medical costs and other extraordinary costs are then added to the basic child support amount. Each parent's percentage of the obligation due is then determined (with credit for times of temporary physical custody).

Agency: Department of Social Services, Division of Child Support Enforcement, P.O. Box 2320, Jefferson City, MO 65102-2320; (573) 751-4301; (1-800-859-7999).

MONTANA

Law: Montana Code Annotated, Title 40, Chapter 4, Section 40-4-212 (M.C.A. § 40-4-212). Ignore volume numbers; look for "title" numbers.

Custody: M.C.A. § 40-4-212. The court shall determine the parenting plan in accordance with the best interest of the child. The court shall consider: the wishes of the child's parent or parents; the wishes of the child; the interaction and interrelationship of the child with the child's parent or parents and siblings and with any other person who significantly affects the child's best interest; the child's adjustment to home, school, and community; the mental and physical health of all individuals involved; physical abuse or threat of physical abuse by one parent against the other parent or the child; chemical dependency or abuse on the part of either parent; continuity and stability of care; developmental needs of the child; whether a parent has knowingly failed to pay birth-related costs that the parent is able to pay, which is considered to be not in the child's best interests; whether a parent has knowingly failed to financially support a child that the parent is able to support, which is considered to be not in the child's best interests; whether the child has frequent and continuing contact with both parents, which is considered to be in the child's best interests unless the court determines, after a hearing, that contact with a parent would be detrimental to the child's best interests. In making that determination, the court shall consider evidence of physical abuse or threat of physical abuse by one parent against the other parent or the child, including but not limited to whether a parent or other person residing in that parent's household has been convicted of certain crimes; and adverse effects on the child resulting from continuous and vexatious parenting plan amendment actions.

Good faith efforts must be made to comply with a parenting plan or obtain dispute resolution before seeking to amend the plan. Also, it is presumed that if a case seeking to change the parenting plan is filed within 6 months after a child support action is brought against that parent, it is vexatious.

Child Support: Administrative Rules of Montana 37.62.101 et seq. Child support may be determined by agreement of the parties but may depart from the guidelines only if sufficient justification in writing is presented, and the parties acknowledge the amount that would be required under the guidelines. Income used is actual income from all sources except certain public assistance grants; deductions from income are permitted for court-ordered alimony (maintenance) and child support, health insurances, taxes, social security and certain other allowable expenses. Child support is determined by combining the parents' incomes then applying a standard basic multiplier as listed in the rules and adding certain supplemental amounts (for example, for child care and health insurance), then factoring in a standard of living allowance (to ensure a child's minimum standard of living is maintained). Child support amounts are adjusted for extended time spent with both parents (at least 110 days). Deviation is permitted if application of the guidelines would be unjust or inappropriate.

Agency: Child Support Enforcement Division, Department of Public Health and Human Services, P.O. Box 202943, Helena, MT 59620; (406) 442-7278; (1-800-346-5437 in Montana only).

Note: The Child Support Enforcement Division has developed a worksheet with the financial affidavit, tables and guidelines needed to calculate child support. Contact them at the address above, or contact any regional office for a copy of these materials.

Nebraska

The Law: Revised Statutes of Nebraska, Chapter 42, Section 42-364 (R.S.N. § 42-364). Ignore volume numbers; look for "chapter" numbers.

Custody: R.S.N. § 42-364. In a dissolution of a marriage or legal separation, the court may include a parenting plan developed under the Parenting Act. Custody and time spent with each parent shall be determined on the basis of the best interests of the minor child with the objective of maintaining the ongoing involvement of both parents in the minor child's life. The best interests of the minor child include consideration of: (1) the relationship of the minor child to each parent prior to the commencement of the action or any subsequent hearing; (2) the desires and wishes of the minor child if of an age of comprehension regardless of chronological age, when such desires and wishes are based on sound reasoning; (3) the general health, welfare, and social behavior of the minor child; and (4)any credible evidence of abuse inflicted on any family or household member. Shared or joint custody is permitted where both parents agree to such an arrangement or the court finds it is in the best interests of a child.

Child Support: Nebraska Child Support Guidelines. The court shall consider the earning capacity of each parent and the guidelines provided by the Supreme Court pursuant to section 42-364.16 for the establishment of child support obligations. Income less taxes, social security deductions, health insurance, mandatory retirement contributions, and child support is combined (except public assistance benefits and payments received for children of prior marriages). The total amount is then matched to the support table based on the number of children, then the percentage of contribution of each parent is determined. Visitation adjustments or direct cost sharing is permitted as an adjustment to the guidelines. Special worksheets are available for joint physical and split custody situations. If there is evidence of an abusive disregard of the use of child support money paid by one party to the other, the court may require the party receiving such payment to file a verified report with the court, as often as the court requires, stating the manner in which such money is used.

Deviations from the guidelines are permissible when: there are extraordinary medical costs of either parent or child; special needs of a disabled child exist; if total net income exceeds $10,000 monthly; or the application of the guidelines in an individual case would be unjust or inappropriate.

Modification is permitted for a material change in circumstances such as a variation by at least 10% of the current child support obligation as a result of the application of the guidelines.

Agency: Child Support Enforcement Office, Department of Social Services P.O. Box 95044, Lincoln, NE 68509; (402) 471-9160; (1-800-831-4573 in Nebraska only).

NEVADA

Law: Nevada Revised Statutes Annotated, Chapter 125, Section 125.480 (N.R.S.A. § 125.480). Ignore volume numbers; look for "chapter" numbers.

Custody: N.R.S.A. § 125.480. In determining custody, the sole consideration of the court is the best interest of the child. If it appears to the court that joint custody would be in the best interest of the child, the court may grant custody to the parties jointly. When awarding custody to either parent, the court shall consider, among other factors, which parent is more likely to allow the child to have frequent associations and a continuing relationship with the noncustodial parent. The court can also order custody to a person in whose home the child has been living and where the child has had a wholesome and stable environment or to a relative whom the court finds suitable and able to provide proper care and guidance for the child, regardless of whether the relative resides within the state or to any other person or persons whom the court finds suitable and able to provide proper care and guidance for the child.

In determining the best interest of the child, the court shall consider: the wishes of the child if the child is of sufficient age and capacity to form an intelligent preference as to his custody; any nomination by a parent of a guardian for the child; and whether either parent or any other person seeking custody has engaged in an act of domestic violence against the child, a parent of the child or any other person residing with the child.

Child Support: N.R.S.A. §§ 125B.070 to 125B.080. The guidelines are factored on the gross income of the parent without custody based on the following percentages of income: one child (18%), two children (25%) three children (29%), four children (31%), and an additional two percent for each additional child. If the parties agree as to the amount of support required, and certify that their agreement is consistent with the appropriate statutory formula or justify why the support deviates from the formula, a court will enter that order. Deviations are permitted for health care, child care and educational expenses, and other extraordinary expenses as listed in the statute.

Amounts not paid become judgments for the sum due. Past due sums must be paid even if the child reaches the age of 18. Handicapped children are entitled to be supported until the handicap is removed or the child becomes self-supporting.

A request for modification may be made every 3 years or at any time on the basis of changed circumstances.

Agency: Child Support Enforcement Program, Nevada State Welfare Division, 2527 North Carson Street, Carson City, NV 89706-0113; (702) 687-4744; (1-800-992-0900 in Nevada only).

New Hampshire

The Law: New Hampshire Revised Statutes Annotated, Chapter 458, Section 458:17 (N.H.R.S.A. § 458:17). Ignore "title numbers; look for "chapter" numbers.

Custody: N.H.R.S.A. § 458:17. There is a presumption that joint legal custody is in the best interest of minor children where the parents have agreed to an award of joint legal custody. The court may take into consideration the child's preference. The presence of abuse is considered harmful to children and the court shall make custody and visitation orders that best protect the children or the abused spouse or both. If joint legal custody is granted despite evidence of abuse, the court shall provide written findings to support the joint custody order. Reasonable visitation privileges to a stepparent of the children or to the grandparents of the children may be entered.

Repeated interference with visitation or custodial rights of the other parent shall be a basis for modifying physical custody without the necessity of showing harm to the child if the court finds that a change of physical custody would be in accordance with the best interests of the child.

Decree must state reasons if joint custody is not ordered. N.H.R.S.A. 458:17

Child Support: N.H.R.S.A. §§ 458-C: 1-7. Child support is determined by multiplying the parents' combined net income, as defined in the statute, by the appropriate percentage which is derived from the table and based on the number of children. That amount is divided between the parents in proportion to their respective incomes (as adjusted). Adjustments to the guidelines are made under special circumstances (such as for extraordinary medical expenses). Deviation is permitted where application of the guidelines would be unjust or inappropriate in a particular case.

Each child support order shall include the court's determination and findings relative to health insurance and the payment of uninsured medical expenses for the children. All will provide for the assignment of the wages of the responsible parent. All support payments are considered judgments when due and payable and a lien shall be automatic against real and personal property for child support arrearages owed by an obligor who resides or owns property in the state and shall incorporate any unpaid child support which may accrue in the future.

Modification requests are permitted 3 years after the entry of the last order for support, without the need to show a substantial change of circumstances. No modification of a support order shall apply to any past sums due prior to the date of filing the motion for modification.

Agency: Office of Child Support, Division of Human Services, Health and Human Services Building, 6 Hazen Drive, Concord, NH 03301-6531; (603) 271-4427; (1-800-852-3345, ext. 4427 in New Hampshire only).

New Jersey

The Law: New Jersey Statutes Annotated, Title 9, Chapter 2, Section 9:2-4 (N.J.S.A. § 9:2-4). Ignore "article" numbers.

Custody: N.J.S.A. § 9: 2-4. In custody proceedings, the rights of both parents shall be equal. The court will order any custody arrangement which is agreed to by both parents unless it is contrary to the best interests of the child. If the parties cannot agree, the court may require each parent to submit a custody plan which it shall consider. A court can order joint custody (legal or physical) with sole or alternating residential arrangements in accordance with the needs of the parents and child, and provisions for consultation between the parents in making major decisions regarding the child's health, education and general welfare or sole custody to one parent with appropriate parenting time for the noncustodial parent; or any other custody arrangement as the court may determine to be in the best interests of the child.

The court shall consider: (1) the parents' ability to agree, communicate, and cooperate in matters relating to the child; (2) the parents' willingness to accept custody and any history of unwillingness to allow parenting time not based on substantiated abuse; (3) the interaction and relationship of the child with its parents and siblings; the history of domestic violence, if any; (4) the safety of the child and the safety of either parent from physical abuse by the other parent; (5) the preference of the child when of sufficient age and capacity to reason so as to form an intelligent decision; (6) the needs of the child; the stability of the home environment offered; (7)the quality and continuity of the child's education; (8) the fitness of the parents; (9) the geographical proximity of the parents' homes; (10) the extent and quality of the time spent with the child prior to or subsequent to the separation; (11) the parents' employment responsibilities; and (12) the age and number of the children.

Child Support: N.J. Rules of Court Appendix IX. This state combines each parent's net income, then apportions the percentage of each parent's share based on tables. In sole-parenting situations, the custodial parent's share of the child-rearing expenses is assumed to be spent directly on the child. The non-custodial parent's share of child-rearing costs represents the support order that is paid to the custodial parent for the benefit of the child. In situations involving visitation or shared-parenting, both parents make direct expenditures for the child while the child resides in their homes. Certain expenses such as health, education and child care expenses and other extraordinary expenses may be added to the basic child support obligation. Adjustments are also made for extended visitation and shared parenting time. Deviations are permitted to accomodate the needs of the children or the parents' circumstances.

Agency: Division of Family Development, Department of Human Services Bureau of Child Support and Paternity Programs, P.O. Box 716 Trenton, NJ 08625-0716; (609) 588-2915; (1-800-621-5437).

NEW MEXICO

The Law: New Mexico Statutes 1978 Annotated, Chapter 40, Section 40-4-9 (N.M.S.A. § 40-4-9). Ignore volume numbers; look for "chapter" numbers.

Custody: N.M.S.A. § 40-4-9. Custody in cases where a child is under fourteen will be determined in accordance with the best interests of the child. The court shall consider: (1) the wishes of the child's parent or parents as to his custody; (2) the wishes of the child as to his/her custodian; (3) the interaction and interrelationship of the child with the parents, siblings and any other person who may significantly affect the child's best interest; (4) the child's adjustment to home, school and community; and (5) the mental and physical health of all individuals involved. If the child is fourteen years of age or older, the court shall consider the desires of the minor as to with whom he or she wishes to live before awarding custody of such minor.

Child Support: N.M. Stat. Ann.§§ 40-4-11.1–11.6. The guidelines are based on the proportionate share of the combined actual gross income of both parents less public assistance and child support received as applied to the schedule of support for the correct number of children. In shared custody cases, each parent's responsibility for direct expenses is deducted from that parent's basic obligation and the difference, if any, is the support due and owing. In sole custody situations, adjustments may be made for extended visitation. Deviations from the guidelines are permitted if application would produce unjust or inappropriate results.

Modification is permitted upon a showing of material and substantial changes in circumstances, such as a 20% or more change in the order based upon application of the guidelines.

Agency: Child Support Enforcement Bureau, Department of Human Services, P.O. Box 25109, Santa Fe, NM 87504. Street Address: 2025 S. Pacheco, Santa Fe, NM; (505) 827-7200; (1-800-432-6217 in New Mexico only).

New York

The Law: McKinney's Consolidated Laws of New York Annotated, Domestic Relations Law, Section 240 (C.L.N.Y., D.R.L. § 240). Be sure you use the volumes marked "Domestic Relations."

Custody: C.L.N.Y., D.R.L. § 240(a). Custody shall be awarded in the court's discretion having regard to the circumstances of the case and of the respective parties and to the best interests of the child. Visitation may be ordered.

Child Support: C.L.N.Y., D.R.L. § 240(1-b). The proportionate percentage of combined parental income is determined by the guidelines based on the number of children to be supported. Child support percentages are: 17% (1 child), 25% (2 children) 29% (3 children), 31% (4 children), and no less than 35% for five or more children. To this is added health care, child care and certain other expenses in prorated amounts. Deviations may be made if the guideline amounts are unjust or inappropriate. The parties may agree to child support; any agreement must include a provision stating that the parties have been advised of the guidelines, and that they are presumptively correct. If the agreement deviates from the guideline amounts, the agreement must specify the guideline amount and the reason or reasons that the agreement does not provide for payment of that amount. Any court order or judgment incorporating a validly executed agreement which deviates from the basic child support obligation must set forth the court's reasons for doing so.

Agency: Office of Child Support Enforcement, Department of Social Services, P.O. Box 14, One Commerce Plaza, Albany, NY 12260-0014; (518) 474-9081; (1-800-343-8859 in New York only).

North Carolina

The Law: General Statutes of North Carolina, Chapter 50, Section 50-13.2 (G.S.N.C. § 50-13.2). Ignore volume numbers; look for "chapter" numbers. Contrary to the title that appears on the covers of the books, these are commonly called "North Carolina General Statutes."

Custody: G.S.N.C. § 50-13.2. Custody of a child to a person, agency, organization or institution will be ordered to best promote the interest and welfare of the child. The court shall consider: domestic violence between the parties, the safety of the child, and the safety of either party from domestic violence by the other party and shall make findings accordingly. Joint custody to the parents shall be considered upon the request of either parent. Any order for custody must include visitation as will best promote the interest and welfare of the child (and may grant grandparent visitation in the court's discretion). In domestic violence cases, the court will enter orders that best protect the children and other victims, including a designation of time and place for the exchange of children away from the abused party, the participation of a third party, or supervised visitation. Absent an order of the court to the contrary, each parent shall have equal access to the records of the minor child involving the health, education, and welfare of the child.

Child Support: North Carolina Child Support Guidelines. The guidelines are based on a shared parental obligation which is determined by the combined adjusted gross income applied to a support table listing the number of children. Child, health and extraordinary costs may be added. Deviation from the Guidelines is permitted where application would be inequitable to one of the parties or to the child.

Modification is permitted upon a showing that there has been a substantial change of circumstances, or for an order which is at least three years old, a deviation of 15% or more between the amount of the existing order and the amount of child support resulting from application of the guidelines will warrant modification.

Agency: Child Support Enforcement Office, Division of Social Services, Department of Human Resources, 100 East Six Forks Road, Raleigh, NC 27609-7750; (919) 571-4114; (1-800-992-9457 in North Carolina only).

NORTH DAKOTA

The Law: North Dakota Century Code Annotated, Title 14, Chapter 14-09, Section 14-09-06 (N.D.C.C. § 14-09-06). Ignore volume numbers; look for "title" numbers.

Custody: N.D.C.C. § 14-09-06.2. The best interests and welfare of the child is determined by the court's consideration and evaluation of all factors affecting the best interests and welfare of the child including:(1) the love, affection, and other emotional ties existing between the parents and child; (2) the capacity and disposition of the parents to give the child love, affection, and guidance and to continue the education of the child; (3) the disposition of the parents to provide the child with food, clothing, medical care, or other remedial care recognized and permitted under the laws of this state in lieu of medical care, and other material needs; (4) the length of time the child has lived in a stable satisfactory environment and the desirability of maintaining continuity; the permanence, as a family unit, of the existing or proposed custodial home; (5) the moral fitness of the parents; (6) the mental and physical health of the parents; (7) the home, school, and community record of the child; (8) the reasonable preference of the child, if the court deems the child to be of sufficient intelligence, understanding, and experience to express a preference;(9) any evidence of domestic violence; (10) the interaction and interrelationship of the child with any person who resides in, is present, or frequents the household of a parent and who may significantly affect the child's best interests; (11) false allegations not made in good faith of harm to a child; and (12) any other factors considered by the court to be relevant to a particular child custody dispute. *N.D.C.C. §§ 14-05-22 and 14-09 et seq.

Child Support: North Dakota Administrative Code §§ 75-02-04.1 et seq. Child support is determined based on the net income of the noncustodial parent matched to a support schedule for the correct number of children to be supported. Deviations are permitted based on the factors identified in the code.

Agency: Department of Human Services, Child Support Enforcement Agency, P.O. Box 7190, Bismarck, ND 58507-7190; (701) 328-3582; (1-800-755-8530 in North Dakota only).

OHIO

The Law: Page's Ohio Revised Code Annotated, Title 31, Section 3109.04 (O.R.C. § 3109.04)

Custody: O.R.C. § 3109.04. The court shall allocate the parental rights and responsibilities based on what is in the best interests of the child. Upon request, and if it is in the best interests of a child, a shared parenting order requiring the parents to share all or some of the aspects of the physical and legal care of the children pursuant to the parties approved plan for shared parenting will be entered. If neither parent requests joint parenting or the court finds that it would not be in the best interests of the child, the court will allocate the parental rights and responsibilities for the care of the children primarily to one of the parents, designate that parent as the residential parent and the legal custodian of the child, and divide between the parents the other rights and responsibilities for the care of the children, including, but not limited to, the responsibility to provide support for the children and the right of the parent who is not the residential parent to have continuing contact with the children.

In determining the best interest of a child, the court shall consider: (1) the wishes of the parents and the child regarding the child's care; (2) the child's interaction and interrelationship with parents, siblings, and any other person who may significantly affect the child's best interest; (3) the child's adjustment to home, school, and community; (4) the mental and physical health of all persons involved in the situation; (5) the parent more likely to honor and facilitate visitation and companionship rights approved by the court; (6) whether either parent has failed to make court-ordered child support payments; (7) either parent's criminal history involving child abuse neglect; (8) whether a parent has continuously and willfully denied the other parent court-ordered visitation; and (9) whether either parent has established a residence, or is planning to establish a residence, outside this state.

For shared parenting, the court will also consider: the ability of the parents to cooperate and make decisions jointly, with respect to the children; the ability of each parent to encourage the sharing of love, affection, and contact between the child and the other parent; any history of, or potential for, child abuse, spouse abuse, other domestic violence, or parental kidnapping by either parent; the geographic proximity of the parents to each other, as the proximity relates to the practical considerations of shared parenting; and the recommendation of the child's guardian ad litem. A shared parenting plan will include: physical living arrangements, child support obligations, provision for the children's medical and dental care, school placement, and the parent with which the children will be physically located during legal holidays, school holidays, and other days of special importance.

No modifications will be granted unless the court finds, based on facts that have arisen since the prior decree or that were unknown to the court at the time of the prior decree, that a change has occurred in the circumstances of the child or either of the parents, and that the modification is necessary to serve the best interest of the child. However, under a shared parenting decree, both parents may agree at any time to modify the terms of the plan by filing the modifications with the court. Courts may also modify the terms of the plan for shared parenting at any time if the court determines that the modifications are in the best interest of the children.

Child Support: O.R.C. §§ 3113.215 et seq. The guidelines are based on proportionate percentages of adjusted gross income (excluding public assistance and prior child support received)of both parents. Adjustments permit deductions for taxes, social security, prior support orders paid (child and spouse). The guideline schedule is then applied to the income amount to determine the basic child support obligation. To that amount is added health insurance expenses and certain child care expenses. Except when the parents have split parental rights and responsibilities, a parent's child support obligation for a child for whom the parent is the residential parent and legal custodian shall be presumed to be spent on that child and shall not become part of a child support order, and a parent's child support obligation for a child for whom the parent is not the residential parent and legal custodian shall become part of a child support order. If the parents have split parental rights and responsibilities, the child support obligations of the parents shall be offset, and the court shall issue a child support order requiring the parent with the larger child support obligation to pay the net amount pursuant to the child support order. There are special worksheets to be used when determining the guideline amounts.

A court may deviate from the guidelines where they would be unjust or inappropriate and not be in the best interest of the child (such as for special needs or extraordinary obligations related to the child or for extended visitation). Modifications requests are permitted if the application of the guidelines would result in a 10% change in support or upon proof of a substantial change in circumstances.

Agency:	Office of Family Assistance and Child Support Enforcement, Department of Human Services, 30 East Broad Street - 31st Floor, Columbus, OH 43266-0423; (614) 752-6561; (1-800-686-1556).

OKLAHOMA

The Law:	Oklahoma Statutes Annotated, Title 43, Section 109 (43 O.S.A. § 109).
Custody:	43 O.S.A. § 109, 112. The court shall consider the best interests of the physical and mental and moral welfare of the child. Children of sufficient age are permitted to express a parent preference. There is no preference for or against joint legal custody, joint physical custody, or sole custody. Custody is awarded based on a preference first for parents, then grandparents, then to third parties according to the best interests of the child. In cases of domestic abuse, it is presumed that it is not in the best interests of the child to have custody, guardianship or unsupervised visitation granted to the abusive person.

Parents may request or agree to joint custody, and the court shall order that if it is in the best interests of the child. The parents may submit a plan jointly, or either parent or both parents may submit separate plans. Any parenting plan shall include provisions detailing the physical living arrangements for the child, child support obligations, medical and dental care for the child, school placement, and visitation rights. In sole custody cases, any order providing for the visitation of a noncustodial parent must provide a specified minimum amount of visitation between the noncustodial parent and the child unless the court determines otherwise. Except for good cause shown and when in the best interests of the child, the order shall encourage additional visitations of the noncustodial parent and the child and in addition encourage liberal telephone communications between the noncustodial parent and the child.

Child Support:	43 O.S.A. § 118-120. Child support is computed as a percentage of the combined gross income of both parents. Certain adjustments to gross income are permitted. The adjusted gross income of both parents is added together and the Child Support Guideline Schedule (43 O.S.A. § 119) is used to compute the support amount. Additions to the support amount for health care expenses and certain child care expenses are also prorated between the parents. The noncustodial parent's share is paid to the custodial parent. There are additional special computations for split custody or extended visitation.

The court may deviate from the guidelines where their application would be unjust, inequitable, unreasonable or inappropriate under the circumstances, or not in the best interests of the children. Modifications may be made if the support amount is not in ccordance with the child support guidelines or upon other material change in circumstances.

Agency: Child Support Enforcement Division, Department of Human Services P.O. Box 53552, Oklahoma City, OK 73152. Street Address: 2409 N. Kelley Avenue, Annex Building, Oklahoma City, OK 73111; (405) 522-5871; (1-800-522-2922).

OREGON

The Law: Oregon Revised Statutes Annotated, Chapter 107, Section 107.137 (O.R.S. § 137). Ignore volume numbers; look for "chapter" numbers.

Custody: O.R.S. §§ 107.105 and 107.137. The court shall give primary consideration to the best interests and welfare of the child and will consider:(1) the emotional ties between the child and other family members; (2) the interest of the parties in and attitude toward the child; (3) the desirability of continuing an existing relationship; (5) any abuse of one parent by the other; (6) and the willingness and ability of each parent to facilitate and encourage a close and continuing relationship between the other parent and the child. The court shall consider the conduct, marital status, income, social environment or life style of either party only if it is shown that any of these factors are causing or may cause emotional or physical damage to the child.

Child Support: Oregon Administrative Regulation 137-50-320–490. The guidelines are based on the combined adjusted gross income of the parents. Gross income is adjusted by child or spousal support obligations. The percentage contribution of each parent to the combined adjusted gross income is determined by dividing the combined adjusted gross income into each parent's adjusted gross income. Next, the basic child support obligation is determined by application of the guideline percentage amounts. Added to that are health care and certain child care expenses. Although a monetary obligation is computed for each parent, only the non-custodial parent will be ordered to pay support except in shared custody and split custody cases. Special computations are made for split or shared custody (at least 35% parenting time) or for significant parenting time (at least 25%).

Deviations from the guidelines are permitted upon a finding that the amount is unjust or inappropriate (such as special hardships or extraordinary needs).

Agency: Recovery Services Section, Adult and Family Services Division, Department of Human Resources, 260 Liberty Street N.E., Salem, OR 97310; (503) 378-5567; (1-800-850-0228 in Oregon only).

PENNSYLVANIA

The Law: Purdon's Pennsylvania Consolidated Statutes Annotated, Title 23, Section 5303 (23 Pa.C.S.A. § 5303).

Custody: 23 Pa.C.S.A. §§ 5303 and 5304. The court must consider the preference of the child as well as any other factor which legitimately impacts the child's physical, intellectual, and emotional well-being. An order for shared custody may be awarded by the court when it is in the best interest of the child; upon application of one or both parents; when the parties have agreed to an award of shared custody; or in the discretion of the court. In a sole custody or visitation order the court must consider which parent is more likely to encourage, permit, and allow frequent and continuing contact and physical access between the noncustodial parent and the child. However, a court will consider each parent and adult household member's present and past violent or abusive conduct in making an award of custody.

Child Support: Pennsylvania Rules of Civil Procedure 1910.16-1 to -5. The guidelines are based on a percentage of adjusted net income of the parents. Certain proportional adjustments are made based on permitted additional expenses (such as health care. There are currently five percentages applicable in the guidelines based on number of children and income level. The proportionate percentage of each parent's obligation is then determined, and the noncustodial parent pays his or her share to the custodial parent. There are special guideline calculations for divided or split custody arrangements.

Deviations are permitted under certain circumstances (e.g., for unusual needs or certain medical expenses). Modifications are permitted upon a material and substantial change in the support amount.

Agency: Bureau of Child Support Enforcement, Department of Public Welfare, P.O. Box 8018, Harrisburg, PA 17105; (717) 787-3672; (1-800-932-0211).

RHODE ISLAND

The Law: General laws of Rhode Island, Section 15-5-16 (G.L.R.I. § 15-5-16). Ignore "title" and "chapter numbers; look for "section" numbers.

Custody: G.L.R.I. § 15-5-16. In regulating the custody of the children, the court shall provide for the reasonable right of visitation by the natural parent not having custody of the children except upon the showing of cause why the right should not be granted. Upon a finding by the court that its order for visitation has not been complied with, the court shall exercise its discretion in providing a remedy, and define the noncustodial parent's visitation in detail. However, if a second finding of noncompliance by the court is made the court shall consider this to be grounds for a change of custody to the noncustodial parent. Domestic violence will be considered.

Child Support: G.L.R.I. § 15-5-16.-2; Child Support Guidelines. The court shall order either or both parents owing a duty of support to a child to pay an amount based upon a formula and guidelines adopted by an administrative order of the family court. Support may be ordered through age 18 (or up to 90 days after graduation or age 19 whichever comes first). For children with a severe physical or mental impairment, support may be ordered until the child turns 21.

Modification is permitted every 3 years, unless the court finds that a substantial change in circumstances has occurred. Child support may be modified retroactively only to the date that the other parent was notified that a petition requesting the modification was filed.

Agency: Child Support Services, Division of Administration and Taxation, 77 Dorrance Street, Providence, RI 02903; (401) 277-2847; (1-800-638-5437 in Rhode Island).

SOUTH CAROLINA

The Law: Code of Laws of South Carolina 1976, Title 20, Section 20-3-160 (C.L.S.C. § 20-3-160). Ignore volume numbers; look for "title" numbers.

Custody: C.L.S.C. § 20-3-160. In any action for divorce from the bonds of matrimony the court may at any stage of the cause, or from time to time after final judgment, make such orders touching the care, custody and maintenance of the children of the marriage and what, if any, security shall be given for the same as from the circumstances of the parties and the nature of the case and the best spiritual as well as other interests of the children may be fit, equitable and just.

Child Support: South Carolina Social Services Regulation 114-4710 to -4750. The guidelines are based on the combined adjusted gross income of the parents. The adjustments permit deductions for child support and alimony, and additions for medical expenses and child care. Then each the combined income is factored using the guideline schedule based on income and number of children. The parent's proportionate share of support is then determined and the noncustodial parent pays his or her share of support to the custodial parent who is presumed to pay his or her share directly. There are special calculations for shared parenting and split custody.

Deviations from the guidelines are permitted where application would be inappropriate (such as by agreement of the parties where in the best interests of the child).

Agency: Department of Social Services, Child Support Enforcement Division, P.O. Box 1469, Columbia, SC 29202-1469; (803) 737-5875; (1-800-768-5858).

SOUTH DAKOTA

The Law: South Dakota Codified Laws Annotated, Title 25, Chapter 4, Section 25-4-45 (S.D.C.L. §25-4-45). Ignore volume numbers; look for "title" numbers.

Custody: S.D.C.L. § 25-4-45. In an action for divorce, the court may, before or after judgment, give such direction for the custody, care, and education of the children of the marriage as may seem necessary or proper, and may at any time vacate or modify the same. In awarding the custody of a child, the court shall be guided by consideration of what appears to be for the best interests of the child in respect to the child's temporal and mental and moral welfare. If the child is of a sufficient age to form an intelligent preference, the court may consider that preference in determining the question. Neither parent may be given preference over the other in determining custody.

Child Support: S.D.C.L. §§ 25-7-6.1. The guidelines are factored on the combined net income of both parents. Allowable deductions include: income taxes withheld, FICA taxes withheld, retirement contributions and payments for child or spouse support. The combined net amount is then applied to the guidelines schedules based on number of children and each parent's proportionate share is determined. The share of the custodial parent is presumed to be spent directly for the benefit of the child. The share of the noncustodial parent establishes the amount of the child support order.

Deviations are permitted. Among others, deviations may be based on special needs of the child or substantial sharing of parenting time or other agreement of the parties.

Modifications are permitted for orders entered prior to July 1, 1997, without a showing of change of circumstances.

Agency: Office of Child Support Enforcement, Department of Social Services, 700 Governor's Drive, Pierre, SD 57501-2291; (605) 773-3641 (no toll-free number).

TENNESSEE

The Law: Tennessee Code Annotated, Title 36, Section 36-6-101 (T.C.A. § 36-6-101). Ignore volume numbers; look for "section" numbers.

Custody: T.C.A. § 36-6-101. In a suit for annulment, divorce or separate maintenance, where the custody of a minor child or minor children is a question, the court may award the care, custody and control of such child or children to either of the parties to the suit or to both parties in the instance of joint custody or shared parenting, or to some suitable person, as the welfare and interest of the child or children may demand. There is a presumption that joint custody is in the best interest of a minor child where the parents have agreed to it. If there is no agreement, there is no preference and either joint or sole custody may be ordered in the court's discretion.

Unless otherwise agreed (or when the court finds it not to be in the best interests of the child), each order pertaining to the custody or possession shall grant to each parent: the right to unimpeded telephone conversations with the child at least twice a week at reasonable times and for reasonable durations; the right to send mail to the child which the other parent shall not open or censor; the right to receive notice and relevant information as soon as practicable but within twenty-four hours of any event of hospitalization, major illness or death of the child; the right to receive directly from the child's school upon written request which includes a current mailing address and upon payment of reasonable costs of duplicating, copies of the child's report cards, attendance records, names of teachers, class schedules, standardized test scores and any other records customarily made available to parents; the right to receive copies of the child's medical records directly from the child's doctor or other health care provider upon written request which contains a current mailing address and upon payment of reasonable costs of duplication; and the right to be free of unwarranted derogatory remarks made about such parent or such parent's family by the other parent to or in the presence of the child.

The order will remain within the control of the court and be subject to such changes or modification as the exigencies of the case may require.

Child Support: Tenn. Comp. Rules & Regulations, Department of Human Services §§ 1240-2-4-.01. Child support is based on a flat percentage of the noncustodial parent s net income as defined in the rules depending on the number of children to be supported. The percentages are: 1 child (21%), 2 children (32%), 3 children (41%), 4 children (46%), and 5 or more children (50%). The amounts may be adjusted upward to reflect additional expenses for child health care, extended visitation, shared parenting time or other extraordinary expenses. The formula presumes that the both parents will expend an equal percentage of their net income for support. However, the parent with custody will pay that amount directly while the parent who does not have custody will pay the support to the other parent.

The parties may agree on a child support amount, however, in cases where the guidelines are not met the parties must provide a justification for the deviation which takes into consideration the best interest of the child and must state the amount which would have been required under the guidelines.

Modifications are permitted upon a showing of significant variance of at least 15% if the current support is $100 or more per month and at least fifteen dollars ($15) if the current support is less than $100 per month, unless, where a downward modification is sought, the payor parent is willfully and voluntarily unemployed or under employed.

Agency: Child Support Services, Department of Human Services, Citizens Plaza Building - 12th Floor, 400 Deadrick Street, Nashville, TN 37248-7400; (615) 313-4880; (1-800-838-6911 in Tennessee only).

TEXAS

The Law: Vernon's Texas Codes Annotated, Family Code, Section 153.002 (T.C.A., Fam. Code § 153.002).

Custody: T.C.A., Fam. Code § 153.002, 153.007. The best interest of the child shall always be the primary consideration of the court in determining the issues of conservatorship and possession of and access to the child.

The parties may enter into a written agreement containing provisions for conservatorship and possession of the child and for modification of the agreement, including variations from the standard possession order. The court will approve an agreement that is in the child's best interest.

Child Support: T.C.A., Fam. Code §§ 154.001. Either or both parents may be ordered to support a child in the manner until the child is 18 (or graduates from high school), is emancipated, marries, or dies (a disabled child may be supported for an indefinite period). The guidelines calculate support based on net monthly income of the noncustodial parent. The percentages are: one child (20%), two children (25%), three children (30%), four children (35%), five children (40%), and six or more children (not less than the amount for five children).

The parties may enter into a written support agreement. Variations from the child support guidelines will be permitted if the court finds that the agreement is in the child's best interest.

Deviations are permitted if application of the guidelines would be unjust or inappropriate under the circumstances (such as based on extensive time of possession and access to a child).

Agency: Office of the Attorney General, State Office Child Support Division, P.O. Box 12017, Austin, TX 78711-2017; (512) 460-6000; (1-800-252-8014).

UTAH

The Law: Utah Code Annotated, Title 30, Chapter 2, Section 30-2-10 (U.C. § 30-2-10). Ignore volume numbers; look for "title" numbers.

Custody: U.C. §§ 30-2-10 and 30-3-10. The court must order either joint or sole custody for the future care and custody of the minor children as it considers appropriate. In determining custody, the court must consider the best interests of the child and the past conduct and demonstrated moral standards of each of the parties. The court may inquire of the children and take into consideration the children's desires regarding the future custody, but the expressed desires are not controlling and the court may determine the children's custody otherwise. The court must also consider: which parent is most likely to act in the best interests of the child, including allowing the child frequent and continuing contact with the noncustodial parent as the court finds appropriate. There are special provisions for visitation in sole custody cases.

For joint custody, the parties may agree, or the court may order it if both parents are suitable for joint custody considering: the benefits to the child; the abilities of the parents to cooperate; the geographic distance between the parents' homes; the preference of the child (if old enough); and other factors deemed relevant by the court.

Child Support: U.C. §§ 78-45-7. Child support is based on adjusted gross income and determined by use of the Child Support Obligation table (§ 78-45-7.14) which includes income and number of children levels. Adjusted gross income is gross income less alimony previously ordered and paid and child support previously ordered. The parents' child support obligation is divided between them in proportion to their adjusted gross incomes. There are special calculations for split or joint physical custody cases. Child support also may be reduced by 50% for each child for time periods during which the child is with the noncustodial parent 25 of any 30 consecutive days.

Parties may agree if the amount equals or exceeds the guidelines amount. In such cases, parties must submit a completed child support worksheet, financial verification required by § 78-45-7.5 (5), and a written statement indicating whether or not the amount of child support requested is consistent with the guidelines.

Medical expenses and income withholding are required. Deviation from the guidelines is permitted upon consideration of the ages, standard of living and situation of the parties; the wealth and income of the parties; the needs and earning ability of the parties; and the responsibilities of the parents for the support of others.

Modification requests are permitted at any time if there has been a substantial change in circumstances (at least 15% difference required), or if at least 3 years have passed since the last order, when the application of the guidelines would cause a 10% change in the amount.

Agency: Office of Recovery Services, P.O. Box 45011, Salt Lake City, UT 84145-0011; (801) 536-8500 (1-800-257-9156).

VERMONT

The Law: Vermont Statutes Annotated, Title 15, Section 665 (15 V.S.A. § 665). Ignore "chapter" numbers; look for "title" numbers.

Custody: 15 V.S.A. § 665. The court may order parental rights and responsibilities to be divided or shared between the parents on such terms and conditions as serve the best interests of the child. When the parents cannot agree to divide or share parental rights and responsibilities, the court shall award parental rights and responsibilities primarily or solely to one parent. The court will consider: (1) the relationship of the child with each parent and the ability and disposition of each parent to provide the child with love, affection and guidance; (2) the ability and disposition of each parent to assure that the child receives adequate food, clothing, medical care, other material needs and a safe environment; (3) the ability and disposition of each parent to meet the child's present and future developmental needs; (4) the quality of the child's adjustment to the child's present housing, school and community and the potential effect of any change; (5) the ability and disposition of each parent to foster a positive relationship and frequent and continuing contact with the other parent, including physical contact, except where contact will result in harm to the child or to a parent; (6) the quality of the child's relationship with the primary care provider, if appropriate given the child's age and development; (7) the relationship of the child with any other person who may significantly affect the child; and (8) the ability and disposition of the parents to communicate, cooperate with each other and make joint decisions concerning the children where parental rights and responsibilities are to be shared or divided. In addition, the court shall consider evidence of abuse.

Child Support: 15 V.S.A.§§ 653-657. The guidelines are based on available income which means gross income, less spousal child support actually paid; the cost of health insurance for the children; FICA and income taxes withheld. Except in cases of shared or split physical custody, the total child support obligation shall be divided between the parents in proportion to their respective available incomes and the noncustodial parent shall be ordered to pay his or her share to the custodial parent. The custodial parent shall be presumed to spend his or her share directly on the child.

Deviations are permitted if the court finds that application of the guidelines is unfair to the child or to any of the parties (such as resources, needs, education or travel-related expenses).

Modifications are permitted upon a showing of a real, substantial and unanticipated change of circumstances. A variance from the guidelines of 10% is considered a substantial change of circumstances. If the child support order has not been modified by the court for at least three years, the court may waive the requirement of a showing of a real, substantial and unanticipated change of circumstances. Modifications may be made only as to future support installments and installments which came due after the date of notice of the motion to modify to the other party.

Agency: Office of Child Support, 103 South Main Street, Waterbury, VT 05671-1901; (or call toll-free 1-800- 786-3214).

VIRGINIA

The Law: Annotated Code of Virginia 1950, Title 20, Section 20-124.2 (C.V. § 20-124.2). Ignore "chapter" numbers; look for "title" and "section" numbers.

Custody: C.V. § 20-124.2, 3. In determining custody, the court shall give primary consideration to the best interests of the child. The court shall assure minor children of frequent and continuing contact with both parents, when appropriate, and encourage parents to share in the responsibilities of rearing their children. There is no presumption favoring either parent as to custody. The court shall give due regard to the primacy of the parent-child relationship but may upon a showing by clear and convincing evidence that the best interest of the child would be served thereby award custody or visitation to any other person with a legitimate interest. The court may award joint custody or sole custody. Mediation shall be used as an alternative to litigation where appropriate. When mediation is used in custody and visitation matters, the goals may include development of a proposal addressing the child's residential schedule and care arrangements, and how disputes between the parents will be handled in the future.

Best interest of child includes: (1) age, physical and mental condition of the child and parties; (2) relationship between the child and each parent; (3) needs of the child; (4) the role each parent played, and will play, in the child's upbringing and care; (5) the parent's role in caring for child; (6) the willingness of each parent to maintain a close relationship and cooperate and resolve disputes; (7) the preference of the child if child is of sufficient age, intelligence, understanding, and experience; (8) any history of family abuse; and (9) any other relevant factor.

Child Support: C.V. §§ 20-108.1–108.2. The court may order that support be paid for any child of the parties. The guidelines are based on combined gross income of the parties (excluding child support and certain other benefits) and determined according to the number of children on the statutory table (§ 20-108.2). Additions for health care coverage and extraordinary medical expenses will be made to the basic support amount, and certain child care expenses may also be added. The total monthly child support obligation is divided proportionately between the parents. The monthly obligation of each parent is computed by multiplying each parent's percentage of the parents' combined gross income by the total child support obligation (monthly). Special calculations are made in split custody or shared custody cases.

The court may require a life insurance policy be maintained for the benefit of the children. Parties may agree to support a child over the age of 18. Support may also be ordered continued for any child up to 19 who is a full-time high school student, not self-supporting, and living in the home of a party. The court may also order the continuation of support for any child over 18 severely and permanently mentally or physically disabled, unable to live independently and support himself, and resides in the home of a parent.

Deviations from the guidelines are permitted where there is a finding that they would be unjust or inappropriate in a particular case (such as based upon the terms of the custody agreement).

Agency: Division of Child Support Enforcement, Department of Social Services, 730 East Broad Street, Richmond, VA 23219; (804) 692-1428; (1-800-468-8894 in Virginia only).

WASHINGTON

The Law: West's Revised Code of Washington Annotated, Title 26, Chapter 26.09, Section 26.09.002 (R.C.W.A. § 26.09.002).

Custody: R.C.W.A. § 26.09.002. The best interests of the child shall be the standard by which the court determines and allocates the parties' parental responsibilities. The policy of this state is that the best interests of the child are served by a parenting arrangement that best maintains a child's emotional growth, health and stability, and physical care. Further, the best interest of the child is ordinarily served when the existing pattern of interaction between a parent and child is altered only to the extent necessitated by the changed relationship of the parents or as required to protect the child from physical, mental, or emotional harm.

Parties are encouraged to develop an agreed parenting plan. The plan must contain provisions for resolution of future disputes between the parents, allocation of decision-making authority, and residential provisions for the child. The plan will allocate decision-making authority to one or both parties regarding the children's education, health care, and religious upbringing. The parties may incorporate an agreement related to the care and growth of the child in these specified areas, or in other areas, into their plan. Regardless of the allocation of decision-making in the parenting plan, either parent may make emergency decisions affecting the health or safety of the child. The plan will include a residential schedule which designates in which parent's home each minor child shall reside on given days of the year, including provision for holidays, birthdays of family members, vacations, and other special occasions. Each parent may make decisions regarding the day-to-day care and control of the child while the child is residing with that parent. When mutual decision making is designated but cannot be achieved, the parties shall make a good-faith effort to resolve the issue through the dispute resolution process.

Best interest factors include: (1) each party's relative strength, nature and stability of the relationship with the child, including which party has taken greater responsibility for the child; (2) any agreement of the parties; (3) each party's past and potential for future performance of parenting functions; (4) child's emotional needs and development; (5) the child's relationship with siblings and any other significant adults, and involvement in his or her physical surroundings, school, and other activities; (6) the wishes of the parties and the child; and (7) each party's employment schedule. The greatest weight is given to factor (1) above. R.C.W.A. §26.09.187.

Child Support: R.C.W.A. §§ 26.19.001–19-100. The child support obligation is to be equitably apportioned between the parents. The guidelines are based on combined monthly net income and the ages and number of children for whom support is owed. Gross income is adjusted to exclude child support and other designated benefits received. Taxes, FICA, pension, mandatory union dues, and spousal support paid are items deducted from gross income to reach the net income amount.

Deviations may be made upon a showing, among other things, of extraordinary expenses or if the child spends a significant amount of time with the parent who would otherwise owe support. An agreement of the parties is not by itself adequate reason for any deviations from the standard calculation. Written findings are required for deviations from the guidelines.

Modifications are permitted where at least 3 years have passed since the last order was entered, and the proposed change in child support is at least a 25% and $100 per month difference from the current support amount.

Agency: Division of Child Support, Department of Social Health Services, P.O. Box 9162, Olympia, WA 98504-9162. Street Address: 712 Pear St., S.E., Olympia, WA 98504; (360) 586-3162; (1-800-457-6202).

WEST VIRGINIA

The Law: West Virginia Code, Chapter 48, Article 2, Section 48-2-15 (W.V.C. § 48-2-15). Ignore volume numbers; look for "chapter" numbers.

Custody: W.V.C. §48-2-15. Custody and visitation will be ordered as may be appropriate under the circumstances. Visitation must be specified in a schedule for the noncustodial parent. Unless it is not in the best interests of the child, all custody orders must provide for the following: the custodial parent shall be required to authorize the child's school to release to the noncustodial parent copies of information concerning the child which would be released to the custodial parent; the custodial parent shall transmit to the noncustodial parent a copy of the child's grades or report card and copies of any other status or progress reports of the child; when practicable the custodial parents will schedule parent-teacher conferences at a time when the noncustodial parent can be present; the custodial parent shall authorize medical providers to release to the noncustodial parent copies of medical care information which would otherwise be released to the custodial parent; the custodial parent shall promptly inform the noncustodial parent of any illness of the child which requires medical attention; or, if the child is in the actual physical custody of the noncustodial parent during a period of visitation, the noncustodial parent shall promptly inform the custodial parent of any illness of the child which requires medical attention; the custodial parent shall consult with the noncustodial parent prior to any elective surgery being performed on the child; and in the event emergency medical procedures are undertaken for the child which require the parental consent of either parent, if time permits, the other parent shall be consulted, or if time does not permit such consultation, the other parent shall be promptly informed of such emergency medical procedures: the same duty to inform the custodial parent applies to the noncustodial parent in the event that the emergency medical procedures are required while the child is in the physical custody of the noncustodial parent during a period of visitation.

Child Support: W.V.C. §§ 48A-1A-1 & 48A-1B-1. The guidelines are based on adjusted gross income which means gross income less the payment of previously ordered child or spousal support. Unreimbursed child health care expenses, work-related child care expenses and any other extraordinary expenses agreed to by the parents or ordered less any extraordinary credits agreed to by the parents or ordered are added to the basic child support obligation to determine the total child support obligation. The child support order is determined by dividing the total child support obligation between the parents in proportion to their income. Washington provides separate worksheets to be used in determining child support in sole and joint custody cases.

Deviations from the guidelines are permitted if the guidelines are inappropriate in a specific case to accommodate the needs of the child or the circumstances of the parent or parents (such as special needs, educational expenses or long-distance visitation costs). The reason for the deviation and the amount of the calculated guidelines award must be stated on the record (preferably in writing on the worksheet or in the order).

Modification requests require a substantial change of circumstances. If application of the guideline would result in a new order that is more than 15% different, then the circumstances are considered to be a substantial change.

Agency: Child Support Enforcement Division, Department of Health & Human Resources, 1900 Kanawha Boulevard East, Capitol Complex, Building 6, Room 817, Charleston, WV 25305; (304) 558-3780; (1-800-249-3778).

Wisconsin

The Law: West's Wisconsin Statutes Annotated, Section 767.24 (W.S.A. § 767.24). Ignore "chapter" numbers; look for "section" numbers.

Custody: W.S.A. § 767.24. In an annulment, divorce, legal separation, or custody case, the court shall determine the legal custody and physical placement of a child based on the best interest of the child. Joint legal custody or sole legal custody of a minor child may be ordered. For joint legal custody, the parties may agree, or if one party requests it, the court must find that both parties are capable of performing parental duties and responsibilities and wish to have an active role in raising the child; no conditions exist at that time which would substantially interfere with the exercise of joint legal custody; and the parties will be able to cooperate in the future decision making required under an award of joint legal custody. In joint legal custody orders, the court may specify one parent as the primary caretaker of the child and one home as the primary home of the child and give one party sole power to make specified decisions, while both parties retain equal rights and responsibilities for other decisions. Evidence of domestic abuse is presumed to show that the parties will not be able to cooperate in the future decision making required.

In either sole or joint legal custody cases, the court shall allocate periods of physical placement between the parties. In determining the allocation of periods of physical placement, the court shall consider: (1) the wishes of the child's parent or parents; (2) the wishes of the child, which may be communicated by the child or through the child's guardian ad litem or other appropriate professional; (3) the interaction and interrelationship of the child with his or her parent or parents, siblings, and any other person who may significantly affect the child's best interest; (4) the child's adjustment to the home, school, religion and community; (5) the mental and physical health of the parties, the minor children and other persons living in a proposed custodial household; (6) the availability of public or private child care services; (7) whether one party is likely to unreasonably interfere with the child's continuing relationship with the other party; (8) whether there is evidence that a party engaged in domestic or child abuse; (9) whether either party has or had a significant problem with alcohol or drug abuse; and (10) such other factors as the court may in each individual case determine to be relevant.

A child is entitled to periods of physical placement with both parents unless, after a hearing, the court finds that physical placement with a parent would endanger the child's physical, mental or emotional health. Access to a child's medical, dental and school records is available to a parent regardless of whether the parent has legal custody of the child.

Child Support: Wisconsin Administrative Code (HHS) 80.02. The court may order either or both parents to pay an amount reasonable or necessary for child support. The guidelines are based on a percentage of gross income standard: 17% (1 child), 25% (2 children), 29% (3children); 31% (4 children), and 34% (5 or more children). The guidelines presume that the parent with whom the child usually lives shares income directly with the child, and that the other parent pays a set percentage of income for the well-being of the child. The support amount may be expressed as a percentage of parental income or as a fixed sum, or as a combination of both in the alternative by requiring payment of the greater or lesser of either a percentage of parental income or a fixed sum

Deviations are permitted where the court finds that use of the percentage standard is unfair to the child or to any of the parties (such as when there are substantial periods of physical placement of the child to both parents).

Modifications are permitted if there has been an unusual change in circumstances or if it has been at least 3 years since the last order was entered.

Agency: Bureau of Child Support, Division of Economic Support, P.O. Box 7935, Madison, WI 53707-7935. Street Address: 201 E. Washington Ave., Room 271, Madison, WI 53707; (608) 266-9909 (no toll-free number).

WYOMING

The Law: Wyoming Statutes Annotated, Title 20, Chapter 2, Section 20-2-113 (W.S.A. § 20-2-113). Ignore volume numbers; look for "title" numbers.

Custody: W.S.A. § 20-2-113. The court may make any disposition of the children that appears most expedient and beneficial for the well-being of the children. The court shall consider the relative competency of both parents and no award of custody shall be made solely on the basis of gender of the parent. If the court finds that both parents have shown the ability to act in the best interest of the child, the court may order any arrangement that encourages parents to share in the rights and responsibilities of rearing their children after the parents have separated or dissolved their marriage. The court shall order custody in well defined terms to promote understanding and compliance by the parties.

The court shall consider evidence of spouse abuse or child abuse as being contrary to the best interest of the child. If the court finds that family violence has occurred, the court shall make arrangements for visitation that best protect the child and the abused spouse from further harm.

Child Support: W.S.A. §§ 20-6-301. The guidelines are based on net income for both parents which is gross income less personal income taxes, social security deductions, cost of dependent health care coverage for dependent children, actual payments being made under preexisting support orders for current support of other children, other court-ordered support obligations currently being paid and mandatory pension deductions. The total income is then compared to the guidelines by number of children to be supported. There are special calculations for shared custody cases, and in sole custody cases, where the noncustodial parent has custody of the child for more than fourteen consecutive days, support will be reduced by 50%.

Parties may agree to child support. All agreements must be accompanied by a financial affidavit on a form approved by the Wyoming Supreme Court (available at the office below) which fully discloses the financial status of the parties. The court will compare the guidelines to review the adequacy of child support agreements negotiated by the parties. If the agreed amount departs from the guidelines, the parties must justify the departure on the forms filed with the court.

Deviations are permitted if application of the guidelines would be unjust or inappropriate in that particular case (such as age of child or health, child or education expenses).

In any case in which child support has been ordered to be paid to the clerk of the court, any payment becomes a judgment on the date it is due. A parent owed support may recover from the owing parent reasonable attorney's fees and other costs of enforcing any judgment for child support.

Modification requests are permitted upon a substantial change of circumstances, at any time. Alternatively, a party may seek modification no earlier than 6 months after the order was entered if the application of the guidelines would result in a 20% change in the amount. An order for child support is not subject to retroactive modification except: upon agreement of the parties; or after the date of a party receives notice that a petition for modification has been filed.

Agency: Child Support Enforcement, Department of Family Services, 2300 Capital Avenue, 3rd Floor, Cheyenne, WY 82002-0490; (307) 777-6948 (no toll-free number).

REGIONAL OFFICES OF THE
FEDERAL OFFICE OF CHILD SUPPORT ENFORCEMENT

REGION I: **Connecticut, Maine, Massachusetts, New Hampshire, Rhode Island, and Vermont**

>OCSE Program Manager, Administration for Children and Families
>John F. Kennedy Federal Building, Room 2000
>Boston, MA 02203
>(617) 565-2478

REGION II: **New York, New Jersey, Puerto Rico, and Virgin Islands**

>OCSE Program Manager, Administration for Children and Families
>Federal Building, Room 4048
>26 Federal Plaza
>New York, NY 10278
>(212) 264-2890

REGION III: **Delaware, Maryland, Pennsylvania, Virginia, West Virginia, and District of Columbia**

>OCSE Program Manager, Administration for Children and Families
>P.O. Box 8436
>Philadelphia, PA 19104
>(215) 596-4370

REGION IV: **Alabama, Florida, Georgia, Kentucky, Mississippi, North Carolina, and South Carolina, and Tennessee**

>OCSE Program Manager, Administration for Children and Families
>101 Marietta Tower, Suite 821
>Atlanta, GA 30323
>(404) 331-2180

REGION V: **Illinois, Indiana, Michigan, Minnesota, Ohio, and Wisconsin**

>OCSE Program Manager, Administration for Children and Families
>105 W. Adams Street, 20th Floor
>Chicago, IL 60603
>(312) 353-4237

REGION VI: Arkansas, Louisiana, New Mexico, Oklahoma, and Texas

> OCSE Program Manager, Administration for Children and Families
> 1301 Young Street, Room 945 (ACF-3)
> Dallas, TX 75202
> (214) 767-3749

REGION VII: Iowa, Kansas, Missouri, and Nebraska

> OCSE Program Manager, Administration for Children and Families
> Federal Building, Suite 276
> 601 East 12th Street
> Kansas City, MO 64106
> (816) 426-3584

REGION VIII: Colorado, Montana, North Dakota, South Dakota, Utah, and Wyoming

> OCSE Program Manager, Administration for Children and Families
> Federal Office Building, Room 325
> 1961 Stout Street
> Denver, CO 80294-3538
> (303) 844-3100

REGION IX: Arizona, California, Hawaii, Nevada, and Guam

> OCSE Program Manager, Administration for Children and Families
> 50 United Nations Plaza, Room 450
> San Francisco, CA 94102
> (415) 437-8459

REGION X: Alaska, Idaho, Oregon, and Washington

> OCSE Program Manager, Administration for Children and Families
> 2201 Sixth Avenue
> Mail Stop RX-70
> Seattle, WA 98121
> (206) 615-2547

Appendix B
Sample Completed Forms

This appendix contains some forms which have been completed for a fictional case in a fictional state. This will give you further assistance in preparing the forms for your state. Below, under the heading "Factual Scenario" are the basic facts of the case. Under the heading "Table of Forms" is a list of the forms that are included in this appendix, along with the page on which each form begins.

Factual Scenario

Twenty-two year old Susan Smith and twenty-five year old John Jones have a child, Carrie Smith, whose date of birth is June 20, 1995. For two years after Carrie was born, the couple lived together at 222 Main Street, in the City of Happytown, which is in Bliss County, in the State of Utopia. They never married. John, however, has never contested the fact that he is the father. He acknowledged paternity when Carrie was born and consented to have his name appear on the birth certificate. In May, 2000, the couple's relationship began to deteriorate, and John moved into his own apartment at 1 Northwood Street, #3, Happytown, which he shares with two of his co-workers. Susan remains in the Main Street apartment with her daughter Carrie. Susan's sister has moved into the apartment with Susan and pays part of the expenses there.

Both Susan's and John's families live nearby and babysit frequently for Carrie. Although John contributed to Carrie's support from her birth, he has not paid any support since he moved out in May, 2000, except for $200, which he gave to Susan for Carrie's birthday party in June.

Susan attends college part-time; and works part-time as an administrative assistant, earning approximately $11,000 annually. John just secured a new job full-time as an entry-level computer technician for a large company. He earns approximately $22,000 annually but potentially will see significant increases in his salary as he gains seniority with the company. Susan's health benefits are provided through the local college. John has health benefits through his employer, and Carrie has been insured on his policy.

In early July, 2000, Susan contacted her local Child Support Enforcement Agency to learn of the services available, but due to the agency's current backlog for non public aid cases, she has decided to file a petition for custody and child support on her own. In her petition, Susan seeks sole custody and child support, but when the case was referred for mandatory mediation, both parties agreed to joint legal custody, keeping primary physical custody with Susan and providing liberal parenting time for John. The state's guidelines are followed to establish child support. This example calculates the monthly support sum due for child support in a combined adjusted gross income state. The judgment incorporates the agreement of the parties.

Note: Although Carrie's expenses are low, as she gets older, they can be expected to increase. Additionally, it is likely that both Susan's and John's income levels will change considerably as Susan completes her education and can seek full-time employment in her field, and as John advances in his career. These changes should trigger a review and adjustment upon a request for modification.

TABLE OF FORMS

The following forms are included in this appendix:

IN THE CIRCUIT COURT
BLISS COUNTY, UTOPIA

SUSAN SMITH,   )
    Petitioner,   )
  v.   ) Case No. _____
)
JOHN JONES,   )
    Respondent.)

PETITION TO ESTABLISH PATERNITY, CUSTODY AND TIME-SHARING, AND FOR CHILD SUPPORT

NOW COMES _____ SUSAN SMITH _____, petitioner, and states as follows:

1. The Petitioner is a resident of _____ Bliss _____ County.

2. _____ The Petitioner _____ is the mother of the minor child(xxx).

3. _____ The Respondent _____ is the father of the minor child(xxx).

4. The name, date of birth, and age of the minor child(xxx) is/xxx

Name	Date of Birth	Age
CARRIE SMITH	JUNE 20, 1995	5

PATERNITY [Choose 1]

☐ 5. Paternity has not been established.
☒ 5. Paternity has been established by:
 ☒ Respondent has acknowledged his paternity of the minor child(xxx) in writing filed with the Department of Vital Statistics in the State in which the child(xxx) was/xxx born.
 ☐ Respondent has consented to paternity and is named as father on the minor child(xxx)'s birth certificate.
 ☐ Paternity of the minor child(xxx) has been established by blood tests.
 ☒ Respondent has openly held out the minor child(xxx) as his natural child(xxx) and established a personal, financial, or custodial relationship with the child(xxx).

HOME STATE AND RESIDENCE OF CHILDREN

6. The child(ren)'s home state is _____ **UTOPIA** _____ because:
   [Select one]
   ☒ the child(ren) lived in this state with a parent or a person acting as a parent for at least six consecutive months immediately preceding the commencement of this proceeding.
   ☐ the child(ren) is/are less than six months old and lived in this state with a parent or a person acting as parent since birth.
   ☐ any absences from this state have been only temporary.
   ☐ this was the home state of the child(ren) within six months before the commencement of this proceeding and the children's absence from the state is because of removal or retention by a person claiming custody or for other reasons.

7. During the past five years, the minor child(ren) have lived with the following persons, at the following places, and for the following periods of time:

With	Address	Dates
Petitioner	222 Main Street Happytown, Utopia	Birth - Present
Petitioner & Respondent	222 Main Street Happytown, Utopia	Birth - May,2000

PRIOR LITIGATION

8. Petitioner knows of no other litigation concerning custody or visitation involving the minor child(ren) of the parties in this state or in any other state in which Petitioner has participated as a party, as a witness, or in any other capacity; EXCEPT {if any, state case name, case number, and name and location of court}:

Case Name	Case Number	Name and Location of Court

PENDING LITIGATION

9. Petitioner has no information of any proceeding that is pending in a court in this state or in any other state involving visitation or custody with the parties' minor child(xxx); EXCEPT *{if any, state case name, case number, and name and location of court}*:

Case Name	Case Number	Name and Location of Court

OTHER CUSTODY AND VISITATION CLAIMS

10. Petitioner knows of no persons other than the parties who have physical custody of the minor child(xxx) or who claim to have custody or visitation rights to the minor child(xxx); EXCEPT *{if any, state name and residence}*:

Name	Residence

CUSTODY OPTIONS [Choose 1]

☐ 11. The parties should be awarded joint legal custody of the minor child(ren), with primary physical custody in and periods of care and responsibility consistent with the best interests of the child(ren).

☒ 11. Petitioner should be awarded sole legal and physical custody of the child(xxx) subject to the respondent's reasonable rights of visitation. Sole legal and physical custody is in the best interests of the minor child(xxx) because:

```
Petitioner is the primary caretaker of the minor
child, and can provide a stable, consistent residence
for the child.
```

CHILD SUPPORT

☒ 12. Child support should be set according to this state's support guidelines and the Respondent should be ordered to pay child support the amount determined by the child support guidelines. A worksheet form and financial affidavit will be timely filed and served on respondent.

☒ 13. Petitioner requests temporary child support during the pendency of this case, in accordance with this state's child support guidelines.

☒ 14. Petitioner requests that child support be retroactive to the birth of the child(xxx), and that the amount of child support be in accordance with this state's child support guidelines.

LIFE INSURANCE

☒ 15. Respondent should be ordered to purchase life insurance with a benefit amount of $____250,000____, naming the petitioner as trustee for the benefit of the minor child(xxx) to pay the child support obligation upon the respondent's death.

MEDICAL INSURANCE

☒ 16. ____Respondent_____ should provide health and dental insurance for the minor child(xxx).

MEDICAL EXPENSES [Choose 1]

☐ 17. _____should pay 100% of the minor child(ren)'s health and dental expenses not paid by insurance.

☐ 17. The parties should each pay one-half of the child(ren)'s health and dental expenses not paid by insurance.

☒ 17. The parties should pay the children(xxx)'s health and dental expenses not paid by insurance in the income percentages shown on the child support worksheet.

SCIENTIFIC TESTING

☒ 18. Petitioner requests scientific paternity testing be ordered if Respondent denies paternity of the child(xxx), with blood or other bodily tissue or fluid samples to be sent for testing to a qualified blood testing laboratory and DNA tests, HLA tests, and any other tests the testing facility recommends to be performed. Petitioner requests that court costs, scientific testing costs, and expert witness fees should be ordered to be paid by Respondent.

BIRTH RECORD

☒ 19. Upon determination of paternity, the Department of Vital Statistics should be ordered to change the birth record of the minor child(~~ren~~) to reflect the paternity as determined by this court.

WHEREFORE, Petitioner asks the Court to:

1. Establish the paternity of the minor child(ren).
2. Award child custody in accordance with this Petition.
3. Order child support according to the Child Support Guidelines.
4. Grant such other and further relief as the Court deems just and equitable.

RESPECTFULLY SUBMITTED:

Susan Smith
_____
Signature of Petitioner
Print Name: __Susan Smith__
Address: __222 Main Street__
__Happytown, Utopia__
Telephone: __(555) 444-4444__

ACKNOWLEDGEMENT

STATE OF _____UTOPIA_____)
) SS.
COUNTY OF _____BLISS_____)

I,_____Susan Smith_____, being first duly sworn upon my oath, depose and state that I am the Petitioner in the above-entitled cause. I have read the attached PETITION TO ESTABLISH PATERNITY, CUSTODY AND TIME-SHARING, AND FOR CHILD SUPPORT. I state that the contents thereof are true and correct, except to the matters stated on information and belief, and those matters I believe to be true.

Susan Smith
_____
Signature of Petitioner

SUBSCRIBED AND SWORN TO before me on
this __15th__ day of _____July_____, __2000__.

C. U. Sine
_____
NOTARY PUBLIC
My Commission Expires: __May 5, 2002__

IN THE CIRCUIT COURT
BLISS COUNTY, UTOPIA

SUSAN SMITH,	)	
Petitioner,	)	
v.	)	Case No. _____
	)	
JOHN JONES,	)	
Respondent.	)	

SUMMONS

TO THE RESPONDENT:
    Name of Respondent: _____John Jones_____
    Address: __16 Northwood Street, #3, Happytown, Utopia____

GREETINGS:
You are hereby directed to serve a pleading or motion in response to the petition filed in the above-captioned case within __30__ days after service of this summons and petition, and file the same, as provided by law. A letter or phone call will not protect your rights.

You are notified that, unless you serve and file a responsive pleading or motion, the petitioner will apply to the court for the relief demanded in the petition, and a court may enter orders affecting the custody, visitation or support of your child(ren).

The name and address of the court is: ____Circuit Court of Bliss County,____
____454 South Washington Street, Happytown, Utopia_____
Petitioner's name : _____Susan Smith_____
Address: __222 Main Street, Happytown, Utopia_____

ISSUED this _____ day of _____, _____

_____
Clerk of the District Court

By _____

IN THE CIRCUIT COURT
BLISS COUNTY, UTOPIA

SUSAN SMITH,   )
        Petitioner,   )
    v.   )   Case No. 99-12345
)
JOHN JONES,   )
        Respondent.   )

RESPONSE TO PETITION TO ESTABLISH PATERNITY, CUSTODY AND TIME-SHARING, AND FOR CHILD SUPPORT

    I, _____ JOHN JONES _____, being the Respondent herein certify that the following information is true:

    1.   I admit the allegations contained in the following numbered paragraphs in the Petition *{indicate paragraph number(s)}*: _____ 1 - 10, 14, and 17 _____
_____.

    2.   I deny the allegations contained in the following numbered paragraphs in the Petition *{indicate paragraph number(s)}*: __ 11, 13, 15, and 16; as to __
__ paragraph 18, I deny testing is needed _____.

    3.   I currently am unable to admit or deny the allegations contained in the following paragraphs due to lack of information *{indicate paragraph number(s)}*: 12 and 19
_____.

    4.   Since this case involves a minor child(~~ren~~), a completed Uniform Child Custody Jurisdiction Act Affidavit is filed with this Response.

    5.   Child support should be determined in accordance with the worksheet form which ☐ is filed with this Response or ☒ will be filed after the other party serves his or her financial affidavit.

    6.   A completed Financial Affidavit form ☐ is filed with this Response or ☒ will be timely filed after the other party serves his or her financial affidavit.

RESPECTFULLY SUBMITTED:

John Jones
_____
Signature of Respondent
Print Name: <u>John Jones</u>
Address: <u>16 Northwood Street, #3</u>
<u>Happytown, Utopia</u>
Telephone: <u>(555) 433-3333</u>

ACKNOWLEDGEMENT

STATE OF <u>UTOPIA</u>   )
) SS.
COUNTY OF <u>BLISS</u>   )

I, <u>JOHN JONES</u>   , being first duly sworn upon my oath, depose and state that I am the Respondent in the above-entitled cause. I have read the attached RESPONSE TO PETITION TO ESTABLISH PATERNITY, CUSTODY AND TIME-SHARING, AND FOR CHILD SUPPORT. I state that the contents thereof are true and correct.

          John Jones
          _____
          Signature of Respondent

SUBSCRIBED AND SWORN TO before me on
this <u>27th</u> day of <u>August</u>, <u>2000</u>.

Whit Ness
_____
NOTARY PUBLIC
My Commission Expires: <u>October 23, 2002</u>

IN THE CIRCUIT COURT
BLISS COUNTY, UTOPIA

SUSAN SMITH,   )
            Petitioner,   )
    v.   )   Case No. 99-12345
)
JOHN JONES,   )
            Respondent.   )

UNIFORM CHILD CUSTODY JURISDICTION ACT AFFIDAVIT

1.   The name, date of birth and age of the minor child(ren) is/are:

Name	Date of Birth	Age
Carrie Smith	June 20, 1995	5

2.   The child(ren)'s home state is _____Utopia_____.

3.   During the past five years, the minor child(ren) have lived with the following persons, at the following places, and for the following periods of time:

With	Address	Dates
Petitioner	222 Main Street Happytown, Utopia	Birth - Present
Petitioner & Respondent	222 Main Street Happytown, Utopia	Birth - May, 2000

4.   I know of no other litigation concerning custody or visitation involving the minor child(ren) of the parties in this state or in any other state in which I have participated as a party, as a witness, or in any other capacity, except: None

Case Name	Case Number	Name and Location of Court

5. I have no information of any proceeding that is pending in a court in this state or in any other state involving visitation or custody with the parties' minor child(~~ren~~) except:

Case Name   Case Number   Name and Location of Court

None

6. The proceeding identified in paragraph 5 above ☐ is pending ☐ has been stayed by a court in this state or in another state involving visitation or custody with the parties' minor child(~~ren~~).   N/A

Case Name   Case Number   Name and Location of Court

7. I know of no persons other than the parties who have physical custody of the minor child(ren) or who claim to have custody or visitation rights to the minor child(~~ren~~) except: None

Name   Residence

I acknowledge that if I obtain information regarding any custody or visitation proceeding concerning the child(~~ren~~) in this state or any other state, I have a continuing duty to advise this court of such proceeding.

Dated: __August 27, 2000__   *John Jones*
                                              Signature of Respondent

SUBSCRIBED AND SWORN TO before me on
this __27th__ day of _____August_____, __2000__.

_____*Whit Ness*_____
NOTARY PUBLIC
My Commission Expires: __October 23, 2002__

207

IN THE CIRCUIT COURT
BLISS COUNTY, UTOPIA

SUSAN SMITH,   )
        Petitioner,   )
   v.   )   Case No. 99-12345
)
JOHN JONES,   )
        Respondent.   )

CERTIFICATE OF SERVICE

I HEREBY CERTIFY that a copy of <u>**Response to Petition to Establish**</u>
<u>**Paternity, Custody and Time-Sharing, and for Child Support; and**</u>
<u>**Uniform Child Custody Jurisdiction Act Affidavit**</u>
_____ *{name of document(s) served}* was:

   ☒ mailed   ☐ telefaxed and mailed   ☐ hand-delivered

to   <u>**Susan Smith, 222 Main Street, Happytown, Utopia**</u>

_____*{name and address*

of person being served}, on <u>**August 27, 2000**</u> *{date}*.

Dated: <u>**August 27, 2000**</u>

John Jones
_____
Signature of ☒   Respondent or ☐ Petitioner
Print Name: <u>**John Jones**</u>
Address: <u>**16 Northwood Street, #3**</u>
            <u>**Happytown, Utopia**</u>
Telephone: <u>**555-433-3333**</u>

IN THE CIRCUIT COURT
BLISS COUNTY, UTOPIA

SUSAN SMITH,   )
            Petitioner,   )
      v.   )   Case No. 99-12345
)
JOHN JONES,   )
            Respondent.   )

NOTICE OF HEARING

TO: [Enter Names and Addresses of the Parties/Attorneys to notify]

        John Jones
        1 Northwood Street, #3
        Happytown, Utopia

YOU ARE HEREBY NOTIFIED that the above cause is set for hearing as follows:

DATE: <u>September 25, 2000</u>   TIME: <u>9:30</u>   <u>A</u>.M.

COURTHOUSE: <u>454 South Washington, Happytown, Utopia</u>

JUDGE: <u>Barry D. Hatchett</u>

SPECIFIC MATTER to be heard <u>Petitioner's Motion for Temporary Support</u>

    <u>and Custody</u>

NOTICED, DATED, AND MAILED this date: <u>August 31</u>, <u>2000</u>

                                    _Susan Smith_____
                                    Signature of party

IN THE CIRCUIT COURT
BLISS COUNTY, UTOPIA

SUSAN SMITH,	)	
Petitioner,	)	
v.	)	Case No. 99-12345
	)	
JOHN JONES,	)	
Respondent.	)	

MOTION FOR TEMPORARY RELIEF

NOW COMES _____ Susan Smith _____, petitioner and states as follows:

1. That Petitioner filed her/XXXPetition for _____ Paternity, Custody and _____ Time-sharing, and for Child Support on _____ July 15, 2000 _____.

2. That Respondent filed a response to the petition on __ August 27, 2000 __.

3. That __1__ child(XXX) was/XXX born to the parties, namely:

Name	Date of Birth	Age
Carrie Smith	June 20, 1995	5
XXX		

   who is/are currently residing with Petitioner.

4. That Petitioner is presently ☐ unemployed ☒ employed and has a net income of approximately $___700___ per month, and is without sufficient funds with which to support the minor child(XXX).

5. That Petitioner has received no direct support from Respondent, except:
   for one $200 payment toward the minor child's birthday party, held on June 20, 2000.

6. That Respondent is presently gainfully employed and has a net income of approximately $1,400__ per month, and has assets totaling in excess of $__10,000__ and is well able to contribute to the support of the parties' minor child(XXX); and Respondent has sufficient funds with which to pay for a just portion of the expenses of filing and maintaining this suit.

7. Attached to this Motion is the Petitioner's financial affidavit setting forth his/XXr financial circumstances.

WHEREFORE, petitioner herein requests:

A. That Petitioner be granted temporary child support and temporary custody of the minor child(~~ren~~).

B. That Respondent be ordered to maintain existing comprehensive major medical and health care insurance coverage on the minor child(~~ren~~) and to pay the premiums on that insurance, and to provide Petitioner with a copy of the insurance policy.

C. That the Respondent be ordered to pay a portion of the expenses of filing and maintaining this suit.

D. That petitioner be granted such other and further relief as the court may deem just.

RESPECTFULLY SUBMITTED:

Susan Smith
Signature of Petitioner
Print Name: Susan Smith
Address: 222 Main Street
  Happytown, Utopia
Telephone: 555-444-4444

ACKNOWLEDGEMENT

STATE OF   UTOPIA   )

    SS

COUNTY OF   BLISS   )

I,   Susan Smith   , being first duly sworn upon my oath, depose and state that I am the Petitioner in the above-entitled cause. I have read the attached Motion . I state that the contents thereof are true and correct.

Susan Smith
Signature of Petitioner

Subscribed and sworn to before me this

31st day of August , 2000 .

C. U. Sine
NOTARY PUBLIC
My Commission Expires: May 5, 2002

IN THE CIRCUIT COURT
BLISS COUNTY, UTOPIA

SUSAN SMITH,	)	
Petitioner,	)	
v.	)	Case No. 99-12345
	)	
JOHN JONES,	)	
Respondent.	)	

FINANCIAL AFFIDAVIT

THE AFFIANT, BEING DULY SWORN, SAYS UNDER PENALTY OF PERJURY THAT AFFIANT IS THE ☒ PETITIONER OR ☐ RESPONDENT IN THE ABOVE-CAPTIONED CASE, HAS PREPARED THIS FINANCIAL STATEMENT, KNOWS THE CONTENTS THEREOF, AND THAT IT IS TRUE AND CORRECT.

Name: __Susan Smith__   Date of Birth: __3-1-77__

Social Security Number: __333-33-3333__

I. PERSONAL INFORMATION

1.   Occupation: __Administrative Assistant (part-time)__

2.   The highest year of education completed: __High School; currently freshman at Happytown College__

3.   Are you presently employed? ☒ Yes ☐ No

    a. If yes: (1)   Where do you work (name and address)?
            __Gem Temporary Services__
            __333 Main Street__
            __Happytown, Utopia__

            (2)   When did you start work there (month/year)?
               __9/98__

    b. If no: (1)   When did you last work (month/year)?

            (2)   What were your gross monthly earnings? $_____

            (3)   Why are you presently unemployed?

II. INCOME INFORMATION

This information should be tailored and taken from the state's Child Support Worksheet(s).

4.   MONTHLY GROSS/ NET INCOME. $ 887.25 /$ 694.41

5.   MISCELLANEOUS INCOME.

      a.   Child support received from other relationships $ -0-

      b.   Other miscellaneous income (list source and amounts) $ -0-

      c.   Total Miscellaneous Income (add lines 3.4a through 3.4c) $ -0-

6.   Income of Other Adults in Household $ -0-

7.   If the income of either party is disputed, state monthly income you believe is correct and explain below:

III. AVAILABLE ASSETS

8.   Cash on hand $ 25.00

9.   On deposit in banks $ 249.00

10.   Stocks and Bonds, cash value of life insurance $ -0-

11.   Other liquid assets: $ -0-

IV. MONTHLY EXPENSE INFORMATION

Monthly expenses for myself and __1__ dependent(s) are: (Expenses should be calculated for the future, after separation, based on the anticipated residential schedule for the children.)

12.   HOUSING.

Rent, 1st mortgage or contract payments $ 249.00

Installment payments for other mortgages
     or encumbrances $ -0-

Taxes & insurance (if not in monthly payment) $ -0-

     Total Housing $ 249.00

13. UTILITIES.

Heat (gas & oil)	$ -0-	
Electricity	$ 20.00	
Water, sewer, garbage	$ -0-	
Telephone	$ 20.00	
Cable	$ 15.95	
Other	$ -0-	
Total Utilities		$ 55.95

14. FOOD AND SUPPLIES.

Food for __2__ persons	$ 200.00	
Supplies (paper, tobacco, pets)	$ 50.00	
Meals eaten out	$ 20.00	
Other	$ -0-	
Total Food Supplies		$ 270.00

15. CHILDREN.

Day Care/Babysitting	$ -0-	
Clothing	$ 50.00	
Tuition (if any)	$ -0-	
Other child related expenses	$ -0-	
Total Expenses Children		$ 50.00

16. TRANSPORTATION.

Vehicle payments or leases	$ 100.00
Vehicle insurance & license	$ 35.00
Vehicle gas, oil, ordinary maintenance	$ 30.00
Parking	$ 5.00

Other transportation expenses $ -0-

Total Transportation $ 55.95

17. HEALTH CARE. (May be omitted if fully covered)

Insurance $ -0-

Uninsured dental, orthodontic, medical,
    and eye care expenses $ 20.00

Other uninsured health expenses $ -0-

Total Health Care $ 20.00

18. PERSONAL EXPENSES (Not including children).

Clothing $ 50.00

Hair care/personal care expenses $ 20.00

Clubs and recreation $ 7.50

Education $ -0-

Books, newspapers, magazines, photos $ 12.50

Gifts $ 20.00

Other $ 20.00

Total Personal Expenses $ 130.00

19. MISCELLANEOUS EXPENSES.

Life insurance (if not deducted from income) $ 12.00

Other _____ $ -0-

Other _____ $ -0-

Total Miscellaneous Expenses $ 12.00

20. TOTAL HOUSEHOLD EXPENSES $ 1,125.95

V. OTHER EXPENSES

21.   INSTALLMENT DEBTS INCLUDED IN ABOVE PARAGRAPHS. (Include the creditor, balance and last payment amount)

-0-

22.   OTHER DEBTS AND MONTHLY EXPENSES NOT INCLUDED IN ABOVE PARAGRAPHS

-0-

Total Monthly Payments for Other Debts and Monthly Expenses $____-0-____

23.   TOTAL EXPENSES $1,125.95

24.   Other: Cost of filing and expense of maintaining this suit:
        (clerk's fees, sheriff's service fees) $ 200.00

VI. SIGNATURE OF AFFIANT

Dated: ___August 31, 2000___   ___Susan Smith_____

                                       ☒ Petitioner OR ☐ Respondent

SUBSCRIBED AND SWORN TO before me on
this __31st__ day of ____August____, __2000__.

___C. U. Sine_____
NOTARY PUBLIC
My Commission Expires: __May 5, 2002__

IN THE CIRCUIT COURT
BLISS COUNTY, UTOPIA

SUSAN SMITH,	)	
Petitioner,	)	
v.	)	Case No. ___99-12345___
	)	
JOHN JONES,	)	
Respondent.	)	

CHILD SUPPORT CALCULATION WORKSHEET

	Parent to Receive Supt	Parent to Pay Supt	Combined
1. Monthly gross income:	$ 887.25	$1,774.50	$2,661.75
2. Adjustments (per month):			
a. Other court or administratively ordered child support being paid:	($ -0-)	($ -0-)	
b. Court ordered spousal support being paid:	($ -0-)	($ -0-)	
c. Support obligation for children in primary physical custody:	($ -0-)	($ -0-)	
3. Adjusted monthly gross income (Line 1 minus lines 2a, 2b and 2c):	$ 887.25	$1,774.50	$2,661.75
4. Proportionate share of combined adjusted monthly gross income: (Each parent's line 3 divided by combined line 3):	33 %	66 %	

5. Basic child support amount
   (From support chart using
   combined line 3): $ __424.00__

	Parent to Receive Supt	Parent to Pay Supt	Combined

6. Additional child-rearing
   costs (per month):

   a. Reasonable work-
      related child care
      costs of the parent
      receiving support
      ($_____) less
      federal tax credit
      ($_____): $____-0-____

   b. Reasonable work-
      related child care
      costs of the parent
      paying support: $____-0-____

   c. Health insurance
      costs for children who
      are the subject of the
      proceeding: $____-0-____ $____-0-____

   d. Uninsured extraordinary
      medical costs (Agreed
      by parents or ordered
      by court): $____-0-____ $____-0-____

   e. Other extraordinary
      child-rearing costs
      (Agreed by parents
      or ordered by court): $____-0-____ $____-0-____

7. Total additional child
   rearing costs (Sum o lines
   6a, 6b, 6c, 6d and 6e): $____-0-____ $____-0-____ $____-0-____

8. Total combined child
support costs (Sum of
lines 5 and combined 7): $ 424.00

	Parent to Receive Supt	Parent to Pay Supt	Combined

9. Each parent's support
obligation (Multiply
line 8 by each parent's
line 4): $ 141.00 $ 283.00

10. Credit for additional
child-rearing costs
of parent obligated
to pay support: ($ -0-)

11. Credit for a portion of the
amounts expended by parent
obligated to pay support
during periods of temporary
physical custody (Multiply
line 5 by 20%):   ($ 85.00)

12. PRESUMED CHILD SUPPORT AMOUNT
(Line 9 minus lines 10 and 11): $ 198.00

IN THE CIRCUIT COURT
BLISS COUNTY, UTOPIA

SUSAN SMITH,   )
          Petitioner,   )
    v.   )   Case No. 99-12345
)
JOHN JONES,   )
          Respondent.   )

ORDER FOR TEMPORARY RELIEF

This cause having come to be heard on _____ September 25, 2000 _____, upon Petitioner's Motion for Temporary Relief, it is HEREBY ORDERED:

1. That the Court has jurisdiction over the parties and subject matter of this action.

2. That the Respondent shall pay child support in the amount of $___198.00___ per month, beginning ___October 1, 2000___.

3. That allocation of parenting time of the minor child(ꭓꭓꭓ) be as follows:

   ☒ Petitioner ☐ Respondent shall be the primary residential parent, subject to parenting time in ☐ Petitioner ☒ Respondent as follows:

   every Tuesday, 6-9 p.m.; alternating Thursdays, 6-9 p.m.; and alternating weekends from 5 p.m. Friday to 4 p.m. Sunday.

4. That ☐ Petitioner ☒ Respondent shall maintain existing comprehensive major medical and health care insurance coverage on the minor child(ren) and shall pay the premiums on that insurance, and shall provide ☒ Petitioner ☐ Respondent with a copy of the insurance policy.

5. That Respondent shall pay a just portion of the expenses of filing and maintaining this suit in the amount of $___133.00___.

ORDERED on _September 25, 2000_

_____
JUDGE

IN THE CIRCUIT COURT
BLISS COUNTY, UTOPIA

SUSAN SMITH,	)	
Petitioner,	)	
v.	)	Case No. 99-12345
	)	
JOHN JONES,	)	
Respondent.	)	

MOTION AND ORDER FOR REFERRAL TO MEDIATION

NOW COMES _____ Susan Smith _____, petitioner, and states:

1.   That Petitioner filed a <u>Petition to Establish Paternity, Custody and</u> <u>Time-Sharing, and for Child Support</u>   on <u>July 15, 1999</u>.

2.   That Respondent filed a response to the petition on <u>August 27, 1999</u>.

3.   That the following matter(s) is/are at issue in this case and is a/are proper subject(s) for mediation at this time:

☒   custody   ☒   time-sharing   ☒   child support

WHEREFORE, petitioner herein requests:

A.   That the matter(s) stated above be referred for mediation, and that a status date be set for 90 days to permit completion of the mediation sessions.

B.   That the costs of mediation be paid by   ☐   petitioner   ☐   respondent

☒   other: <u>   the parties in proportion to their incomes</u>

C.   That Petitioner be granted such other and further relief as the court may deem just.

Respectfully submitted,

Susan Smith
_____
Signature of Petitioner
Print Name: <u>   Susan Smith</u>
Address: <u>   222 Main Street</u>
<u>   Happytown, Utopia</u>
Telephone: <u>   555-444-4444</u>

221

STATE OF _____UTOPIA_____)
) SS.
COUNTY OF _____BLISS_____)

I,_____Susan Smith_____, being first duly sworn upon my oath, depose and state that I am the Petitioner in the above-entitled cause. I have read the attached MOTION FOR REFERRAL FOR MEDIATION. I state that the contents thereof are true and correct.

_____*Susan Smith*_____
Signature of Petitioner

SUBSCRIBED AND SWORN TO before me on
this **26th** day of __September__, __2000__.

__*C. U. Sine*__
NOTARY PUBLIC
My Commission Expires: ___May 5, 2002___

ORDER

This matter is hereby referred for mediation to: __Bliss County Circuit Court Mediation Services_____, as to the matters of:

☒ custody   ☒ time-sharing   ☒ child support

A status date is set for _____ to permit completion of the mediation sessions.

Costs of mediation shall be paid by: ☐ petitioner   ☐ respondent

☒ other: __the parties in proportion to their incomes_____

ORDERED ON __September 26, 2000__

_____
JUDGE

IN THE CIRCUIT COURT
BLISS COUNTY, UTOPIA

SUSAN SMITH,   )
          Petitioner,)
     v.   )   Case No. 99-12345
)
JOHN JONES,   )
          Respondent.)

PARENTING PLAN

1. Legal Custody

We agree to share joint legal custody of our child(**xxx**); that is, neither of us will make a major change affecting our child(**xxx**) in the areas of religion, residence, non-emergency medical care, education or major recreational activities without consultation with the other. Before such a decision is made, we will discuss the matter and both of us must agree. If we cannot agree, our disagreement will be resolved by the methods we have chosen and set out in this parenting plan.

2. Time-Sharing

We will share time with the child(**xxx**) as follows:

Weekends and Weekdays (check one):

☐ Weekdays: _____

_____.

    Weekends: Weekends begin at _____ ___.M. (Friday) (Saturday) and end at _____ ___.M. (Sunday) (Monday), unless Monday is a legal holiday, in which case the weekend ends at _____ ___.M. (Monday) (Tuesday).

☒ We have attached a calendar for the year(s) _____2000 and 2001_____ to this plan, and have marked in red the days the child(**xxx**) will spend with mother and in blue the days the child(**xxx**) will spend with father. Days for this calendar begin at _9:00_ _A_.M. and end at _6:00_ _P_.M.

Vacations (check one):

☒ Each parent will have uninterrupted time with the child(~~ren~~) for __2__ weeks each summer if that parent gives the other at least __30__ days notice.

☐ Until the youngest child reaches age ___, uninterrupted vacation time with a parent is limited to ___ weeks. Between the ages of ___ and ___, that time will be ___ weeks. Between the ages of ___ and ___, that time will be ___ weeks. After reaching age ___, vacation time will be ___ weeks.

Holidays: Regardless of the day of the week, the child(ren) will spend:

(a) Mother's Day and mother's birthday with mother;

(b) Father's Day and father's birthday with father;

(c) Child(~~ren~~)'s birthdays with _____mother_____ in even-numbered years and with _____father_____ in odd-numbered years.

(d) Child(ren) will spend holidays as follows:

	With Mother (Specify Year Odd/Even/Every)	With Father (Specify Year Odd/Even/Every)
New Year's Day	Odd	Even
Martin Luther King Day	Even	Odd
Presidents Day	Odd	Even
Memorial Day	Even	Odd
July 4th	Odd	Even
Labor Day	Even	Odd
Veterans Day	Odd	Even
Thanksgiving Day	Even	Odd
Christmas Eve	Odd	Even
Christmas Day	Even	Odd
Evening before child's birthday	Even	Odd
Annual church picnic		Every
Annual mother-daughter church breakfast	Every	

224

Telephone: We agree that the child(~~ren~~) has/~~have~~ a right to place phone calls to and receive phone calls from the absent parent.

Changes: Each of us is free to ask for exceptions to this schedule, but we understand that the other parent can say "no," and we will not argue about it.

Transportation: We will divide the responsibility for getting the child(ren) to and from each other's house, day care, school, etc., as follows:

<u>Susan will drop Carrie at John's mother's house for John's</u>
<u>parenting time. John will be present or his mother may receive</u>
<u>Carrie. John will return Carrie to Susan's mother's house.</u>
<u>Susan will be present or her mother may receive Carrie.</u>
_____.

3. Trial Period or Permanent Plan: (Check one)

☐ We have not tried this time-sharing schedule before, so we agree that we will review the time-sharing plan in _____ days and at that time we will make any changes we agree on. If we cannot agree on changes, we will resolve our dispute using the method set forth in paragraph 6 below.

☒ We have already tried this time-sharing schedule, so we intend it to be permanent. We recognize, however, that as our child(~~ren~~) grow(s) and our lives change, it may be necessary to change the schedule from time to time. We agree that this is a major change that we have to discuss and agree on, and if necessary follow the dispute resolution procedures set out in paragraph 6 below.

4. The Status Quo — What we have now:

(a) Doctor <u>Perry's Family Clinic, Happytown</u>
(b) Dentist <u>Doctor Tooth, Happytown</u>
(c) Other medical <u>St. Bernard's Hospital</u>
(d) School <u>Marta Stewart Elementary School</u>
(e) Religion <u>Catholic</u>
(f) Recreation <u>Happytown YMCA</u>

We agree that neither of us will remove, cause to be removed, or permit removal of the child(~~ren~~) from the State of <u>Utopia</u>, except for temporary visits which do not interfere with the time-sharing schedule, without the written consent of the other parent or resolution of the dispute by the method set forth in paragraph 6 below.

5. Emergencies

In case of a medical emergency, if time allows, the parent with that period of responsibility will contact the other parent concerning treatment of the child. If the absent parent cannot be reached, any decision for emergency medical treatment will be made in the best interest of the child by the available parent.

6. Dispute Resolution

We will discuss all major changes in the child(ren)'s lives in order to try to reach agreement. If we cannot agree after discussion, we will participate in counseling, conciliation, or mediation to try to reach agreement. If there is still a dispute, we agree to submit the matter to the Court.

7. General Matters

In order to foster a continuing relationship between our child(ren) and both parents, we both agree:

(a) To be actively involved in the major decisions and legal responsibilities of our child(ren).

(b) To communicate and be flexible about the needs of our child(ren), especially as those needs change due to growth and development.

(c) To be supportive of and positive about the child(ren)'s relationship with the other parent. Each of us will give loving permission to the child(ren) to enjoy the relationship with the other parent and neither of us will interfere with the parent-child relationship of the other.

(d) That neither of us will align the child(ren) against the other parent or the other parent's family.

(e) We agree that each of us is responsible to keep the other parent informed of the child(ren)'s school functions, parent-teacher conferences and recreational activities.

I Agree:

_Susan Smith_____
Mother's Signature

I Agree:

_John Jones_____
Father's Signature

IN THE CIRCUIT COURT
BLISS COUNTY, UTOPIA

SUSAN SMITH,	)	
Petitioner,	)	
v.	)	Case No. 99-12345
	)	
JOHN JONES,	)	
Respondent.	)	

REQUEST FOR HEARING

1. Type of case: ___Custody/Child Support___

2. Judge to whom assigned ___Barry D. Hatchett___

3. Are there any hearings presently set? ___ Yes _X_ No

    If yes, when? _____

4. Specific matters to be heard [for example, petition for custody]:

    ___Agreement to Establish Custody and Time Sharing,___
    ___and for Support___

5. Estimated total time required for hearing all parties and witnesses: ___10 minutes___

6. Names, addresses, and phone numbers of all attorneys or parties to notify:

    None

Hearing requested by: ___Agreement of Petitioner and Respondent___
                Petitioner/Respondent [circle one]

IN THE CIRCUIT COURT
BLISS COUNTY, UTOPIA

SUSAN SMITH,		)	
	Petitioner,	)	
v.		)	Case No. 99-12345
		)	
JOHN JONES,		)	
	Respondent.	)	

FINAL JUDGMENT

THE COURT having read the pleadings, heard the evidence, and being otherwise advised, finds:

FINDINGS OF FACT

1. The Petitioner is a resident of _____ Bliss _____ County, _____ Utopia _____.

2. Petitioner is the mother of the minor child(xxx).

3. Respondent is the father of the minor child(xxx).

4. The name(s), date(s) of birth, and age(s) of the minor child(xxx) is/xxx

Name	Date of Birth	Age
Carrie Smith	June 20, 1995	5

WHEREFORE, THIS COURT ORDERS:

PATERNITY

1. The Respondent is hereby declared to be the natural father of the minor child(xxx).

CUSTODY [Choose One]

☐ 2. Mother is awarded sole legal and physical custody of the minor child(ren) subject to the other parent's reasonable rights of visitation. Sole legal and physical custody is in the best interests of the minor child(ren) because:

☒ 2. Mother and Father are awarded joint legal custody of the minor child(ren), with primary physical custody in ☒ Mother ☐ Father, and periods of care and responsibility consistent with the best interests of the child(ren).

☐ 2. Custody is determined in accordance with the parenting plan attached to this judgment and by agreement of the parties.

CHILD SUPPORT [Check all that apply]

☒ 3. Child support is set according to the Child Support Guidelines and ☐ Mother ☒ Father is ordered to pay child support in the amount of $_____198.00_____ per _____month_____, beginning _____December 1, 2000_____.

☐ 4. Child support in arrears are found to be $ _____ and ☐ Mother ☐ Father is ordered to pay child support arrears by paying an additional amount of $_____ per _____, beginning _____.

LIFE INSURANCE

☒ 5. ☐ Mother ☒ Father is ordered to purchase life insurance with a benefit amount of $_____125,000_____, naming the ☒ Mother ☐ Father as trustee for the benefit of the minor child(ren) in order to pay the child support obligation upon the parent's death.

MEDICAL INSURANCE

☒ 6. ☐ Mother ☒ Father is ordered to provide health and dental insurance for the minor child(ren).

MEDICAL EXPENSES [Choose One]

☐ 7. ☐ Mother ☐ Father shall pay 100% of the child(ren)'s health and dental expenses not paid by insurance.

☐ 7. Mother and Father shall each pay one-half of the child(ren)'s health and dental expenses not paid by insurance.

☒ 7. Mother and Father shall pay the child(ren)'s health and dental expenses not paid by insurance in the percentages shown on the child support worksheet.

BIRTH RECORDS

☐ 8. The Department of Vital Statistics should be ordered to change the birth record of the minor child to reflect the paternity as determined by this court.

ENTERED: _____

_____

Judge

AGREED: _____*Susan Smith*_____
           Petitioner

AGREED: _____*John Jones*_____
           Respondent

Appendix C
Forms

How to Use These Forms

The forms in this appendix will serve as guidelines for the more common forms you will need or encounter. They will undoubtedly need to be modified to fit the requirements and practices in the court where you will be filing your case. It is important that you understand the limitations of these forms, and the importance of complying with the requirements of the courts in your area. If you have not already done so, be sure to read "Using Self-Help Law Books," beginning on page 1 of this book.

Some states have standard forms that must be used in custody, visitation, and child support cases. If you are married, you will incorporate custody, visitation, and support requests (or agreements) into the divorce case (or legal separation or annulment). For specifics on forms used in divorce cases, see *How to File Your Own Divorce*, by Edward A. Haman, or one of the state-specific divorce books listed in the back of this book. These books are available through your local bookstore, or directly from Sphinx Publishing by calling 1-800-226-5291.

For each form in this appendix, there is an explanation of the general use of the form. Not all forms are used in every state (or county), and additional forms may be required. Check with your local court clerk to determine which legal forms are required and which are available through the clerk's office. If a form is required, but not available through your court clerk's office, adapt one of the forms from this book, following the formats for your state, or check your local law library for a state family law form book.

Most custody cases follow the same general procedure. A case is started by filing the original of a Petition (form 1) and Summons (form 2) with the clerk of your court and by serving copies of these papers on the other party. The party filing the Petition is usually called the *petitioner* or *plaintiff*. The Petition asks the court to establish paternity (if necessary), and award custody (or visitation) and child support to the petitioner. Many states also require that certain information be filed under the Uniform Child Custody Jurisdiction Act. In some states, this information is included in your Petition; and in others, it will be on a separate form. A Return of Service (form 3) of the petition and summons on the respondent must be filed.

File the documents in the state in which you reside (or the child's state). Check with your clerk's office to determine the filing fee for filing the petition. If you cannot pay, check to determine how a court can waive or defer the fee.

The party responding to the petition is usually called the *respondent* or *defendant*. After being served the summons and petition, the respondent must file a written Response (form 4) with the clerk of the court within a certain number of days (usually twenty to thirty days depending on your state's laws), but may be longer if the respondent is served out of state. With that Response should be filed the relevant Uniform Child Custody Jurisdiction Act Affidavit (form 5). Copies of the written response and affidavit must be sent to the petitioner (or the petitioner's lawyer), and Certificate of Service (form 6) must be filed with the clerk of the court.

To obtain records or the appearance of an individual, a Subpoena (form 7) may be sent. To obtain written answers under oath of the other party, Interrogatories (form 8) may be sent. If paternity must be established (and this has not been requested in the petition), a Motion for Scientific Paternity Testing (form 7) may be filed.

To properly establish child support, all states require some financial information disclosure from the parties, usually on specific forms which may be called "financial affidavit" or "statement of financial means" or something similar (see form 11). Also, each state's child support guidelines are very specific, and nearly all states have adopted child support worksheet forms (form 12) which must be filed prior to obtaining a child support order.

In addition, parties may file motions in court seeking temporary relief (such as temporary custody or support) (see form 13) during the pendency of the case.

Either party may request the court to enter a child support order which deviates from the guideline amount. In some states, this is done by filling in a special section of the child support worksheet. In other states, a separate motion must be filed (form 15).

For parties who agree, a Parenting Plan (form 17 or form 18) should be filed with the court. (In some states, each party may file their own proposed parenting plan if there is no agreement.)

A request for hearing of the petition or a motion (form 19) and a Notice of Hearing form (form 20) with a Certificate of Service upon the other party (form 6) may be sent as necessary to obtain a hearing on the petition or a motion filed.

If the respondent is served with the petition and summons but fails to file a written response within the required time period, the petitioner may file a motion to request the court to enter a default (forms 21 and 22) against the respondent with Certificate of Service (form 6) verifying that a copy was sent to the respondent.

Once the case is resolved a final judgment (form 23) will be entered addressing custody/visitation and support (and paternity if necessary).

If one of the parties disagrees with the trial court's decision, that party may appeal by filing a Notice of Appeal (form 24).

After the judgment is entered, if either party (or both) seeks to have the custody or support amount modified, and state law permits such a request, the party may file a petition or motion to modify the judgment (form 25) and send (or serve) a copy to the other party (form 6, or forms 2,3).

Be sure to make extra copies of all the documents you file with the court and serve on the other parties, and keep a file-stamped copy for your records to prove you actually filed the document. Keep an organized file of all court papers, especially proof that you sent the documents to the other party, along with any letters concerning your case. This is important if a judge in your case needs to see a copy of a document which is not in your court file.

TABLE OF FORMS

The forms listed below, and instructions for completing them, are included in this appendix. You will note that there are two page numbers given for each form. The first page number is for the instructions, and the second number is where the form itself begins.

Form 1: Petition for (Paternity) Custody/Visitation and Support

Instructions

Paragraphs 1–4. These paragraphs ask for general information about the parties and the child(ren) for whom custody is sought.

Paragraph 5. Select the box to indicate whether paternity has already been established. If you check the box stating "Paternity has been established," check one or more of the boxes below that to indicate how paternity has been established.that applies.

Paragraphs 6–10. These paragraphs contain information relating to the Uniform Child Custody Jurisdiction Act. In some states it will be acceptable to include this information in the Petition (and it won't be necessary to file a separate Uniform Child Custody Jurisdiction Act Affidavit), and in other states you will need to file a separate form with this information. In paragraph 6, fill in the name of the state where you will be filing your petition on the line, then check one or more of the boxes below that to show that this state is the child(ren)'s *home state*. Periods of temporary absence from the state are counted as part of the six months. In paragraph 7, fill in the information regarding where the child(ren) has/have lived for the past five years. In paragraph 8, if there were no previous court cases involving custody or visitation, type in the word "none" after the word "EXCEPT." If there were any previous cases, type in the case name (such as "Smith v. Jones"), the case number, and the name and location of the court (such as "Circuit Court, Dade County, Florida"). In paragraph 9, do the same thing relating to cases that are currently pending as you did in paragraph 8 for previous cases. In paragraph 10, if there are no other persons who have physical custody or claim a right to custody or visitation, type in the word "none" after the word "EXCEPT." If there are any other claiming custody or visitation rights, fill in their name and residence address.

Paragraph 11. Check the box which applies regarding custody/visitation.

Paragraphs 12–17. Check each of the boxes that apply to child support, life insurance, and medical care.

Paragraphs 18–19. These paragraphs ask the court to order the blood tests and to change the birth record for the child.

WHEREFORE section. This section summarizes your requests. Once this section is completed, sign and date the Petition. Before a notary public, you should complete and sign the acknowledgement at the end of the Petition to assure the court that the statements made are truthful.

See form A in appendix B for an example of a completed Petition.

PETITION TO ESTABLISH PATERNITY, CUSTODY AND TIME-SHARING, AND FOR CHILD SUPPORT

NOW COMES _____, petitioner, and states as follows:

1. The Petitioner is a resident of _____ County.

2. _____ is the mother of the minor child(ren).

3. _____ is the father of the minor child(ren).

4. The name, date of birth, and age of the minor child(ren) is/are:

   <u>Name</u>   <u>Date of Birth</u>   <u>Age</u>

PATERNITY [Choose 1]

☐ 5. Paternity has not been established.

☐ 5. Paternity has been established by [check all that apply]:

   ☐ Respondent has acknowledged his paternity of the minor child(ren) in writing filed with the appropriate agency in the State in which the child(ren) was/were born.

   ☐ Respondent has consented to paternity and is named as father on the minor child(ren)'s birth certificate.

   ☐ Paternity of the minor child(ren) has been established by blood tests.

   ☐ Respondent has openly held out the minor child(ren) as his natural child(ren) and established a personal, financial, or custodial relationship with the child(ren).

HOME STATE AND RESIDENCE OF CHILDREN

6. The child(ren)'s home state is _____ because: [Select all that apply]

☐ the child(ren) lived in this state with a parent or a person acting as a parent for at least six consecutive months immediately preceding the commencement of this proceeding.

☐ the child(ren) is/are less than six months old and lived in this state with a parent or a person acting as parent since birth.

☐ any absences from this state have been only temporary.

☐ this was the home state of the child(ren) within six months before the commencement of this proceeding and the children's absence from the state is because of removal or retention by a person claiming custody or for other reasons.

7. During the past five years, the minor child(ren) have lived with the following persons, at the following places, and for the following periods of time:

With	Address	Dates

PRIOR LITIGATION

8. Petitioner knows of no other litigation concerning custody or visitation involving the minor child(ren) of the parties in this state or in any other state in which Petitioner has participated as a party, as a witness, or in any other capacity; EXCEPT *{if any, state case name, case number, and name and location of court}*:

PENDING LITIGATION

9. Petitioner has no information of any proceeding that is pending in a court in this state or in any other state involving visitation or custody with the parties' minor child(ren); EXCEPT *{if any, state case name, case number, and name and location of court}*:

OTHER CUSTODY AND VISITATION CLAIMS

10. Petitioner knows of no persons other than the parties who have physical custody of the minor child(ren) or who claim to have custody or visitation rights to the minor child(ren); EXCEPT *{if any, state name and residence}*:

CUSTODY OPTIONS [Choose 1]

☐ 11. The parties should be awarded joint legal custody of the minor child(ren), with primary physical custody in and periods of care and responsibility consistent with the best interests of the child(ren).

☐ 11. Petitioner should be awarded sole legal and physical custody of the child(ren) subject to the respondent's reasonable rights of visitation. Sole legal and physical custody is in the best interests of the minor child(ren) because:

CHILD SUPPORT [Check all that apply]

☐ 12. Child support should be set according to this state's support guidelines and the Respondent should be ordered to pay child support the amount determined by the child support guidelines. A worksheet form and financial affidavit will be timely filed and served on respondent.

☐ 13. Petitioner requests temporary child support during the pendency of this case, in accordance with this state's child support guidelines.

☐ 14. Petitioner requests that child support be retroactive to the birth of the child(ren), and that the amount of child support be in accordance with this state's child support guidelines.

LIFE INSURANCE

☐ 15. Respondent should be ordered to purchase life insurance with a benefit amount of $_____, naming the petitioner as trustee for the benefit of the minor child(ren) to pay the child support obligation upon the respondent's death.

MEDICAL INSURANCE

☐ 16. _____ should provide health and dental insurance for the minor child(ren).

MEDICAL EXPENSES [Choose 1]

☐ 17. _____ should pay 100% of the minor child(ren)'s health and dental expenses not paid by insurance.

☐ 17. The parties should each pay one-half of the child(ren)'s health and dental expenses not paid by insurance.

☐ 17. The parties should pay the children(ren)'s health and dental expenses not paid by insurance in the income percentages shown on the child support worksheet.

SCIENTIFIC TESTING

☐ 18. Petitioner requests scientific paternity testing be ordered if Respondent denies paternity of the child(ren), with blood or other body tissue or fluid samples to be sent for testing to a qualified blood testing laboratory and DNA tests, HLA tests, and any other tests the testing facility recommends to be performed. Petitioner requests that court costs, scientific testing costs, and expert witness fees should be ordered to be paid by Respondent.

BIRTH RECORD

☐ 19. Upon determination of paternity, the Department of Vital Statistics should be ordered to change the birth record of the minor child(ren) to reflect the paternity as determined by this court.

WHEREFORE, Petitioner asks the Court to:

1. Establish the paternity of the minor child(ren).
2. Award child custody in accordance with this Petition.
3. Order child support according to the Child Support Guidelines.
4. Grant such other and further relief as the Court deems just and equitable.

RESPECTFULLY SUBMITTED:

_____

Signature of Petitioner

Print Name: _____

Address: _____

_____

Telephone: _____

ACKNOWLEDGEMENT

STATE OF _____)

) SS.

COUNTY OF _____)

I,_____, being first duly sworn upon my oath, depose and state that I am the Petitioner in the above-entitled cause. I have read the attached PETITION TO ESTABLISH PATERNITY, CUSTODY AND TIME-SHARING, AND FOR CHILD SUPPORT. I state that the contents thereof are true and correct, except to the matters stated on information and belief, and those matters I believe to be true.

_____

Signature of Petitioner

SUBSCRIBED AND SWORN TO before me on

this _____ day of _____, _____.

_____

NOTARY PUBLIC

My Commission Expires: _____

Form 2: Summons

Instructions

> *Caution:* Most, if not all, states have their own requirements for the form of a Summons. For example, some states require the Summons to be printed in two of more languages. Therefore, be sure to find out what form must be used in your state. Only as a last resort, after you are absolutely convinced there is no required form, should you use the form on the next page.

The Summons gives the respondent written notice that he or she is being sued, and provides basic information about what must be done to file a response.

After the words "To the Respondent," fill in the other parent's name and address. This is information the sheriff or other process server will use to try to locate the other parent.

On the short line in the first paragraph below the word "Greetings," fill in the number of days your state allows for filing an answer or response to a petition. In most states, this is twenty or thirty days. You may be able to get this information from the court clerk, or you may need to go to a law library and look it up in your state's the court rules.

You will then fill in the name and address of the court where the other parent must file any response. Finally, fill in your name and address on the lines indicated. If you are a victim of domestic violence and do not want the other parent to know your home address, check with your state laws, the court clerk's office, or your state attorney general's office to see if you can use an alternate address.

The remainder of the Summons form will be filled in by the court clerk when you file your Petition.

See form B in appendix B for an example of a completed Summons.

SUMMONS

TO THE RESPONDENT:

  Name of Respondent: _____

  Address: _____

GREETINGS:

You are hereby directed to serve a pleading or motion in response to the petition filed in the above-captioned case upon the petitioner indicated below within _____ days after service of this summons and petition, and file the same with the court, as provided by law. A letter or phone call will not protect your rights.

You are notified that, unless you serve and file a responsive pleading or motion, the petitioner will apply to the court for the relief demanded in the petition, and a court may enter orders affecting the custody, visitation, or support of your child(ren).

The name and address of the court is: _____

_____

Petitioner's name : _____

Address: _____

ISSUED this _____ day of _____, _____

                    Clerk of the Court

              By _____

Form 3: Return of Service

Instructions

A copy of the Summons and the Petition must be served on the respondent parent.

YOU MAY NOT SERVE THE SUMMONS AND PETITION YOURSELF. In all states it is most common for a law enforcement officer, usually a sheriff's deputy, to serve a Summons and Petition. In some states, service must be either by a law enforcement officer or by someone who is authorized by the court. In other states, service may be made by any competent person eighteen years of age or over who is not a party to the action.

> *Caution:* Many states that have their own Summons form also have their own Return of Service form, either as a part of the Summons itself, or as a separate form. As with the Summons, be sure to use the Return of Service required in your state. Often, the law enforcement officer will provide the Return of Service form. Only use the form on the following page as a last resort, if you are absolutely certain there is no required form for your state or county.

Upon service, the sheriff, deputy, or other process server must complete a Return of Service form (sometimes called an *Affidavit of Service*), which will include the case heading information; the name of the person served; the title of the papers served; and the date, time, place, and manner of service (each state has its own rules on who can be served and how to serve by mail or publication). Then the process server must sign and date the form, and file it with the clerk of the court.

Documents required to be sent to the other party after the petition will be proved by filing a "certificate of service" form (See form 6 below).

RETURN OF SERVICE

I, being duly sworn, on oath, say that I am over the age of eighteen (18) years and not a party to this lawsuit, and that I served the within Summons in said County on the _____ day of _____, _____, by delivering a copy thereof, with copy of Petition attached, in the following manner: (check one box and fill in appropriate blanks)

☐ to Respondent.

☐ to _____, a person over _____ years of age and residing at the residence of Respondent, _____, who was not home at the time of service.

☐ by posting a copy of the Summons and Petition in a public part of the premises of Respondent _____ (used if no person found at dwelling house or usual place of abode, if permitted by state law)

_____   _____

Signature of Person Making Service   Title [if any]

SUBSCRIBED AND SWORN to before me this _____ day of _____, _____.

_____
Notary or Other Officer authorized to Administer Oaths

Form 4: Response to Petition to Establish Paternity, Custody and Time-Sharing, and for Child Support

Instructions

The Response to the Petition for custody is used to admit or deny all of the allegations in the petition, or explain to the court that you do not have sufficient information with which to do so.

After completing the form, sign the form before a notary public, and file the original with the clerk of the circuit court in the county where the petition was filed. A copy of your Response together with any other forms required by your jurisdiction must be served on the petitioner, by mailing a copy to the petitioner at the address given in the Petition and Summons.. Each jurisdiction has a time limit within which the Response must be filed (often twenty to thirty days).

See form C in appendix B for an example of a completed Response.

RESPONSE TO PETITION TO ESTABLISH PATERNITY, CUSTODY AND TIME-SHARING, AND FOR CHILD SUPPORT

I, _____, being the Respondent herein, certify that the following information is true:

    1.   I admit the allegations contained in the following numbered paragraphs in the Petition *{indicate paragraph number(s)}*:_____

_____.

    2.   I deny the allegations contained in the following numbered paragraphs in the Petition *{indicate paragraph number(s)}*: _____

_____.

    3.   I currently am unable to admit or deny the allegations contained in the following paragraphs due to lack of information *{indicate paragraph number(s)}*: _____

_____.

    4.   Since this case involves a minor child(ren), a completed Uniform Child Custody Jurisdiction Act Affidavit is filed with this Response.

    5.   Child support should be determined in accordance with the worksheet which ☐ is filed with this Response, or ☐ will be filed after the other party serves his/her financial affidavit.

    6.   A completed Financial Affidavit form ☐ is filed with this Response, or ☐ will be timely filed after the other party serves his/her financial affidavit.

RESPECTFULLY SUBMITTED:

_____

Signature of Respondent
Print Name: _____
Address: _____
_____
Telephone: _____

ACKNOWLEDGEMENT

STATE OF _____)
) SS.
COUNTY OF _____)

I,_____, being first duly sworn upon my oath, depose and state that I am the Respondent in the above-entitled cause. I have read the attached RESPONSE TO PETITION TO ESTABLISH PATERNITY, CUSTODY AND TIME-SHARING, AND FOR CHILD SUPPORT. I state that the contents thereof are true and correct.

_____

Signature of Respondent

SUBSCRIBED AND SWORN TO before me on
this _____ day of _____, _____.

_____

NOTARY PUBLIC
My Commission Expires: _____

Form 5: Uniform Child Custody Jurisdiction Act Affidavit

Instructions

An affidavit demonstrating the court's jurisdiction over the child(ren) at issue in the case must often be filed by both parties. In some states, this information may be included in the Petition, as it is in form 1 in this appendix.

In paragraph 1, fill in the name, date of birth, and age of each child. In paragraph 2, fill in the name of the state where you will be filing your petition. Periods of temporary absence from the state are counted as part of the six months. In paragraph 3, fill in the information regarding where the child(ren) has/have lived for the past five years.

In paragraph 4, if there were no previous court cases involving custody or visitation, type in the word "none" after the word "except." If there were any previous cases, type in the case name (such as "Smith v. Jones"), the case number, and the name and location of the court (such as "Circuit Court, Dade County, Florida").

In paragraph 5, do the same thing relating to cases that are currently pending as you did in paragraph 8 for previous cases. Paragraph 6 relates to any cases listed in paragraph 5. If no cases are listed in paragraph 5, skip paragraph 6. If a case is listed in paragraph 5, check one of the boxes in paragraph 6 to indicate the current status of that case. If the case listed in paragraph 5 was stayed by a different court, list that case name, number, and the name and location of the court.

In paragraph 7, if there are no other persons who have physical custody or claim a right to custody or visitation, type in the word "none" after the word "except." If there are any other persons claiming custody or visitation rights, fill in their name and residence address.

After completing the affidavit, sign it before a notary public, and file the original with the clerk of the circuit court in the county where the petition was filed. This form should be attached to your Response and together with any other forms required by your jurisdiction must be served on the petitioner.

See form D in appendix B for an example of a completed Uniform Child Custody Jurisdiction Act Affidavit.

UNIFORM CHILD CUSTODY JURISDICTION ACT AFFIDAVIT

1.   The name, date of birth and age of the minor child(ren) is/are:

     <u>Name</u>   <u>Date of Birth</u>   <u>Age</u>

2.   The child(ren)'s home state is _____.

3.   During the past five years, the minor child(ren) have lived with the following persons, at the following places, and for the following periods of time:

     <u>With</u>   <u>Address</u>   <u>Dates</u>

4.   I know of no other litigation concerning custody or visitation involving the minor child(ren) of the parties in this state or in any other state in which I have participated as a party, as a witness, or in any other capacity, except:

     <u>Case Name</u>   <u>Case Number</u>   <u>Name and Location of Court</u>

5.   I have no information of any proceeding that is pending in a court in this state or in any other state involving visitation or custody with the parties' minor child(ren) except:

Case Name   Case Number   Name and Location of Court

6.   The proceeding identified in paragraph 5 above ☐ is pending ☐ has been stayed by a court in this state or in another state involving visitation or custody with the parties' minor child(ren).

Case Name   Case Number   Name and Location of Court

7.   I know of no persons other than the parties who have physical custody of the minor child(ren) or who claim to have custody or visitation rights to the minor child(ren) except:

Name   Residence

I acknowledge that if I obtain information regarding any custody or visitation proceeding concerning the child(ren) in this state or any other state, I have a continuing duty to advise this court of such proceeding.

Dated: _____   _____
                                                              Signature of Respondent

SUBSCRIBED AND SWORN TO before me on
this _____ day of _____, _____.

_____
NOTARY PUBLIC
My Commission Expires: _____

Form 6: Certificate of Service

Instructions

A copy of every document you file must be sent to the other party. A Certificate of Service must be filed with the court as proof that each document has been sent to the other party. After completing the Certificate, file the original with the clerk of the court in the county where the petition was filed.

See form E in appendix B for an example of a completed Certificate of Service.

CERTIFICATE OF SERVICE

I HEREBY CERTIFY that a copy of _____

_____

_____

_____ *{name of document(s) served}* was:

       □ mailed   □ telefaxed and mailed   □ hand delivered

to _____

_____ *{name and address*

of person served}, on _____ *{date}*.

_____

Signature of □ Respondent or □ Petitioner

Print Name: _____

Address: _____

                _____

Telephone: _____

Form 7: Subpoena

Instructions

A Subpoena requests the appearance or of an individual (or an individual as a representative of an institution), to testify at a court hearing. A Subpoena can also require the person to bring specific documents, such as payroll records, medical records, police reports, etc. (this is often called a *subpoena duces tecum*). Many courts have subpoena forms that you may obtain from the court clerk.

After the word "TO," fill in the name and address of the person to whom the subpoena is directed. If you are seeking information from an institution, such as an employer or bank, and do not know th name of the appropriate person, you can indicate their title or position. For example: "Keeper of payroll records, Acme Corporation" or "Medical Records Clerk, City Hospital."

In the paragraph beginning with the words "You are hereby commanded," fill in the name of the judge, and the date, time, and place of the hearing.

If you want the person to bring documents, below the phrase "You are commanded also to bring the following," fill in a description of the documents or other items you want the person to bring. Be as specific and detailed as possible, so there is no doubt what the person is to bring.

SUBPOENA

TO:

YOU ARE HEREBY COMMANDED to appear before the Honorable _____
_____, Judge of the above-entitled court,
on _____ {date}, at _____ {time}, in Courtroom _____, at
the _____ Courthouse located
at:_____

YOU ARE COMMANDED ALSO to bring the following:

**YOUR FAILURE TO APPEAR IN RESPONSE TO THIS SUBPOENA WILL SUBJECT
YOU TO PUNISHMENT FOR CONTEMPT OF THIS COURT.**

ISSUED this _____ day of _____, _____

Clerk of the Court

By _____

PARTY REQUESTING SUBPOENA:
Name: _____
Address: _____

_____
Telephone No. _____

Form 8: Interrogatories

Instructions

Interrogatories are questions required to be answered by a party under oath on issues presented in the case. The number and type of questions may be determined or limited by local rules, but the following form may be adapted to your fact situation as appropriate. Some courts may also require that a certain amount of space be left after each question for the answer. Note that the court will require a certificate showing the date you gave the other party notice of the interrogatories. Also, the interrogatories must state the length of time for answering, which is also determined by court rule.

INTERROGATORIES

TO:

You are hereby requested to answer the following under oath within _____ days of the date of the service hereof:

1.   State your full name, current address, date of birth, and social security number.

2.   List your education by school, date and degree.

3.   State the number, age, and relationship of all persons presently residing with you.

4.   List all employment held by you during the preceding three years. With regard to each employment, state the name and address of each employer; your position, job title, or job description; if you had an employment contract; the date on which you commenced your employment and, if applicable, the date and reason for the termination of your employment; your current gross and net income per pay period; your gross income and social security wages as shown on the last W-2 tax and wage statement received by you, and the deductions shown thereon; and all additional benefits received from your employment stating the type and value thereof.

5.   During the preceding three years, have you had any source of income other than from your employment listed above? If so, with regard to each source of income, state the following: the source of income, including the type of income and the name and address of the source; the frequency with which you receive income from the source; the amount of income received by you from the source during the immediately preceding three years; and the amount of income received by you from the source for each month during the immediately preceding three years.

6.   State your monthly expenses for the previous 12 months, including living, personal, entertainment, stating to whom and the amount paid.

7.   State the name, address, and phone number of all mental and physical health care providers you and/or your child(ren) have seen in the past three years, including the date and nature of service and the amount paid.

8.   Do you own any life, annuity, or endowment insurance policies? If so, with regard to each such policy, state: the name, address, and phone number of the company; the policy number; the face value of the policy; the present value of the policy; the amount of any loan or encumbrance on the policy; the date of acquisition of the policy; and the beneficiary or beneficiaries.

9.   Do you have any right, title, claim, or interest in or to a pension plan, retirement plan, or profit sharing plan, including, but not limited to, individual retirement accounts (IRAs), 401(k) plans, and deferred compensation plans? If so, with regard to each such plan or account, state: the name and address of the entity providing the plan; the date of your initial participation in the plan; and the amount of funds currently held on your behalf under the plan.

10.   State the name and address of any accountant, tax preparer, bookkeeper, and other person, firm, or entity who has kept or prepared books, documents, and records with regard to your income, property, business, or financial affairs during the past three years.

11.   State the name and address of each witness who will testify at trial, and state the subject of each witness' testimony.

12.   List every document you intend to produce at trial.

13.   State the name and address of each expert or opinion witness who will offer any testimony, and state: the subject matter on which the witness is expected to testify; the conclusions and/or opinions of the witness and the basis therefor, including reports of the witness, if any; the qualifications of each opinion witness, including a *curriculum vitae* and/or resumé, if any; and the identity of any written reports of the witness regarding an issue in this suit.

14.   Has/have the child(ren) made statements to you that reveal attitudes toward custody/visitation? If so, state the contents of the statements, to whom made, and date made.

15.   State all acts committed, and words spoken, by the other parent which adversely affected the child(ren) by dates, nature, persons present, and how it affected the child(ren).

16.   If you had primary care of the child(ren), what are your goals and plans for the next 24 months? State the name, address, and phone number of persons who would be involved in the daily care of the child(ren).

17.   To what extent do you contribute to the care of the with whom you live, and his/her child support?

18.   Specify all vacations, or other trips taken with the person you live with since _____ (date) by nature, date, and source of funds.

19.   List all sums you spend on the person you live with and his/her child(ren) for Christmas, holidays, and birthdays since _____ (date).

20.   Have you used an illegal or controlled substance in the past three years? If so, state type, amount, and duration of use by date.

21.   Why do you believe it is in the child(ren)'s best interest for you to be custodian/joint custodian of the child(ren), and why it would not be in the child(ren)'s best interests for the other parent to be?

To the person answering: Furnish all information available to you. Answer every portion you can, and provide an explanation of your efforts if you cannot answer. These interrogatories are continuing and you must supplement your answers as necessary. You are reminded that your answers are under oath and subject to penalties for perjury.

_____
Signature of Sending Party

Certificate of Service

A true and accurate copy of this notice and attachments was ☐ hand-delivered or ☐ faxed to _____ or ☐ placed in the United States mail, postage prepaid, to the above party on the following date: _____.

Dated: _____   _____
                                                            Signature of ☐ Petitioner ☐ Respondent

SUBSCRIBED AND SWORN TO before me this _____ day of _____, _____.

_____
NOTARY PUBLIC
My Commission Expires: _____.

Attestation (for answering party)

STATE OF   )
) SS.

COUNTY OF   )

_____, being first duly sworn on oath, deposes and states that he/she is a ☐ petitioner ☐ respondent in the above-captioned matter, that he/she has read the foregoing document, and the answers made herein are true, correct, and complete to the best of his/her knowledge and belief.

_____

Signature

SUBSCRIBED AND SWORN TO before me this
_____ day of _____, _____.

_____

NOTARY PUBLIC
My Commission Expires: _____.

Form 9: Motion for Scientific Paternity Testing

Instructions

If you have asked the court to determine paternity in your case, you may use this motion to request the court to order a paternity test to determine the legal fatherhood for the child. Complete the motion, then sign it before a notary public. File the original with the clerk of the court in the county where the petition was filed and keep a copy for your records. Also, a copy of this form must sent to the other party in your case. (See form 6)

Form 10: Order for Scientific Paternity Testing

Instructions

If the judge orders paternity testing, you will usually need to submit a written order for the judge to sign. To complete form 10, you need to fill in the date of the hearing on your motion on the line in the first, unnumbered paragraph. Then check boxes and fill in information as appropriate to reflect what the judge orders. The judge will date and sign the form.

MOTION FOR SCIENTIFIC PATERNITY TESTING

☐ Petitioner ☐ Respondent certifies that the following information is true:

1.   At this time, other than testimony, very little or no substantial proof of paternity or nonpaternity is available in this action.

2.   I request that the Court enter an order for appropriate scientific testing of the biological samples of Petitioner and Respondent, and the minor child(ren) listed below, so that a determination of paternity of the minor child(ren) can be made to a reasonable degree of medical certainty:

<u>Name</u>   <u>Birth date</u>

3.   I request that the costs of the scientific testing initially be borne by:

☐ Petitioner ☐ Respondent ☐ both Petitioner and Respondent.

Dated: _____

_____
Signature of Party
Printed Name: _____
Address: _____
City, State, Zip: _____
Telephone Number: _____

ORDER FOR SCIENTIFIC PATERNITY TESTING

This cause having come to be heard on _____, on the Motion for Scientific Paternity Testing, and the Court being fully advised in the premises,

IT IS HEREBY ORDERED:

1.   That the above motion is GRANTED.

2.   That the Petitioner, Respondent, and the minor child(ren) shall appear for the purpose of appropriate scientific testing: [Select one only]

☐ a. Immediately

☐ b. at _____ a.m./p.m., on _____, at _____ _____.

☐ c. at a time and place to be specified by _____ _____. Appropriate scientific testing on Petitioner, Respondent, and the minor child(ren) shall be at _____ _____, with at least 30 days advance written notice.

3.   The costs of the scientific paternity testing shall be assessed:

☐   at a later date   ☐   against Petitioner   ☐   against Respondent

☐   Other {explain} _____

4.   The test results, opinions, and conclusions of the test laboratory shall be filed with the Court. Any objection to the test results must be made in writing and must be filed with the Court at least 10 days before the hearing. If no objection is filed, the test results shall be

admitted into evidence. Nothing in this paragraph prohibits a party from calling an outside expert witness to refute or support the testing procedure or results, or the mathematical theory on which they are based.

5.   Test results are admissible in evidence and should be weighed along with other evidence of the paternity of the alleged father unless the statistical probability of paternity equals or exceeds 95 percent. A statistical probability of 95 percent or more creates a rebuttable presumption that the alleged father is the biological father of the child(ren). If the party fails to rebut the presumption of paternity, the Court may enter a summary judgment of paternity. If the test results show the alleged father cannot be the biological father, the case shall be dismissed with prejudice.

6.   The Court reserves jurisdiction over the parties and the subject matter of this action to enforce the terms and provisions of this and all previous orders as well as to enter such other orders as may be just.

ORDERED ON _____

_____

JUDGE

Form 11: Financial Affidavit

Instructions

Every state requires that both parties disclose certain financial information to properly determine the issue of child support. Most states have adopted a form for this purpose. Some states require an exchange of tax return information or other documents verifying various financial matters. Once again, this is a matter of court rule or statute.

In completing form 11 (or the Financial Affidavit specific to your state or court), you may want to refer to your state's child support guidelines. You will want to be sure that any income or expense items mentioned in the guidelines are included in your Financial Affidavit.

Section I of form 11 asks for personal information about your education and employment. In Section II, fill in your income. Be sure to use monthly figures, using the most current, relevant figures. Also, the exact figures will depend on those required by the state's child support guidelines. Section III requests available asset information. In Sections IV and V, fill in the expense items listed. Finally, Section VI is the affiant's signature.

After completing the Financial Affidavit, sign it before a notary public, and file the original with the clerk of the circuit court in the county where the petition was filed.

Proof of service that the Financial Affidavit has been sent to the other party is required to be filed with the clerk of the court.

See form H in appendix B for an example of a completed Financial Affidavit.

FINANCIAL AFFIDAVIT

THE AFFIANT, BEING DULY SWORN, SAYS UNDER PENALTY OF PERJURY THAT AFFIANT IS THE ☐ PETITIONER OR ☐ RESPONDENT IN THE ABOVE-CAPTIONED CASE, HAS PREPARED THIS FINANCIAL STATEMENT, KNOWS THE CONTENTS THEREOF, AND THAT IT IS TRUE AND CORRECT.

Name:_____ Date of Birth: _____

Social Security Number: _____

I. PERSONAL INFORMATION

1. Occupation: _____

2. The highest year of education completed: _____

3. Are you presently employed? ☐ Yes ☐ No

    a. If yes: (1)   Where do you work (name and address)?

                                 _____

                                 _____

                                 _____

                (2)   When did you start work there (month/year)?

                      _____

    b. If no: (1)   When did you last work (month/year)?

                      _____

                (2)   What were your gross monthly earnings? $_____

                (3)   Why are you presently unemployed?

II. INCOME INFORMATION

4.   MONTHLY GROSS/ NET INCOME. $_____

5.   MISCELLANEOUS INCOME.

      a.   Child support received from other relationships $_____

      b.   Other miscellaneous income (list source and amounts) $_____

      c.   Total Miscellaneous Income (add lines 3.4a through 3.4c) $_____

6.   Income of Other Adults in Household $_____

7.   If the income of either party is disputed, state monthly income you believe is correct and explain below:

III. AVAILABLE ASSETS

8.   Cash on hand $_____

9.   On deposit in banks $_____

10.   Stocks and Bonds, cash value of life insurance $_____

11.   Other liquid assets: $_____

IV. MONTHLY EXPENSE INFORMATION

Monthly expenses for myself and _____ dependents are: (Expenses should be calculated for the future, after separation, based on the anticipated residential schedule for the children.)

12.   HOUSING.

Rent, 1st mortgage or contract payments $_____

Installment payments for other mortgages or encumbrances $_____

Taxes & insurance (if not in monthly payment) $_____

      Total Housing $_____

13.   UTILITIES.

      Heat (gas & oil) $_____

      Electricity $_____

      Water, sewer, garbage $_____

Telephone $_____

Cable $_____

Other $_____

Total Utilities $_____

14. FOOD AND SUPPLIES.

Food for _____ persons $_____

Supplies (paper, tobacco, pets) $_____

Meals eaten out $_____

Other $_____

Total Food Supplies $_____

15. CHILDREN.

Day Care/Babysitting $_____

Clothing $_____

Tuition (if any) $_____

Other child related expenses $_____

Total Expenses Children $_____

16. TRANSPORTATION.

Vehicle payments or leases $_____

Vehicle insurance & license $_____

Vehicle gas, oil, ordinary maintenance $_____

Parking $_____

Other transportation expenses $_____

Total Transportation $_____

17. HEALTH CARE. (May be omitted if fully covered)

Insurance $_____

Uninsured dental, orthodontic, medical, eye care expenses $_____

Other uninsured health expenses $_____

Total Health Care $_____

18. PERSONAL EXPENSES (Not including children).

Clothing $_____

Hair care/personal care expenses $_____

Clubs and recreation $_____

Education $_____

Books, newspapers, magazines, photos $_____

Gifts $_____

Other $_____

Total Personal Expenses $_____

19. MISCELLANEOUS EXPENSES.

Life insurance (if not deducted from income) $_____

Other _____ $_____

Other _____ $_____

Total Miscellaneous Expenses $_____

20. TOTAL HOUSEHOLD EXPENSES $_____

V. OTHER EXPENSES

21. INSTALLMENT DEBTS INCLUDED IN ABOVE PARAGRAPHS. (Include the creditor, balance and last payment amount)

22. OTHER DEBTS AND MONTHLY EXPENSES NOT INCLUDED IN ABOVE PARAGRAPHS

Total Monthly Payments for Other Debts and Monthly Expenses $_____

23. TOTAL EXPENSES $_____

24. Other:

VI. SIGNATURE OF AFFIANT

Dated: _____   _____

                                               ☐ Petitioner OR ☐ Respondent

SUBSCRIBED AND SWORN TO before me on
this _____ day of _____, _____.

_____
NOTARY PUBLIC
My Commission Expires: _____

Form 12: Child Support Calculation Worksheet

Instructions

This example calculates the monthly support sum due for child support in a combined adjusted gross income state. Note that every state has its own calculation requirements, guidelines and most states have form worksheets for use in the state. Be sure to use the proper guideline amounts for your calculations. The following is a sample only.

Line 1: Enter one-twelfth of the parent's yearly gross income. *Gross income* includes income from all sources except public assistance.

Line 2a: Enter the monthly amount of any other court or administrative order for child support to the extent of the amounts actually being paid toward the current support of any child not the subject of the proceeding.

Line 2b: Enter the monthly amount of any court order for spousal support to the extent of the amounts actually being paid toward current spousal support.

Line 2c: Enter the monthly amount of the support obligation of the parent for any children in his or her primary physical custody and not the subject of the proceeding.

Line 3: Enter the monthly amount calculated by subtracting from the parent's monthly gross income on line 1 the sum of that parent's adjustments from lines 2a, 2b, and 2c. If the resulting figure is negative, enter "0." The combined adjusted monthly gross income is calculated by adding together the adjusted monthly gross incomes of both parents.

Line 4: Enter the percentage calculated by dividing the parent's adjusted monthly gross income from line 3 by the combined adjusted monthly gross income from line 3.

Line 5: Enter the monthly amount from the schedule of basic child support obligations for the parents' combined adjusted monthly gross income from line 3, which, whenever necessary, shall be rounded to the nearest gross income amount on the schedule of basic child support obligations prior to determining the amount to be entered on line 5.

Line 6a: Enter the monthly amount of any reasonable work-related child care costs incurred or to be incurred for the children who are the subject of the proceeding by the parent entitled to receive support to earn the monthly gross income on line 1.

Line 6b: Enter the monthly amount of any reasonable work-related child care costs incurred or to be incurred for the children who are the subject of the proceeding by the parent obligated to pay support to earn the monthly gross income on line 1.

Line 6c: Enter the monthly amount of any premium paid or to be paid by the parent or deducted or to be deducted by an employer from the parent's gross monthly income for a policy of health insurance for the children who are the subject of the proceeding.

Line 6d: Enter the monthly amount of any extraordinary medical costs paid or to be paid by the parent by agreement or pursuant to court order for the children who are the subject of the proceeding. *Extraordinary medical costs* are reasonable and necessary medical and dental expenses for a long-term recurring health condition, such as dental treatment, orthodontic treatment, asthma treatment and physical therapy, that are not covered or fully paid under any policy of medical insurance.

Line 6e: Enter the monthly amount of any other extraordinary child-rearing costs paid or to be paid by the parent by agreement or pursuant to court order for the children who are the subject of the proceeding. *Other extraordinary child-rearing costs* may include, but are not limited to, the cost of tutoring sessions, special or private elementary and secondary schooling to meet the particular educational needs of a child, camps, lessons, travel or other activities intended to enhance the athletic, social or cultural development of a child.

Line 7: Enter the monthly amount calculated by adding together the parent's additional child- rearing costs from lines 6a, 6b, 6c, 6d and 6e. The combined additional child-rearing costs is calculated by adding together the monthly additional child-rearing costs of both parents.

Line 8: Enter the monthly amount calculated by adding together the basic child support amount from line 5 and the combined additional child-rearing costs from line 7.

Line 9: Enter the monthly amount calculated by multiplying the combined child support costs from line 8 by each parent's proportionate share of the combined adjusted monthly gross income from line 4.

Line 10: Enter the monthly amount of the additional child-rearing costs from line 7 paid or to be paid by the parent obligated to pay support for any children who are the subject of the proceeding.

Line 11: Enter the monthly amount of the credit of the parent obligated to pay support for a portion of the amounts expended during that parent's periods of regular overnight visitation or custody, which shall be calculated by multiplying the basic child support amount from line 5 by twenty percent.

Line 12: Enter the monthly amount calculated by subtracting from the child support obligation of the parent obligated to pay support from line 9, that parent's credit for additional child-rearing costs from line 10 and that parent's credit for a portion of the amounts expended during periods of regular overnight visitation or custody from line 11.

See form I in appendix B for an example of a completed Child Support Calculation Worksheet.

CHILD SUPPORT CALCULATION WORKSHEET

	Parent to Receive Supt	Parent to Pay Supt	Combined
1. Monthly gross income:	$_____	$_____	
2. Adjustments (per month):			
a. Other court or administratively ordered child support being paid:	($_____)	($_____)	
b. Court ordered spousal support being paid:	($_____)	($_____)	
c. Support obligation for children in primary physical custody:	($_____)	($_____)	
3. Adjusted monthly gross income (Line 1 minus lines 2a, 2b and 2c):	$_____	$_____	$_____
4. Proportionate share of combined adjusted monthly gross income: (Each parent's line 3 divided by combined line 3):	____%	____%	
5. Basic child support amount (From support chart using combined line 3):			$_____

	Parent to Receive Supt	Parent to Pay Supt	Combined
6. Additional child-rearing costs (per month):			
a. Reasonable work-related child care costs of the parent receiving support ($_____) less federal tax credit ($_____):	$_____		
b. Reasonable work-related child care costs of the parent paying support:		$_____	
c. Health insurance costs for children who are the subject of the proceeding:	$_____	$_____	
d. Uninsured extraordinary medical costs (Agreed by parents or ordered by court):	$_____	$_____	
e. Other extraordinary child-rearing costs (Agreed by parents or ordered by court):	$_____	$_____	
7. Total additional child rearing costs (Sum o lines 6a, 6b, 6c, 6d and 6e):	$_____	$_____	$_____

	Parent to Receive Supt	Parent to Pay Supt	Combined
8. Total combined child support costs (Sum of lines 5 and combined 7):			$_____
9. Each parent's support obligation (Multiply line 8 by each parent's line 4):	$_____	$_____	
10. Credit for additional child-rearing costs of parent obligated to pay support:		($_____)	
11. Credit for a portion of the amounts expended by parent obligated to pay support during periods of temporary physical custody (Multiply line 5 by 20%):		($_____)	
12. PRESUMED CHILD SUPPORT AMOUNT (Line 9 minus lines 10 and 11):		$_____	

Form 13: Motion for Temporary Relief

Instructions

Most court proceedings take time. It may be weeks or months before you can get a court hearing on your Petition. If you are in immediate need of financial help, or are having ongoing arguments with the other parent about custody or visitation, you can seek a temporary court order. To do so, you will need to file the appropriate motion with the court clerk. Such a motion is commonly called a Motion for Temporary Relief. You may also see this called by other names, such as *Motion for Temporary Custody* or *Motion for Support Pendente Lite* (this is a Latin term, roughly meaning "pending th litigation").

See form G in appendix B for an example of a completed Motion for Temporary Relief.

Form 14: Order for Temporary Relief

Instructions

If the judge grants your motion, you will need to prepare an order for the judge to sign. Form 14 is such an order. You simply fill in the blanks to reflect what the judge orders, then give it to the judge to sign and fill in the date.

See form J in appendix B for an example of a completed Order for Temporary Relief.

MOTION FOR TEMPORARY RELIEF

NOW COMES _____, petitioner and states as follows:

1. That Petitioner filed her/his Petition for _____
_____ on _____.

2. That Respondent filed a response to the petition on _____.

3. That _____ child(ren) was/were born to the parties, namely:

   Name   Date of Birth   Age

   who is/are currently residing with Petitioner.

4. That Petitioner is presently ☐ unemployed ☐ employed and has a net income of approximately $_____ per month, and is without sufficient funds with which to support the minor child(ren).

5. That Petitioner has received no direct support from Respondent, except:

6. That Respondent is presently gainfully employed and has a net income of approximately $_____ per month, and has assets totaling in excess of $_____, and is well able to contribute to the support of the parties' minor child(ren); and Respondent has sufficient funds with which to pay for a just portion of the expenses of filing and maintaining this suit.

7. Attached to this Motion is the Petitioner's financial affidavit setting forth his/her financial circumstances.

WHEREFORE, petitioner herein requests:

A. That Petitioner be granted temporary child support and temporary custody of the minor child(ren).

B. That Respondent be ordered to maintain existing comprehensive major medical and health care insurance coverage on the minor child(ren) and to pay the premiums on that insurance, and to provide Petitioner with a copy of the insurance policy.

C. That Respondent be ordered to pay a just portion of the expenses of filing and maintaining this suit.

D. That petitioner be granted such other and further relief as the court may deem just.

RESPECTFULLY SUBMITTED:

_____

Signature of Petitioner

Print Name: _____

Address: _____

_____

Telephone: _____

ACKNOWLEDGEMENT

STATE OF _____)

                            SS

COUNTY OF _____)

I,_____, being first duly sworn upon my oath, depose and state that I am the Petitioner in the above-entitled cause. I have read the attached Motion. I state that the contents thereof are true and correct.

_____

Signature of Petitioner

Subscribed and sworn to before me this

_____ day of _____, _____.

_____

Notary Public

My Commission expires: _____

ORDER FOR TEMPORARY RELIEF

This cause having come to be heard on _____, upon Petitioner's Motion for Temporary Relief, it is HEREBY ORDERED:

1. That the Court has jurisdiction over the parties and subject matter of this action.

2. That the Respondent shall pay child support in the amount of $_____ per month, beginning _____.

3. That allocation of parenting time of the minor child(ren) be as follows:

   ☐ Petitioner ☐ Respondent shall be the primary residential parent, subject to parenting time in ☐ Petitioner ☐ Respondent as follows:

4. That ☐ Petitioner ☐ Respondent shall maintain existing comprehensive major medical and health care insurance coverage on the minor child(ren) and shall pay the premiums on that insurance, and shall provide ☐ Petitioner ☐ Respondent with a copy of the insurance policy.

5. That Respondent shall pay a just portion of the expenses of filing and maintaining this suit in the amount of $_____.

ORDERED on _____

_____
JUDGE

Form 15: Motion to Deviate from Child Support Guidelines

Instructions

In every state, a court may deviate from the child support guidelines under certain circumstances. In some states, you will simply raise this issue at the hearing. In other states, you will need to file a motion and state the specific reasons for deviating from the guideline amount. Form 15 includes many of the more common reasons for deviating form the child support guideline amount. Some of these reasons may not be recognized in your state, or you may find that your state law includes reasons not listed in form 15. Therefore, remember to review your state's guidelines to determine the exact factors upon which a deviation may be based. Once you have completed your motion, it must be filed with the clerk where you filed your previous documents. You will also need to file a Certificate of Service (form 6) verifying that you sent a copy of your motion to the other party. And remember to keep a file-stamped copy for your own records.

Form 16: Order to Deviate from Child Support Guidelines

Instructions

If the judge approves your request to deviate form the guideline amount, you will need to prepare an order for the judge to sign. In paragraph 1, fill in the amount of support that would be called for under your state's guidelines. In paragraph 2, fill in the reasons the judge agreed justify deviating from the guideline. Fill in paragraph 3 according to what the judge ordered. The judge will then sign and date the form.

MOTION TO DEVIATE FROM CHILD SUPPORT GUIDELINES

☐ Petitioner or ☐ Respondent requests that the Court enter an order granting the following:

SECTION I

[✔ one only (a or b)]

☐ a. MORE child support than the amount required by the child support guidelines. The Court should order MORE child support than the amount required by the child support guidelines because of:

[✔ all that apply to your situation]

☐ 1. Extraordinary medical, psychological, educational, or dental expenses.

☐ 2. Seasonal variations in one or both parent's income.

☐ 3. Age(s) of the child(ren), taking into consideration the greater needs of older child(ren).

☐ 4. Special needs that have been met traditionally within the family budget even though the fulfilling of those needs will cause support to exceed the guidelines.

☐ 5. Refusal of the nonresidential parent to become involved in the activities of the child(ren).

☐ 6. Due consideration given to the primary residential parent's homemaking services.

☐ 7. Total available assets of mother, father, and child(ren).

☐ 8. Impact of IRS dependency exemption and waiver of that exemption.

☐ 9. Residency of subsequently born or adopted child(ren) with the obligor, including consideration of the subsequent spouse's income.

☐ 10. Any other adjustment that is needed to achieve an equitable result, which may include reasonable and necessary expenses jointly incurred during the marriage.

Explain any items marked above:

☐ b. LESS child support than the amount required by the child support guidelines. The Court should order LESS child support than the amount required by the child support guidelines because of:

[✔ all that apply to your situation]

☐ 1. Extraordinary medical, psychological, educational, or dental expenses.

☐ 2. Independent income of child(ren), excluding the child(ren)'s SSI income.

☐ 3. Payment of both child support and spousal support to a parent that regularly has been paid and for which there is a demonstrated need.

☐ 4. Seasonal variations in one or both parent's income.

☐ 5. Age of the child(ren), taking into consideration the greater needs of older child(ren).

☐ 6. The child(ren) spend(s) a substantial amount of time with the nonresidential parent, thereby reducing expenses of the primary residential parent.

☐ 7. Due consideration given to the primary residential parent's homemaking services.

☐ 8. Visitation with nonresidential parent for more than 28 consecutive days.

☐ 9. Total available assets of obligee, obligor, and child(ren).

☐ 10. Impact of IRS dependency exemption and waiver of that exemption.

☐ 11. Application of the child support guidelines requires the obligor to pay more than 55% of gross income for a single support order.

☐ 12. Any other adjustment that is needed to achieve an equitable result, which may include reasonable and necessary expenses jointly incurred during the marriage.

Explain any items marked above:

SECTION II. INCOME AND ASSETS OF CHILD(REN) COMMON TO BOTH PARTIES

List the total of any independent income or assets of the child(ren) common to both parties (income from Social Security, gifts, stocks/bonds, employment, trust fund(s), investment(s), etc.). Attach an explanation.

TOTAL VALUE OF ASSETS OF CHILD(REN) $_____

TOTAL MONTHLY INCOME OF CHILD(REN) $_____

SECTION III. EXPENSES FOR CHILD(REN) COMMON TO BOTH PARTIES

1.   Monthly babysitting, or other child care $_____

2.   Monthly after-school care $_____

3.   Monthly school tuition $_____

4.   Monthly school supplies, books, and fees $_____

5.   Monthly after-school activities $_____

6.   Monthly lunch money $_____

7.   Monthly private lessons/tutoring $_____

8.   Monthly allowance $_____

9.   Monthly clothing $_____

10.   Monthly uniforms $_____

11.   Monthly entertainment (movies, birthday parties, etc.) $_____

12.   Monthly health and dental insurance premiums $_____

13.   Monthly medical, dental, prescription charges (unreimbursed) $_____

14.   Monthly psychiatric/psychological/counselor (unreimbursed) $_____

15.   Monthly orthodontic (unreimbursed) $_____

6.   Monthly grooming $_____

17.   Monthly non-prescription medications/cosmetics/toiletries/sundries $_____

18.   Monthly gifts from children to others (other children, relatives, teachers, etc.) $_____

19.   Monthly camp or other summer activities $_____

20.   Monthly clubs (Boy/Girl Scouts, etc.) or recreational fees $_____

21.   Monthly visitation expenses (for nonresidential parent) $_____

        Explain:

22.   Monthly insurance (life, etc.) {explain}: $_____

Other {explain}:

23.   _____ $_____

24.   _____ $_____

25.   _____ $_____

26. TOTAL EXPENSES FOR CHILD(REN) COMMON TO
       BOTH PARTIES (add lines 1 through 25) $_____

_____

Signature of Party

Printed Name: _____

Address: _____

City, State, Zip: _____

Telephone Number: _____

Fax Number: _____

ORDER PERMITTING DEVIATION FROM CHILD SUPPORT GUIDELINES

THE COURT, having reviewed the Motion for Deviation from Child Support Guidelines, any response which may have been filed, and otherwise being fully advised in the premises, HEREBY ORDERS:

1.   Based on the calculations derived from the child support guidelines, the presumed amount of child support under the guidelines is $_____.

2.   Deviation from the child support guidelines is appropriate because:

3.   The ☐ Petitioner ☐ Respondent is ordered to pay child support in the amount of $_____ per month, beginning on _____.

ORDERED ON _____

_____
JUDGE

Form 17 and Form 18: Parenting Plans

Instructions

In some states you may be required to come up with a written parenting plan, which is basically your agreement regarding custody and visitation. Some courts have standard parenting plans that automatically apply unless the parties agree to something different. The intent of a parenting plan is to make both parents understand exactly how custody and visitation will work, and to reduce or eliminate problems and disagreements. Form 17 and form 18 are two examples of parenting plans which cover most of the potential problem areas. Neither form is considered best in all situations, and you may also use parts from both of these forms to create your own customized plan.

See form L in appendix B for an example of a completed Parenting Plan.

PARENTING PLAN

I. GENERAL INFORMATION

This parenting plan applies to the following children:

<u>Name</u>   <u>Birthdate</u>

II. RESIDENTIAL SCHEDULE

These provisions set forth where the child(ren) shall reside each day of the year and what contact the child(ren) shall have with each parent.

A. PRE-SCHOOL SCHEDULE

☐ There are no children of preschool age.

☐ Prior to enrollment in school, the child(ren) shall reside with the

☐ mother   ☐ father,   except for the following days and times when the child(ren) will reside with or be with the other parent:

from: _____[day and time]

to: _____[day and time]

☐ every week   ☐ every other week   ☐ the first and third week of the month

☐ the second and fourth week of the month   ☐ other:

from: _____[day and time]

to: _____[day and time]

☐ every week   ☐ every other week   ☐ the first and third week of the month

☐ the second and fourth week of the month   ☐ other:

B. SCHOOL SCHEDULE

Upon enrollment in school, the child(ren) shall reside with the ☐ mother ☐ father, except for the following days and times when the child(ren) will reside with or be with the other parent:

from: _____[day and time]

to: _____[day and time]

☐ every week   ☐ every other week   ☐ the first and third week of the month

☐ the second and fourth week of the month   ☐ other:

from: _____[day and time]

to: _____[day and time]

☐ every week   ☐ every other week   ☐ the first and third week of the month

☐ the second and fourth week of the month   ☐ other:

☐ The school schedule will start when each child begins

☐ kindergarten   ☐ first grade   ☐ other: _____

C. SCHEDULE FOR WINTER VACATION

The child(ren) shall reside with the ☐ mother ☐ father during winter vacation, except for the following days and times when the child(ren) will reside with or be with the other parent:

D. SCHEDULE FOR SPRING VACATION

The child(ren) shall reside with the ☐ mother ☐ father during spring vacation, except for the following days and times when the child(ren) will reside with or be with the other parent:

E. SUMMER SCHEDULE

Upon completion of the school year, the child(ren) shall reside with the ☐ mother ☐ father, except for the following days and times when the child(ren) will reside with or be with the other parent:

☐ Same as school year schedule.

☐ Other:

F. VACATION

☐ Does not apply.

☐ The schedule for vacation with parents is as follows:

G. SCHEDULE FOR HOLIDAYS

The residential schedule for the child(ren) for the holidays listed below is as follows:

	With Mother (Specify Year Odd/Even/Every)	With Father (Specify Year Odd/Even/Every)
New Year's Day	_____	_____
Martin Luther King Day	_____	_____
Presidents Day	_____	_____
Memorial Day	_____	_____
July 4th	_____	_____
Labor Day	_____	_____
Veterans Day	_____	_____
Thanksgiving Day	_____	_____
Christmas Eve	_____	_____
Christmas Day	_____	_____
_____	_____	_____
_____	_____	_____
_____	_____	_____
_____	_____	_____

☐ For purposes of this parenting plan, a holiday shall begin and end as follows (set forth times):

☐ Holidays which fall on a Friday or a Monday shall include Saturday and Sunday.

☐ Other:

H. SCHEDULE FOR SPECIAL OCCASIONS

The residential schedule for the child(ren) for the following special occasions (i.e., birthdays) is as follows:

Occasion	With Mother (Specify Year Odd/Even/Every)	With Father (Specify Year Odd/Even/Every)

☐ Other:

I. PRIORITIES UNDER THE RESIDENTIAL SCHEDULE

☐ Does not apply.

☐ For purposes of this parenting plan the following days shall have priority:

☐ Parent's vacations have priority over holidays. Holidays have priority over other special occasions. Special occasions have priority over school vacations.

☐ Other:

J. TRANSPORTATION ARRANGEMENTS

Transportation arrangements for the child(ren), other than costs, between parents shall be as follows:

K. DESIGNATION OF CUSTODIAN

The children named in this parenting plan are scheduled to reside the majority of the time with the ☐ mother ☐ father. This parent is designated the custodian of the child(ren) solely for purposes of all other state and federal statutes which require a designation or determination of custody. This designation shall not affect either parent's rights and responsibilities under this parenting plan.

III. DECISION MAKING

A. DAY-TO-DAY DECISIONS

Each parent shall make decisions regarding the day-to-day care and control of each child while the child is residing with that parent. Regardless of the allocation of decision making in this parenting plan, either parent may make emergency decisions affecting the health or safety of the children.

B. MAJOR DECISIONS

Major decisions regarding each child shall be made as follows:

Education decisions	☐ mother	☐ father	☐ joint
Non-emergency health care	☐ mother	☐ father	☐ joint
Religious upbringing	☐ mother	☐ father	☐ joint
	☐ mother	☐ father	☐ joint
	☐ mother	☐ father	☐ joint
	☐ mother	☐ father	☐ joint
	☐ mother	☐ father	☐ joint
	☐ mother	☐ father	☐ joint
	☐ mother	☐ father	☐ joint

IV. DISPUTE RESOLUTION

Disputes between the parties, other than child support disputes, shall be submitted to (list person or agency):

- ☐ counseling by _____
- ☐ mediation by _____
- ☐ arbitration by _____

The cost of this process shall be allocated between the parties as follows:

- ☐ _____% mother _____% father.
- ☐ based on each party's proportional share of income from the child support worksheets.
- ☐ as determined in the dispute resolution process.

The counseling, mediation, or arbitration process shall be commenced by notifying the other party by ☐ written request ☐ certified mail ☐ other:

In the dispute resolution process:

(a) Preference shall be given to carrying out this Parenting Plan.

(b) Unless an emergency exists, the parents shall use the designated process to resolve disputes relating to implementation of the plan, except those related to financial support.

(c) A written record shall be prepared of any agreement reached in counseling or mediation and of each arbitration award and shall be provided to each party.

(d) If the court finds that a parent has used or frustrated the dispute resolution process without good reason, the court shall award attorneys' fees and financial sanctions to the other parent.

(e) The parties have the right of review from the dispute resolution process to the superior court.

V. OTHER PROVISIONS

☐ There are no other provisions.

☐ There are the following other provisions:

VI. SIGNATURES FOR PARENTING PLAN

_____

Mother
Date and Place of Signature

_____

Father
Date and Place of Signature

PARENTING PLAN

1. Legal Custody

We agree to share joint legal custody of our children; that is, neither of us will make a major change affecting our children in the areas of religion, residence, non-emergency medical care, education, or major recreational activities without consultation with the other. Before such a decision is made, we will discuss the matter and both of us must agree. If we cannot agree, our disagreement will be resolved by the methods we have chosen and set out in this parenting plan.

2. Time-Sharing

We will share time with the children as follows:

Weekends and Weekdays (check one):

☐ Weekdays: _____

_____.

Weekends: Weekends begin at _____ ___.M. (Friday) (Saturday) and end at _____ ___.M. (Sunday) (Monday), unless Monday is a legal holiday, in which case the weekend ends at _____ ___.M. (Monday) (Tuesday).

☐ We have attached a calendar for the year(s) _____ to this plan, and have marked in red the days the children will spend with mother and in blue the days the children will spend with father. Days for this calendar begin at _____ ___.M. and end at _____ ___.M.

Vacations (check one):

☐ Each parent will have uninterrupted time with the children for _____ weeks each summer if that parent gives the other at least _____ days notice.

☐ Until the youngest child reaches age ___, uninterrupted vacation time with parent is limited to ___ weeks. Between the ages of ___ and ___, that time will be ___ weeks. Between the ages of ___ and ___, that time will be ___ weeks. After reaching age ___, vacation time will be ___ weeks.

Holidays: Regardless of the day of the week, the children will spend:

(a) Mother's Day and mother's birthday with mother;

(b) Father's Day and father's birthday with father;

(c) Children's birthdays with _____ in even-numbered years and with _____ in odd-numbered years.

(d) Children will spend their time on holidays as follows:

	With Mother (Specify Year Odd/Even/Every)	With Father (Specify Year Odd/Even/Every)
New Year's Day	_____	_____
Martin Luther King Day	_____	_____
Presidents Day	_____	_____
Memorial Day	_____	_____
July 4th	_____	_____
Labor Day	_____	_____
Veterans Day	_____	_____
Thanksgiving Day	_____	_____
Christmas Eve	_____	_____
Christmas Day	_____	_____
_____	_____	_____
_____	_____	_____
_____	_____	_____
_____	_____	_____
_____	_____	_____

Telephone: We agree that the children have a right to place phone calls to and receive phone calls from the absent parent.

Changes: Each of us is free to ask for exceptions to this schedule, but we understand that the other parent can say "no," and we will not argue about it.

Transportation: We will divide the responsibility for getting the child(ren) to and from each other's house, day care, school, etc., as follows:

_____

_____

_____

_____

_____.

3. Trial Period or Permanent Plan: (Check one)

☐ We have not tried this time-sharing schedule before, so we agree that we will review the time-sharing plan in _____ days and at that time we will make any changes we agree on. If we cannot agree on changes, we will resolve our dispute using the method set forth in paragraph 6 below.

☐ We have already tried this time-sharing schedule, so we intend it to be permanent. We recognize, however, that as our children grow and our lives change, it may be necessary to change the schedule from time to time. We agree that this is a major change that we have to discuss and agree on, and if necessary follow the dispute resolution procedures set out in paragraph 6 below.

4. The Status Quo — What we have now:

(a) Doctor _____

(b) Dentist _____

(c) Other medical _____

(d) School _____

(e) Religion _____

(f) Recreation _____

We agree that neither of us will remove, cause to be removed, or permit removal of the children from the State of _____, except for temporary visits which do not interfere with the time-sharing schedule, without the written consent of the other parent or resolution of the dispute by the method set forth in paragraph 6 below.

5. Emergencies

In case of a medical emergency, if time allows, the parent with that period of responsibility will contact the other parent concerning treatment of the child. If the absent parent cannot be reached, any decision for emergency medical treatment will be made in the best interest of the child by the available parent.

6. Dispute Resolution

We will discuss all major changes in the children's lives in order to try to reach agreement. If we cannot agree, after discussion, we will participate in counseling, conciliation or mediation to try to reach agreement. If there is still a dispute, we agree to submit the matter to the Court.

7. General Matters

In order to foster a continuing relationship between our children and both of their parents, we both agree:

(a) To be actively involved in the major decisions and legal responsibilities of our child(ren).

(b) To communicate and be flexible about the needs of our child(ren), especially as those needs change due to growth and development.

(c) To be supportive of and positive about the child(ren)'s relationship with the other parent. Each of us will give loving permission to the child(ren) to enjoy the relationship with the other parent and neither of us will interfere with the parent-child relationship of the other.

(d) That neither of us will align the children against the other parent or the other parent's family.

(e) We agree that each of us is responsible to keep the other parent informed of the child(ren)'s school functions, parent-teacher conferences and recreational activities.

I Agree: I Agree:

_____   _____
Mother's Signature   Father's Signature

FORM 19: REQUEST FOR HEARING

and

FORM 20: NOTICE OF HEARING

Instructions

Once all the required documents are filed with the clerk's office, and the time has passed for the other parent to file a Response, you may request a hearing on your Petition. To do this, you can use form 16 and form 17. In some courts, you can call the court clerk or the judge's secretary or assistant and arrange for a hearing date. In such cases, you will not need to file a Request for Hearing (form 19). In other courts, hearings are only scheduled as a result of a written request, in which case you will need to file the proper document (usually called a *Request for Hearing*, or *Motion to Set Final Hearing*, or some similar name).

See form M in appendix B for an example of a completed Request for Hearing.

Once the hearing date is set, you will need to notify the other party. Sometimes the court clerk will send out the notice, and other times you will need to do this. The Notice of Hearing (form 20) informs the other party of the date, time, and place of the hearing.

See form F in appendix B for an example of a completed Notice of Hearing.

REQUEST FOR HEARING

1. Type of case: _____

2. Judge to whom assigned _____

3. Are there any hearings presently set? ___ Yes ___ No

   If yes, when? _____

4. Specific matters to be heard [for example, petition for custody]:

   _____

5. Estimated total time required for hearing all parties and witnesses: _____

6. Names, addresses, and phone numbers of all attorneys or parties to notify:

Hearing requested by: _____
                    Petitioner/Respondent [circle one]

NOTICE OF HEARING

TO: [Enter Names and Addresses of the Parties/Attorneys to notify]

YOU ARE HEREBY NOTIFIED that the above cause is set for hearing as follows:

DATE: _____   TIME: _____ ____.M.

COURTHOUSE: _____

JUDGE: _____

SPECIFIC MATTER to be heard _____

_____

NOTICED DATED AND MAILED this date: _____, _____

_____
Signature of party

Form 21: Motion for Default

Instructions

A Motion for Default (form 21) is used when the respondent fails to respond to your Petition within the required time period. This is the means to get the court to officially take notice of the fact that the other party did not respond. The required time period varies from state to state, so check your state's law for the period. Remember that if the parent was served out of state, the parent may have up to sixty days to respond, not including the date of service. In some states, after a default is entered by the court, you can go to the hearing and simply present a judgment to the judge for signing that states what you requested in your Petition. You will not need to call any witnesses or present any more documents. In other states, defaults are not permitted in some cases (such as divorce), and you may still need to present all of your testimony and other evidence. To complete the Motion for Default (form 21), you will need to fill in the date you filed your Petition, and the date it was served on the other party, in the main paragraph. Then sign your name and fill in your name, address, and telephone information.

Form 22: Default

Instructions

The Default (form 22) is the form the judge or court clerk signs to officially declare that the respondent is in default for failing to respond to the Petition. You will fill in the other party's name on the line in the main paragraph, and submit this form to the clerk along with the Motion for Default (form 21).

MOTION FOR DEFAULT

Petitioner hereby requests this court to enter a default against the respondent for failure to respond to the petition filed on _____ and served upon respondent on _____.

RESPECTFULLY SUBMITTED:

_____

Signature of Petitioner

Print Name: _____

Address: _____

Telephone: _____

ORDER OF DEFAULT

A default is hereby entered against the Respondent, _____,
for failure to serve or file a response in this action as required by law.

DATED: _____

_____

Form 23: Judgment

Instructions

The judgment is the final determination of your rights to custody, visitation, and support. In some states, this will be called a *decree*, a *final order*, or some similar name. The court (or where permitted by state law, an administrative officer) will enter the judgment, which may incorporate the terms of your parenting plan if you have submitted one. Make sure you obtain a certified copy of this Judgment as it will be needed throughout the child(ren)'s minority. After the hearing, you will fill out the Judgment (form 23) to reflect what the judge ordered. Most of the more common matters are covered in form 23; however, you may need to substantially modify this form in order to comply with the requirements of your court. Some states have lengthy notices that are required to be in all judgments. Other states require detailed findings of fact. Therefore, be sure to do some research to find out what is required for judgments in your court.

See form N in appendix B for an example of a completed Judgment.

FINAL JUDGMENT

THE COURT having read the pleadings, heard the evidence, and being otherwise advised, finds:

FINDINGS OF FACT

    1. The Petitioner is a resident of _____, County,

_____.

    2. Petitioner is the mother of the minor child(ren).

    3. Respondent is the father of the minor child(ren).

    4. The name(s), date(s) of birth, and age(s) of the minor child(ren) is/are:

Name	Date of Birth	Age

WHEREFORE, THIS COURT ORDERS:

PATERNITY

    1. The Respondent is hereby declared to be the natural father of the minor child(ren).

CUSTODY [Choose One]

☐ 2. Mother is awarded sole legal and physical custody of the minor child(ren) subject to the other parent's reasonable rights of visitation. Sole legal and physical custody is in the best interests of the minor child(ren) because:

☐ 2. Mother and Father are awarded joint legal custody of the minor child(ren), with primary physical custody in ☐ Mother ☐ Father, and periods of care and responsibility consistent with the best interests of the child(ren).

☐ 2. Custody is determined in accordance with the parenting plan attached to this judgment and by agreement of the parties.

CHILD SUPPORT [Check all that apply]

☐ 3. Child support is set according to the Child Support Guidelines and Father is ordered to pay monthly child support of $_____ to be paid on or before the first of each month, beginning the first month after the entry of this Judgment.

☐ 4. Child support in arrears are found to be $ _____ and Father is ordered to pay child support arrears by paying an additional monthly amount of $_____ to be paid on or before the first of each month, beginning the first month after the entry of this Judgment.

LIFE INSURANCE

☐ 5. Father is ordered to purchase life insurance with a benefit amount of $_____, naming the Mother as trustee for the benefit of the minor child(ren) in order to pay the child support obligation upon the parent's death.

MEDICAL INSURANCE

☐ 6. Father is ordered to provide health and dental insurance for the minor child(ren).

MEDICAL EXPENSES [Choose One]

☐ 7. Father shall pay 100% of the child(ren)'s health and dental expenses not paid by insurance.

☐ 7. Mother and Father shall each pay one-half of the child(ren)'s health and dental expenses not paid by insurance.

☐ 7. Mother and Father shall pay the child(ren)'s health and dental expenses not paid by insurance in the percentages shown on the child support worksheet.

BIRTH RECORDS

☐ 8. The Department of Vital Statistics should be ordered to change the birth record of the minor child to reflect the paternity as determined by this court.

ENTER:

_____

Judge

AGREED: _____
                 Petitioner

AGREED: _____
                 Respondent

Form 24: Notice of Appeal

Instructions

If either party believes that the court abused its discretion or made its decision contrary to the law, that party may file an appeal. The Notice of Appeal is a form used to officially provide notice to the court and the other party that you have filed the appeal. There are strict timelines within which you must act to appeal your case, so act promptly if you intend to appeal. Usually, you will have no more than thirty days after the Judgment is issued in which to file your appeal. This is done by filing a Notice of Appeal. You must also file a Certificate of Service (form 6) verifying that you served the Notice of Appeal on the other party.

It is strongly suggested that you hire an attorney to handle an appeal. Normally, the attorney will prepare and file the Notice of Appeal, and the actual appeal procedures are beyond the scope of this book. However, if you are quickly approaching the deadline for filing an appeal, or believe you are prepared to handle the appeal yourself, a Notice of Appeal is provided on the following page.

NOTICE OF APPEAL

TO: [Enter Names and Addresses of the Parties/Attorneys to notify]

YOU ARE HEREBY NOTIFIED that on _____{date}, I have filed the within NOTICE of APPEAL against a Judgment entered on: _____.

NOTICED DATED AND MAILED this date: _____

_____

Signature of party

Form 25: Petition to Modify Judgment

Instructions

If, through time or circumstances, state law permits a modification request, then the Petition for Modify Judgment (form 25) may be used to make that request of the court. Ordinarily, you must serve the modification request like your original Petition, even though it may be considered a continuation of the original case. You must also file proof that you served the Petition on the other party (See forms 2,3).

Form 26: Order Modifying Judgment

Instructions

If the judge grants your request to modify the Judgment, you will need to prepare an Order Modifying Judgment (form 26) for the judge to sign.

PETITION FOR MODIFICATION OF CUSTODY AND/OR CHILD SUPPORT

The ☐ Petitioner ☐ Respondent, _____, states as follows:

1.   On _____, _____, Judge _____ entered a Judgment for Custody with a Parenting Plan. A certified copy of the custody decree/parenting plan to be modified is filed with or attached to this petition, if the decree or plan to be modified was entered in another county or state.

2.   The custody judgment/parenting plan should be modified because a substantial change of circumstances has occurred in the circumstances of the children or the other party and the modification is in the best interests of the children and is necessary to serve the best interests of the children. This request is based on the factors below.

    ☐ The parents agree to the modification.

    ☐ The children have been integrated into my family with the consent of the other parent in substantial deviation from the prior decree or parenting plan.

    ☐ The children's present environment is detrimental to the children's physical, mental or emotional health and the harm likely to be caused by a change in environment is outweighed by the advantage of a change to the children.

    ☐ The requested modification or adjustment of the prior custody decree/parenting plan is based upon the following substantial change in circumstance:

3.   The most recent support order was entered in _____ _____{county and state} on _____ {date}. The order requires _____ {name} to pay $_____ per month for the support of {list name(s) of the child(ren)}:

4.   The order of child support should be modified for the following reasons.

  ☐ The previous order was entered more than ___ years ago and there has been a change in the income of the parents.

  ☐ _____ {name of child} is in need of postsecondary educational support because the child is in fact dependent and is relying upon the parents for the reasonable necessities of life.

  ☐ _____ {name of child} is a dependent adult child and support should be extended beyond his or her eighteenth birthday.

  ☐ The previous order was entered by default.

  ☐ The previous order was entered more than a year ago and:

      ☐ The order works a severe economic hardship.

      ☐ The child has moved to a new age category for support purposes.

      ☐ The child is still in high school and there is a need to extend support beyond the child's eighteenth birthday to allow the child to complete high school.

      ☐ Either or both parents should be required to maintain or provide health insurance coverage.

  ☐ There has been the following substantial change of circumstances since the order was entered (explain):

WHEREFORE, ☐ PETITIONER OR ☐ RESPONDENT hereby requests this Court to:

1.   Enter an order establishing child support in conjunction with the proposed parenting plan, the child support worksheet, and financial declaration which have been filed with this petition.

2.   Adopt a temporary parenting plan until further hearing in this matter.

3.   Other:

☐ Ordering child support payments which are based upon the State Child Support Schedule. A copy of the child support worksheet is filed with this action.

☐ Requiring a periodic adjustment of support.

☐ Extending child support beyond _____'s {name of child} eighteenth birthday to allow the child to complete high school.

☐ Extending child support beyond _____'s {name of child} eighteenth birthday until he/she is no longer dependent upon either or both parents and is capable of self-support.

☐ Allowing for postsecondary educational support for _____ _____ {name of child}.

☐ Ordering the payment of day care.

☐ Ordering the payment of educational expenses.

☐ Ordering the payment of long distance transportation expenses.

☐ Ordering the payment of uncovered health care expenses.

☐ Awarding the tax exemption for the children as follows:

Dated: _____   _____
                                        Signature

                                        _____
                                        Print or Type Name

ACKNOWLEDGEMENT

STATE OF _____)

                                                  ss

COUNTY OF _____)

I,_____, being first duly sworn upon my oath, depose and state that I am the Petitioner in the above-entitled cause. I have read the attached PETITION TO MODIFY JUDGMENT OF CUSTODY AND CHILD SUPPORT. I state that the contents thereof are true and correct, except to the matters stated on information and belief, and those matters I believe to be true.

_____
Signature of Party

SUBSCRIBED AND SWORN TO before me on
this _____ day of _____, _____.

_____
NOTARY PUBLIC
My Commission Expires: _____

ORDER MODIFYING JUDGMENT

THE COURT FINDS:

1. This case has come before this Court on a petition to modify the _____ _____, dated _____, regarding the matter(s) of: ☐ Child custody ☐ Visitation ☐ Child support.

2. This Court has jurisdiction to modify the judgment and over the parties.

3. This Order applies to the following child(ren):

    <u>Name</u>   <u>Birth Date</u>   <u>Age</u>

4. Grounds for Changing Custody/Parenting Plan:

    ☐ The parents agree to the modification.

    ☐ The requisite time period has passed and there has been a substantial change in circumstances that make a change in custody/visitation in the best interest of the child(ren) for the reasons described below:

☐ There has been domestic violence, spousal abuse, or child abuse as described below since the date of the earlier order, and it is in the best interest of the child(ren) that the change is made for the reasons described below:

☐ The child(ren)'s current environment may seriously endanger the child(ren)'s physical, mental, moral, or emotional health, the child(ren) is/are at risk under the current order, and it is in the best interest of the child(ren) that custody is changed for the reasons described below:

5.   Grounds for Changing Child Support:

    ☐ The parents agree to the change

    ☐ The requisite time period has passed and there has been a change in circumstances that make changing child support justified for the reasons described below:

WHEREFORE, THE COURT ORDERS that the _____
_____, dated _____, is amended as follows:

ORDERED _____

_____
JUDGE

Form 27: Motion and Order for Referral to Mediation

Instructions

If your court allows for mediation of custody disputes, and you would like to take advantage of this procedure, you may need to file a request for mediation. Form 27 is a motion for referral to mediation and an order all in one document. In some states, mediation is automatically approved if one of the parties asks for it, without a hearing. Therefore, you may or may not need to file a Certificate of Service (form 6) for the motion. You may be able to just submit the motion, get the order portion signed, then send a copy to the other parent and file a Certificate of Service as to the motion and the order.

MOTION AND ORDER FOR REFERRAL TO MEDIATION

NOW COMES _____, petitioner, and states:

1. That Petitioner filed a _____ on _____.

2. That Respondent filed a response to the petition on _____.

3. That the following matter(s) is/are at issue in this case and is a/are proper subject(s) for mediation at this time:

    ☐ custody   ☐ time-sharing   ☐ child support

WHEREFORE, petitioner herein requests:

A. That the matter(s) stated above be referred for mediation, and that a status date be set for 90 days to permit completion of the mediation sessions.

B. That the costs of mediation be paid by   ☐ petitioner   ☐ respondent

    ☐ other: _____

C. That Petitioner be granted such other and further relief as the court may deem just.

Respectfully submitted,

_____
Signature of Petitioner
Print Name: _____
Address: _____
              _____
Telephone: _____

ACKNOWLEDGEMENT

STATE OF _____)

) SS.

COUNTY OF _____)

I,_____, being first duly sworn upon my oath, depose and state that I am the Petitioner in the above-entitled cause. I have read the attached MOTION FOR REFERRAL FOR MEDIATION. I state that the contents thereof are true and correct.

_____

Signature of Petitioner

SUBSCRIBED AND SWORN TO before me on
this _____ day of _____, _____.

_____

NOTARY PUBLIC
My Commission Expires: _____

ORDER

This matter is hereby referred for mediation to: _____
_____, as to the matters of:

    ☐ custody   ☐ time-sharing   ☐ child support

A status date is set for _____ to permit completion of the mediation sessions.

Costs of mediation be paid by   ☐ petitioner   ☐ respondent
    ☐ other: _____

ORDERED ON _____

_____

JUDGE

INDEX

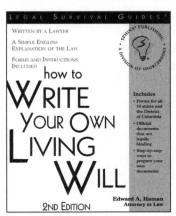

SPHINX® PUBLISHING'S NATIONAL TITLES

Valid in All 50 States

LEGAL SURVIVAL IN BUSINESS

How to Form a Limited Liability Company	$19.95
How to Form Your Own Corporation (2E)	$19.95
How to Form Your Own Partnership	$19.95
How to Register Your Own Copyright (2E)	$19.95
How to Register Your Own Trademark (3E)	$19.95
Most Valuable Business Legal Forms You'll Ever Need (2E)	$19.95
Most Valuable Corporate Forms You'll Ever Need (2E)	$24.95
Software Law (with diskette)	$29.95

LEGAL SURVIVAL IN COURT

Crime Victim's Guide to Justice	$19.95
Debtors' Rights (3E)	$12.95
Defend Yourself against Criminal Charges	$19.95
Grandparents' Rights (2E)	$19.95
Help Your Lawyer Win Your Case (2E)	$12.95
Jurors' Rights (2E)	$9.95
Legal Malpractice and Other Claims against Your Lawyer	$18.95
Legal Research Made Easy (2E)	$14.95
Simple Ways to Protect Yourself from Lawsuits	$24.95
Victims' Rights	$12.95
Winning Your Personal Injury Claim	$19.95

LEGAL SURVIVAL IN REAL ESTATE

How to Buy a Condominium or Townhome	$16.95
How to Negotiate Real Estate Contracts (3E)	$16.95
How to Negotiate Real Estate Leases (3E)	$16.95
Successful Real Estate Brokerage Management	$19.95

LEGAL SURVIVAL IN PERSONAL AFFAIRS

Your Right to Child Custody, Visitation and Support	$19.95
The Nanny and Domestic Help Legal Kit	$19.95
How to File Your Own Bankruptcy (4E)	$19.95
How to File Your Own Divorce (3E)	$19.95
How to Make Your Own Will	$12.95
How to Write Your Own Living Will	$9.95
How to Write Your Own Premarital Agreement (2E)	$19.95
How to Win Your Unemployment Compensation Claim	$19.95
Living Trusts and Simple Ways to Avoid Probate (2E)	$19.95
Neighbor v. Neighbor (2E)	$12.95
The Power of Attorney Handbook (3E)	$19.95
Simple Ways to Protect Yourself from Lawsuits	$24.95
Social Security Benefits Handbook (2E)	$14.95
Unmarried Parents' Rights	$19.95
U.S.A. Immigration Guide (3E)	$19.95
Guia de Inmigracion a Estados Unidos (2E)	$19.95

Legal Survival Guides are directly available from Sourcebooks, Inc., or from your local bookstores.

For credit card orders call 1–800–43–BRIGHT, write P.O. Box 4410, Naperville, IL 60567-4410 or fax 630-961-2168

SPHINX® PUBLISHING ORDER FORM

BILL TO:		SHIP TO:	
Phone #	**Terms**	**F.O.B.** Chicago, IL	**Ship Date**

Charge my: ☐ VISA   ☐ MasterCard   ☐ American Express

☐ **Money Order or Personal Check**

Credit Card Number

Expiration Date

Qty	ISBN	Title	Retail	Ext.
		SPHINX PUBLISHING NATIONAL TITLES		
____	1-57071-166-6	Crime Victim's Guide to Justice	$19.95	____
____	1-57071-342-1	Debtors' Rights (3E)	$12.95	____
____	1-57071-162-3	Defend Yourself against Criminal Charges	$19.95	____
____	1-57248-082-3	Grandparents' Rights (2E)	$19.95	____
____	1-57248-087-4	Guia de Inmigracion a Estados Unidos (2E)	$19.95	____
____	1-57248-103-X	Help Your Lawyer Win Your Case (2E)	$12.95	____
____	1-57071-164-X	How to Buy a Condominium or Townhome	$16.95	____
____	1-57071-223-9	How to File Your Own Bankruptcy (4E)	$19.95	____
____	1-57071-224-7	How to File Your Own Divorce (3E)	$19.95	____
____	1-57248-083-1	How to Form a Limited Liability Company	$19.95	____
____	1-57248-100-5	How to Form a DE Corporation from Any State	$19.95	____
____	1-57248-101-3	How to Form a NV Corporation from Any State	$19.95	____
____	1-57248-099-8	How to Form a Nonprofit Corporation	$24.95	____
____	1-57071-227-1	How to Form Your Own Corporation (2E)	$19.95	____
____	1-57071-343-X	How to Form Your Own Partnership	$19.95	____
____	1-57071-228-X	How to Make Your Own Will	$12.95	____
____	1-57071-331-6	How to Negotiate Real Estate Contracts (3E)	$16.95	____
____	1-57071-332-4	How to Negotiate Real Estate Leases (3E)	$16.95	____
____	1-57071-225-5	How to Register Your Own Copyright (2E)	$19.95	____
____	1-57248-104-8	How to Register Your Own Trademark (3E)	$19.95	____
____	1-57071-349-9	How to Win Your Unemployment Compensation Claim	$19.95	____
____	1-57071-167-4	How to Write Your Own Living Will	$9.95	____
____	1-57071-344-8	How to Write Your Own Premarital Agreement (2E)	$19.95	____
____	1-57071-333-2	Jurors' Rights (2E)	$9.95	____
____	1-57248-032-7	Legal Malpractice and Other Claims against...	$18.95	____
____	1-57071-400-2	Legal Research Made Easy (2E)	$14.95	____
____	1-57071-336-7	Living Trusts and Simple Ways to Avoid Probate (2E)	$19.95	____
____	1-57071-345-6	Most Valuable Bus. Legal Forms You'll Ever Need (2E)	$19.95	____
____	1-57071-346-4	Most Valuable Corporate Forms You'll Ever Need (2E)	$24.95	____
____	1-57248-089-0	Neighbor v. Neighbor (2E)	$12.95	____
____	1-57071-348-0	The Power of Attorney Handbook (3E)	$19.95	____
____	1-57248-020-3	Simple Ways to Protect Yourself from Lawsuits	$24.95	____
____	1-57071-337-5	Social Security Benefits Handbook (2E)	$14.95	____
____	1-57071-163-1	Software Law (w/diskette)	$29.95	____
____	0-913825-86-7	Successful Real Estate Brokerage Mgmt.	$19.95	____
____	1-57248-098-X	The Nanny and Domestic Help Legal Kit	$19.95	____
____	1-57071-399-5	Unmarried Parents' Rights	$19.95	____
____	1-57071-354-5	U.S.A. Immigration Guide (3E)	$19.95	____
____	0-913825-82-4	Victims' Rights	$12.95	____
____	1-57071-165-8	Winning Your Personal Injury Claim	$19.95	____
____	1-57248-097-1	Your Right to Child Custody, Visitation and Support	$19.95	____
		CALIFORNIA TITLES		
____	1-57071-360-X	CA Power of Attorney Handbook	$12.95	____
____	1-57071-355-3	How to File for Divorce in CA	$19.95	____
____	1-57071-356-1	How to Make a CA Will	$12.95	____
____	1-57071-408-8	How to Probate an Estate in CA	$19.95	____
____	1-57071-357-X	How to Start a Business in CA	$16.95	____
____	1-57071-358-8	How to Win in Small Claims Court in CA	$14.95	____
____	1-57071-359-6	Landlords' Rights and Duties in CA	$19.95	____
		FLORIDA TITLES		
____	1-57071-363-4	Florida Power of Attorney Handbook (2E)	$12.95	____
____	1-57248-093-9	How to File for Divorce in FL (6E)	$21.95	____
____	1-57248-086-6	How to Form a Limited Liability Co. in FL	$19.95	____
____	1-57071-401-0	How to Form a Partnership in FL	$19.95	____
____	1-57071-380-4	How to Form a Corporation in FL (4E)	$19.95	____
____	1-57071-361-8	How to Make a FL Will (5E)	$12.95	____
____	1-57248-088-2	How to Modify Your FL Divorce Judgment (4E)	$22.95	____
____		***Form Continued on Following Page***	**SUBTOTAL**	____

To order, call Sourcebooks at 1-800-43-BRIGHT or FAX (630)961-2168 (Bookstores, libraries, wholesalers—please call for discount)

SPHINX® PUBLISHING ORDER FORM

Qty	ISBN	Title	Retail	Ext.
		FLORIDA TITLES (CONT'D)		
	1-57071-364-2	How to Probate an Estate in FL (3E)	$24.95	
	1-57248-081-5	How to Start a Business in FL (5E)	$16.95	
	1-57071-362-6	How to Win in Small Claims Court in FL (6E)	$14.95	
	1-57071-335-9	Landlords' Rights and Duties in FL (7E)	$19.95	
	1-57071-334-0	Land Trusts in FL (5E)	$24.95	
	0-913825-73-5	Women's Legal Rights in FL	$19.95	
		GEORGIA TITLES		
	1-57071-376-6	How to File for Divorce in GA (3E)	$19.95	
	1-57248-075-0	How to Make a GA Will (3E)	$12.95	
	1-57248-076-9	How to Start a Business in Georgia (3E)	$16.95	
		ILLINOIS TITLES		
	1-57071-405-3	How to File for Divorce in IL (2E)	$19.95	
	1-57071-415-0	How to Make an IL Will (2E)	$12.95	
	1-57071-416-9	How to Start a Business in IL (2E)	$16.95	
	1-57248-078-5	Landlords' Rights & Duties in IL	$19.95	
		MASSACHUSETTS TITLES		
	1-57071-329-4	How to File for Divorce in MA (2E)	$19.95	
	1-57248-108-0	How to Make a MA Will (2E)	$12.95	
	1-57248-109-9	How to Probate an Estate in MA (2E)	$19.95	
	1-57248-106-4	How to Start a Business in MA (2E)	$16.95	
	1-57248-107-2	Landlords' Rights and Duties in MA (2E)	$19.95	
		MICHIGAN TITLES		
	1-57071-409-6	How to File for Divorce in MI (2E)	$19.95	
	1-57248-077-7	How to Make a MI Will (2E)	$12.95	
	1-57071-407-X	How to Start a Business in MI (2E)	$16.95	
		MINNESOTA TITLES		
	1-57248-039-4	How to File for Divorce in MN	$19.95	
	1-57248-040-8	How to Form a Simple Corporation in MN	$19.95	
	1-57248-037-8	How to Make a MN Will	$9.95	
	1-57248-038-6	How to Start a Business in MN	$16.95	
		NEW YORK TITLES		
	1-57071-184-4	How to File for Divorce in NY	$19.95	
	1-57248-105-6	How to Form a Corporation in NY	$19.95	
		NEW YORK TITLES (CONT'D)		
	1-57248-095-5	How to Make a NY Will (2E)	$12.95	
	1-57071-185-2	How to Start a Business in NY	$16.95	
	1-57071-187-9	How to Win in Small Claims Court in NY	$14.95	
	1-57071-186-0	Landlords' Rights and Duties in NY	$19.95	
	1-57071-188-7	New York Power of Attorney Handbook	$19.95	
		NORTH CAROLINA TITLES		
	1-57071-326-X	How to File for Divorce in NC (2E)	$19.95	
	1-57071-327-8	How to Make a NC Will (2E)	$12.95	
	1-57248-096-3	How to Start a Business in NC (2E)	$16.95	
	1-57248-091-2	Landlords' Rights & Duties in NC	$19.95	
		OHIO TITLES		
	1-57248-102-1	How to File for Divorce in OH	$19.95	
		PENNSYLVANIA TITLES		
	1-57071-177-1	How to File for Divorce in PA	$19.95	
	1-57248-094-7	How to Make a PA Will (2E)	$12.95	
	1-57248-112-9	How to Start a Business in PA (2E)	$16.95	
	1-57071-179-8	Landlords' Rights and Duties in PA	$19.95	
		TEXAS TITLES		
	1-57071-330-8	How to File for Divorce in TX (2E)	$19.95	
	1-57248-009-2	How to Form a Simple Corporation in TX	$19.95	
	1-57071-417-7	How to Make a TX Will (2E)	$12.95	
	1-57071-418-5	How to Probate an Estate in TX (2E)	$19.95	
	1-57071-365-0	How to Start a Business in TX (2E)	$16.95	
	1-57248-111-0	How to Win in Small Claims Court in TX (2E)	$14.95	
	1-57248-110-2	Landlords' Rights and Duties in TX (2E)	$19.95	

SUBTOTAL THIS PAGE _____

SUBTOTAL PREVIOUS PAGE _____

Illinois residents add 6.75% sales tax _____

Florida residents add 6% state sales tax plus applicable discretionary surtax _____

Shipping— $4.00 for 1st book, $1.00 each additional _____

TOTAL _____